THE DURHAM BOOK OF DAYS

ROBERT WOODHOUSE

I am indebted to my wife, Sally, for her research and unstinting support, and to Liz and Ben Taylorson for their administrative and research skills. My gratitude extends to Bob Eastwood and staff at Durham City Library and Durham University Library.

The Julian calendar was in use until Wednesday, September 2nd 1752. The following day, the Gregorian calendar was adopted, making the date Thursday, September 14th 1752. The dates in this book before and after the shift correspond to the respective calendars.

References for extracts appear in brackets at the end of each entry.

Robert Woodhouse, 2014

First published 2014

The History Press
The Mill, Brimscombe Port
Stroud, Gloucestershire, GL5 2QG
www.thehistorypress.co.uk

British Library Cataloguing in Publication Data.
A catalogue record for this book is available from the British Library.

ISBN 978 0 7524 7647 6

Typesetting and origination by The History Press
Printed in India

– JANUARY 1ST –

1863: Philip Armes became Master of the Choristers on this date. He succeeded William Henshaw and initially received an annual salary of £260 which was increased to £300 in 1870. Soon after moving to Durham, Armes married Emily Jane Davison (in January 1864) and, whilst living first at No. 20 North Bailey (1864–72) and then at No. 17, they had two sons and two daughters.

Philip Armes gained a reputation as 'a martinet and strict disciplinarian' with a habit of carrying a military cane for use when conducting and also as a means of administering punishment. His ability as a musician brought order to the music of the liturgy by arranging two sets of chants for the Psalms and, whilst reviving interest in church music of the sixteenth and seventeenth centuries, Armes edited items from Durham's collection of manuscripts from that period. His scheme for allowing internal students to study for a degree in music was accepted by the University of Durham in 1886. In 1897 he was appointed as the university's first Professor of Music and retired some ten years later in May 1907. Following his death on February 10th 1908, Philip Armes was buried in the cemetery of St Mary le Bow, Durham. (Crosby, Brian, *Come on Choristers! A History of the Chorister School, Durham*, Durham: B. Crosby, 1999)

— JANUARY 2ND —

1875: At about 5 p.m. on this day householders at the higher end of North Road in Durham City were deafened by a gas explosion at the tailor and drapery store owned by William Gray.

After earlier smelling gas Mr Gray had contacted the Gas Company's offices on Framwellgate and a workman had subsequently checked the shop. He reported that no work on the gas pipes was needed before Monday (January 4th). As the smell of gas grew stronger Mr Gray chose to carry out his own investigations. Soon after 5 p.m., leaving gas in the shop unlit, he lit a candle and set out to locate the source of the leak. Having determined that the smell was not coming from gas pipes, Mr Gray was edging across the shop floor towards a party wall with a house at the corner of Atherton Street when a huge explosion hurled him out of his shop.

After temporarily losing consciousness he was able to crawl through an opening before collapsing again. While some neighbours rushed away from the scene others helped to move Mr Gray to the nearby Durham County Hospital. Sadly two young children in the house were fatally injured and at the inquest that followed it was recommended that Durham Gas Company should fit stop valves on mains pipes. (Fordyce, T. (ed.), *Local Records; or, Historical Register of remarkable events which have occurred in Northumberland and Durham … 1833 to [1875], being a continuation of the work published by … Mr. John Sykes*, Newcastle upon Tyne: T. Fordyce, 1867–1876)

— January 3rd —

1644: On this day Francis Walker was on trial at Durham Assizes for stating:

> The Parliament are rogues and traitors. God confound them and the devil confound them; I wish the Parliament house blown up with gunpowder as it should have been once, I hope to see them all hanged, one against another in a short time. Parliament seek to be the King themselves, and they would have the King to be worse than you and I , and that he could not say whether the horse he rode on was his own.

(Dufferwiel, Martin, *Durham: A Thousand Years of History and Legend*, Edinburgh: Mainstream, 1996)

—·—

1953: On this day the wedding took place at Durham Cathedral of Lady Anne Katharine Gabrielle Lumley and Matthew White Ridley, son of Viscount Ridley of Blagdon, Northumberland. The bride was given away by her father the 11th Earl of Scarborough and they were led into the cathedral by the head verger, Mr Frederick Woodward.

The couple lived on the family's 7,000-acre Blagdon estate at Seaton Burn near Stannington and were married for fifty-three years until Lady Anne Katharine's death on October 16th 2006. (*The Journal*, Newcastle upon Tyne, 1958)

‒ JANUARY 4TH ‒

1929: On this day Charles Conlin was hanged at Durham Jail after being found guilty of murdering his grandparents, Thomas and Emily Kirby, in September of the previous year. The tragic series of events began on the early afternoon of Saturday September 22nd 1928 when Annie Maria Stirr of No. 93 Norton Avenue, Norton near Stockton, set out to gather soil in a lane near her home in order to re-pot plants. As she dug at an area of disturbed soil beneath a hedge a human hand poked out of the ground. When police officers arrived at the scene they uncovered the bodies of a man and a woman as well as a discarded spade in a nearby field.

The victims were soon identified as Thomas and Emily Kirby who lived in Victoria Avenue, Norton and suspicion soon focused on their 22-year-old grandson, Charles Conlin. After leaving school at the age of 14 he had worked in a number of jobs but lost some on account of his dishonesty and was serving his notice at a local nitrates factory when the gruesome crime took place. As evidence accumulated against Charles Conlin a grey wallet belonging to Thomas Kirby was found in his possession and, at his trial on November 15th, a guilty verdict was returned. (*The Northern Echo*, Darlington, 1870‒)

─ JANUARY 5TH ─

1681: This date appears in a manuscript contained within an organ book of Durham choristers accompanied by the names of William Greggs and Alixander Shaw. It was at about this time that Greggs replaced Shaw in the combined post of organist and chorister and he continued in this dual role until his death in October 1710. There are several references in Chapter Act Books to William Greggs' duties including 'The completion of Father Smith's new organ, with two extra notes per octave ("quarter tones") which required a person well-acquainted with this peculiar keyboard to avail himself of its use' and in 1686 Greggs was given leave by the chapter on December 1st 'to goe to London to improve himself in the Skill of Musicke'. In 1690 he was granted £10 to allow him to buy the Langley song school and some years later he received payment for composing an anthem to celebrate a national victory. During 1704 he was 'admonished to be more careful in his teaching of the choristers'.

Following his death on October 15th 1710, William Greggs was buried in the church of St Mary the Less at Durham where an epitaph is displayed on the south wall. (Crosby, Brian, *Come on Choristers! A History of the Chorister School, Durham*, Durham: B. Crosby, 1999)

— JANUARY 6TH —

1804: On this day a destructive fire swept through the worsted mill of George and Henry Salvin which covered ground on the south side of St Oswald's church in Durham City. During 1796 the owners had moved machinery from Castle Eden to the factory that was set among housing for the workforce at a time when an ambitious plan had been put forward for a canal and river transport system. The city was also benefitting in the closing decade of the eighteenth century, from improvements to amenities such as lighting and paving as a result of legislation in 1790. A year after the demise of Salvins' business, Durham's weaving industry was dealt another serious blow when John Starforth's factory went bankrupt and closed. With a workforce of around 700, this represented about one tenth of the city's population.

Weaving was prospering in Durham as early as 1243 and by 1450 an active Guild of Weavers had been set up. In addition to regulating the local weaving trade, guild members set up training facilities, firstly for young men and later for women. (Richardson, Michael, *Memory Lane: Durham City*, Derby: Breedon, 2000)

— January 7th —

1873: A daughter, Margaret, was born on this day to Mary Ann Cotton, of West Auckland, in Durham Jail. Although exact details are difficult to establish, it is certain that this was Mary Ann's eighth child and the christening of Margaret Quick-Manning identified her father as John Quick-Manning. He was in all probability the excise officer at West Auckland Brewery and certainly married to someone else. He left the area almost immediately and changed his surname. Some reports suggest that he moved abroad while others indicate that he returned to his hometown of Darlington where he ran a small beerhouse.

Mary Ann Cotton was on a charge of murdering her stepson, Charles, and her trial was postponed for several months to allow her to give birth. She nursed Margaret in her cell and one visitor reported how he had met Mrs Cotton 'sitting on a stool close by a good fire, giving the breast to her baby'. Her trial began on March 3rd and Mary Ann Cotton was found guilty four days later. One week before her execution on March 24th, she handed over baby Margaret for adoption by a couple that she knew in West Auckland, William and Sarah Edwards. (*The Northern Echo*, Darlington, 1870–)

~ January 8th ~

1904: On this day Battersby Brothers' 'Cheap Sale' was advertised in the columns of local newspapers:

CORSET DEPARTMENT

Children's, all sizes 9½d, usual price 1s.

Ladies Corsets 6½d and 11½d; usual price 1s 6d.

Ladies Corsets, 1s 11½d; worth 2s 6d.

BLOUSE DEPARTMENT

We are noted for the best stock of Blouses in the City.

A Grand Line in New Stuff to clear at 11½d each.

Another Line of 2s 6d and 2s 11d. Goods, all at 1s 11d.

Pinafores 6½d, 9d, 11½d, 1s 4d and 1s 9d; the cheapest ever offered.

UNDERCLOTHING DEPARTMENT

Ladies' Flannelette Knickers, 8½d per pair.

Ladies' Flannelette Chemises 11½d each.

Ladies' Flannelette Night Dresses 1s 9½d each.

Ladies' Moreen Skirts were 2s 11½ d; Sale Price 1s 11½d.

Ladies' Divided Skirts, all prices.

} All much under price

Ladies' Woven Combinations, in Pink and Natural, 1s 6d and 1s 11d; worth 2s and 2s 11d.

Children's Woven Combinations, all sizes at 8½d each.

Men's Shetland Under Shirts and Pants, 11½d each.

Men's Natural Wool Shirts and Pants, 1s 11½d; usual price 2s 9d.

Men's Shetland Lamb's Wool Shirts and Pants 1s 6d, usual price 2s.

Our Entire Stock of Ties, 6½d quality, 5d, 1s quality 9½d.

Men's Astrachan and Kid Gloves 2s 6d quality for 1s 6d.

How fashions and prices have changed! (*Durham Chronicle*, 1820–1984)

~ January 9th ~

2013: Renovation works were unveiled on this day at an area in front of the Fergusson building at Durham University's St Mary's College. The site, which had been in use during recent years as a car park, had been restored to its original purpose as a recreation area and the work was commissioned to mark sixty years since the late Queen Mother opened the Fergusson building, off South Road, Durham City, in 1952. The foundation stone had been laid some five years earlier by the queen, then still Princess Elizabeth. Today's unveiling was performed by Professor Chris Higgins, vice-chancellor of Durham University, and represented an integral part of a wider refurbishment of St Mary's College aimed at improving its student accommodation for the twenty-first century.

St Mary's College was founded in 1899 as a pioneering women-only institution and became one of the first places in the United Kingdom where women could study for degrees. Its increasing popularity meant that the college outgrew its first base in what is now the Chorister School, behind Durham Cathedral, and this led to work on a new headquarters which was named after a former college principal, Margaret Fergusson. (*The Northern Echo*, Darlington, 1870–)

~ January 10th ~

2013: On this day a senior United Nations official, Baroness Valerie Amos, was made an honorary Doctor of Civil Law by Durham University at a ceremony held in Durham Cathedral. Currently serving as the UN's under-secretary-general for humanitarian affairs and emergency relief coordinator, Baroness Amos was made a Labour life peer in 1997 and served as Leader of the House of Lords and Secretary of State for International Development. She has also been British High Commissioner to Australia and European Union Special Representative to the African Union.

The honorary degree was presented by Professor Chris Higgins, Durham University's vice chancellor, who replaced the chancellor and opera singer Sir Thomas Allen after illness prevented him from attending. An honour was also presented to Ken West, a pioneer of natural burials, who was made an honorary Master of Arts. Baroness Amos commented, 'It is a great privilege to be honoured by Durham University, a university with a long and proud history where there is a strong commitment to the principles of social justice.' Professor Higgins said, 'All of our honorary degree recipients have made outstanding contributions in their chosen fields and are a real example to our students of what can be achieved with drive, determination and skill.' (*The Northern Echo*, Darlington, 1870–)

~ January 11th ~

1683: On this day the will of Dean John Sudbury of Durham Cathedral was made. It included provision to complete work on a great organ to stand on a screen in the building and to finish work on the cathedral library. He had already spent in excess of £1,000 on rebuilding and fitting out the library and ordered executors of his will to pay out further amounts to complete the project according to his specifications. Appointed as dean in February 1662, John Sudbury died in 1684 and his grave slab is to be seen in the North Quire Aisle of Durham Cathedral. (Stranks, C.J., *This Sumptuous Church: The story of Durham Cathedral*, London: SPCK, 1993)

—

1711: Durham City diarist Jacob Bee was buried in St Margaret's Churchyard on this day. He had also been baptised and married at this church. Although his life was almost entirely unremarkable, much of it spent in 'Bee's Cottage' close to the railway viaduct, his diary entries give a fascinating insight into everyday life in Durham. (*The Northern Echo*, Darlington, 1870–)

—

2012: On this day moves were announced to try to save a house that featured in the cult gangster movie *Get Carter*. Developers wanted to demolish 'Beechcroft' in Broomside Lane, Belmont, on the outskirts of Durham City. (*The Northern Echo*, Darlington, 1870–)

~ January 12th ~

1800: James Cawdell, manager of theatres in Durham and Stockton, died in Durham City on this day. 'His abilities in his profession were generally admitted and admired, and as an intelligent, friendly, social and facetious companion he was almost unrivalled.' (Richmond, Thomas, *The Local Records of Stockton and the Neighbourhood; or, a Register of Memorable Events, Chronologically Arranged, Which Have Occurred in and near Stockton Ward and the North-Eastern Parts of Cleveland*, Stockton: William Robinson, 1868)

———

1951: On this day an advertisement for the Union Surgical Appliances Stores Ltd said:

Have pleasure in announcing a branch has been opened at:
1, Crossgate, Durham City
with a large selection of Steel and Elastic Trusses, Anklets, Kneecaps, Stockings and Two way Stretch Elastic Hosiery.
Air cushions, Bedpans, Rubber Sheeting, Rubber Urinals, Hot Water Bottles, 12in x 8in, and Durex Surgical Rubberware.

(*Durham Chronicle*, 1820–1984)

~ January 13th ~

1610: On this day Ralph Tailor was baptised in St Margaret's parish church in Durham City and probably moved to Newcastle when he was 15 to become a scrivener. This involved a seven-year apprenticeship and when Tailor began his career, in his mid-20s, plague was decimating Newcastle's population. As a scrivener, Ralph Tailor was responsible for most of the wills of plague victims during the summer of 1636 and his signature appears on a quarter of probate documents. (Wrightson, Keith, *Ralph Tailor's Summer : A Scrivener, his City and the Plague*, New Haven: Yale University Press, 2011)

—

1840: Samuel Storey was born on this day at Sherburn, near Durham, the sixth son of Robert Storey who had moved to Sherburn from Monkwearmouth where the family were farmers. Following Robert Storey's death in 1843 Samuel's mother moved the family to Newcastle and Samuel trained as a teacher. He married in 1864 and left teaching to develop business interests and involvement in politics in the Sunderland area. This led to the founding of the *Sunderland Daily Echo* in December 1873 and election as a Liberal MP in 1881. He retained an active interest in political events and newspapers up to his death in 1925. (*North Magazine: A Magazine for Durham, Northumberland and North Yorkshire*, York, 1971–)

— January 14th —

1953: On this day crowds in Durham marketplace watched Field Marshal, Viscount Montgomery of Alamein receive the Honorary Freedom of the City from Durham's mayor, Councillor Gordon McIntyre. Movietone cameras mounted on top of a van recorded the event for cinema audiences and proceedings included the presentation to Viscount Montgomery of an oak casket, made from 800-year-old beams from Durham Cathedral, containing an illuminated manuscript (after 'Monty's' death it was returned to Durham and is displayed in the town hall entrance.) Whilst in the marketplace Viscount Montgomery was given a surprise gift by university policeman, William Plunkett. It was a framed photograph of his brother, Canon Colin Montgomery, and dated from 1926 when he was president of the union during his time as a student at St Chad's College. (Richardson, Michael, *Memory Lane: Durham City*, Derby: Breedon, 2000)

1985: Forty firemen tackled a blaze that spread through St Godric's church at Durham to leave a cloud of smoke over the city on this day. The fire had been started by a 13-year-old boy at the west end of the building some two years after several thousand pounds had been spent on roof repairs. A Harrison organ and a fifteenth-century desk were among furnishings badly damaged. (Richardson, Michael, *Memory Lane: Durham City*, Derby: Breedon, 2000)

~ JANUARY 15TH ~

2002: Durham City's newly-opened Gala Theatre began a season of Alan Ayckbourn's *Damsel's in Distress* trilogy of *Gameplan, Flatspin* and *Role Play*. It ran until January 31st 2002 before setting out on a UK-wide tour. The three plays represent Ayckbourn's 58th, 59th and 60th plays and although they are entirely separate comedies, they were written to be performed by the same cast using the same set (a luxury apartment in the London Docklands). The Gala Theatre was part of a Millennium City development which also includes a cinema, tourist information centre, bars and restaurants. The Gala represented the largest regional theatre in the UK for more than a decade and Durham's first dedicated theatre for fifty years. (www.whatsonstage.com)

2011: On this day a rare Shakespeare First Folio, which was stolen from Durham University some twelve years earlier, formed the centrepiece of an exhibition – *Treasures of Durham University* which opened to the public at the university's Palace Green Library. The exhibition included a number of other university treasures and manuscripts and represented the inaugural exhibition in the new Wolfson Gallery following a £2.3 million programme of refurbishment. (www.dur.ac.uk/news)

— January 16th —

1691: On this day Sir John Duck, former Mayor of Durham City, died. He had arrived in Durham as a young man to take up an apprenticeship as a butcher and in spite of a warning in the books of the Butcher's Company to 'John Heslopp, that he forebear to sett John Duck on work in the trade as a butcher' he established himself in this business. Folklore suggests that he was walking along the riverbank when a raven dropped a gold coin at his feet and this enabled him to build up his business. Although his methods were suspect at times, Sir John Duck reached the top of his trade and amassed considerable wealth. In 1680 he was Mayor of Durham City. Lord Crewe appointed him a Commissioner of the Peace and during 1686 he became a baronet. He owned property in several parts of County Durham as well as a house on the north side of Silver Street in the city. John Duck married Anne Heslop at St Nicholas' church in 1665 and in 1681 he and his wife gave to the church a velvet pulpit cloth and eight velvet cushions 'to be made use of at all times when sermons are preached'. He was buried in St Margaret's Churchyard. (www.stnics.org.uk)

⁓ January 17th ⁓

1776: Jane Porter, novelist and dramatist, was born at Durham on this day. She soon became a keen reader and is said to have risen at 4 a.m. in order to read and write, and, whilst still in her childhood, reputedly read the whole of Edmund Spenser's *The Faerie Queene*. As she matured into a tall and beautiful woman, her aloof manner earned Jane the nickname of 'La Penserosa' meaning 'a melancholy or brooding person'. Following her father's death the Porter family moved to Edinburgh where Walter Scott was a regular visitor and another move, this time to London, brought her into contact with contemporary literary figures. Jane Porter's novel *Thaddeus of Warsaw*, published in 1803, represents one of the earliest examples of the historical novel and was set during the Polish independence struggle of the 1790s. A novel about William Wallace, *The Scottish Chiefs*, brought further success and Jane Porter also wrote several plays as well as contributing to periodicals. She died on May 24th 1850. (en.wikipedia.org/wiki/Jane_Porter)

———

2009: On this day Ushaw College at Bearpark, near Durham City, a Roman Catholic seminary announced that it was opening its doors for guided group tours. (*The Northern Echo*, Darlington, 1870–)

~ January 18th ~

1796: On this day Reynold Gideon Bowyer, Canon of Durham Cathedral, invited the lay clerks to dinner. In addition to the seven clerks who attended, the party included Mr Morpeth, the chapter's architect; Mr Shields, the registrar's clerk; Mr and Mrs Bowyer; Mr and Mrs Perigal and Edmund Hastings. Seated around a table, the food on offer included soup, roast pork, celery, 'fowls', mashed potatoes, fricassee, stewed celery, apple tart, turnips, veal collops, beetroot, tongue and roast beef. The removes were partridges and ducks but no dessert.

The origin of residence dinners was in statutes issued to the dean and chapter by Queen Mary in 1555 but they fell out of use during the second quarter of the nineteenth century. At Durham the dean and every cannon who had £40 or more each year from a source outside the cathedral, was required to maintain a separate household, to keep the residence and to provide hospitality. (Mussett, P., 'Hospitality residence at Durham Cathedral' *Transactions of the Architectural and Archaeological Society of Durham and Northumberland*, new series, Vol. 6, 1982)

1939: Herbert Hensley Henson, the Bishop of Durham, carried out his last official act as bishop when he laid the foundation stone of the second chapel at Bede College on this day. (Richardson, Michael, *Memory Lane: Durham City*, Derby: Breedon, 2000)

~ January 19th ~

1627: A dispute between John Richardson of the Bailey, Durham City and Dr John Cradock, Vicar of Gainford and Chancellor to the Bishop of Durham, reached a dramatic climax in Durham Cathedral on this day. During the early 1600s Dr Cradock had accumulated considerable property and influence in County Durham and Northumberland. This led to an accusation in the House of Commons that he had abused his offices, extorted money and ransacked people's properties. The leading figure behind these accusations was John Richardson and, on December 22nd 1625, Dr Cradock's sons called at his house at the Bailey in Durham City. During the altercation that followed they 'frightened his wife' and assaulted one of Mr Richardson's staff. Some thirteen months later, on January 19th 1627, Richardson gained revenge. Along with a group of friends, he loitered in Durham Cathedral as Dr Cradock made his way down the aisle during the singing of the litany. About halfway down Mr Richardson's gang leapt out on Cradock 'in contempt of the place, the person and the tyme' and arrested him. Before he could face trial Dr Cradock died suddenly at Woodhorn, near Ashington. His wife, Margaret, was accused of poisoning him but then acquitted at her trial. (*The Northern Echo*, Darlington, 1870–)

— January 20th —

1973: On this day Forbes Henderson, the first prize winner of the international Open Classical Guitar Competition at the 1972 Lanchester Arts Festival in Coventry, gave a recital in the Great Hall of Durham Castle under the auspices of the Durham University Classical Guitar Society.

With encouragement from his father, Forbes Henderson played the guitar from an early age and during schooldays in York he was tutored by Gordon Crosskey. His studies continued at the Royal Academy of Music with Hector Quine and then at the Royal Manchester College of Music. He gained further experience during a summer course at Nice with Alexandre Lagoya and two seasons with the Wavendon Allmusic Plan where John Williams provided tuition. Early concert performances by Forbes Henderson included venues in Coventry, Sheffield, York and Edinburgh. In Sheffield he played Rodrigo's *Fantasia para un Gentilhombre* for guitar and orchestra under conductor Antony Hopkins. His first recital in Durham included music ranging from Bach's Cello Suite No. 1 in the arrangement for guitar, as made famous by an early John Williams recording, to Richard Rodney Bennett's *Five Impromptus*. (*North Magazine: A Magazine for Durham, Northumberland and North Yorkshire*, York, 1971–)

~ January 21st ~

2013: An obituary was published on this day by the Royal Society of Tropical Medicine and Hygiene outlining the lifetime achievements of Dr Andrew Davis in dealing with tropical diseases. Born January 31st 1928 at Washington, Tyne and Wear, he was educated at Johnston School, Durham City and then Durham Medical School. Following National Service, Andrew Davis was appointed director of the World Health Organisation (WHO) Bilharziasis Chemotherapy Centre in what is now Tanganyika in 1962, and between 1971 and 1974 he was director of the Medical Research Council's epidemiological research unit in Jamaica. A move to WHO in Geneva as senior medical officer (schistosomiasis) brought appointment as one of the few British scientists to be made director of a major programme – the parasitic disease programme. In 1980 Andrew Davis was elected a life member of the Swiss Tropical Medicine Society and nine years later he was awarded the silver medal of the Society of Tropical Medicine of France. In 2003 he received the Sir Rickard Christophers Medal from the Royal Society of Tropical Medicine and Hygiene. (www.rstmh.org/node/609)

~ January 22nd ~

2013: Artwork produced by pupils from thirteen Roman Catholic schools across north-east England was featured in an exhibition that began on this day in the Galilee Chapel of Durham Cathedral. Under the title, *The Gospel Stories*, the display was made up of a range of items completed by more than 150 pupils from schools and sixth-form colleges in the Hexham and Newcastle Catholic Partnership. The wide-ranging exhibition included artworks in paint, textiles, ceramics, print and photography and was said by organisers to reflect how young artists had interpreted Biblical events, messages and themes.

The director of the Partnership, Sara Crawshaw, said, 'Through this exhibition students have had some very precious time with their Gospel and like numerous artists before them have found the Bible to be a source of enormous inspiration.' Schools involved in the exhibition were drawn from a wide geographical area ranging from North Shields on Tyneside to Stockton and Billingham and westwards to Bishop Auckland and Lanchester. A student from St Leonard's Catholic School in Durham City, Sophie McNay, summed up the feelings of exhibitors when she said: 'This is a great opportunity for me and it's a real privilege to have my painting shown in Durham Cathedral.' (*Durham Times*, Durham: Newsquest, 2007–)

– January 23rd –

1557: On this day sessions of the peace were held at Durham where officials and jurors heard eight cases covering incidents committed between October 18th 1556 and January 20th 1557. Several of the cases involved 'unlawful and riotous assembly' at locations including Beckley, Heugh near Lanchester, Team Bridge and Darlington. During the riot at Beckley the mob 'violently entered the house of Robert Porter of Shield Row, expelled the same and continued in possession until the present and with their animals consumed his grass'.

Another case involved Anthony Coot of Durham City, a slater, who 'with force and arms broke and entered the close of Christopher Hochenson, at Durham and stole a wainload of stones worth 2*s*' and a group of men were in court because 'having neither land nor tenements worth 40*s* a year, on 20 January 1557 kept greyhounds contrary to the statute'. At the same hearing were 'John Crawe, of Durham city, fisher, William Watson of the same, fisher, John Watson of the same, fisher, Richard Jakson of Sunderland, fisher, Richard Morey of the same, fisher, and Roland Ledebeater of the same, fisher, [as they] on 20 January 1557 and some days earlier forestalled fish coming to the lord's market, contrary to divers statutes.' (Fraser, C.M. (ed.), *Durham Quarter Sessions Rolls 1471–1625*, Durham: Surtees Society, 1991)

— January 24th —

1463: On this day the Prior of Durham granted his licence to John Etrick and Thomas Jonson of Gretham, to go to the Holy Land upon a pilgrimage against the Turks, having previously branded them upon the right side of their naked breasts with a hot iron shaped like a cross before the shrine of St Cuthbert. (Sykes, John, *Local records; or, Historical register of Northumberland and Durham, Newcastle-upon-Tyne, and Berwick-upon-Tweed*, Stockton-on-Tees: Patrick and Shotton, 1973)

1958: This day saw the closure of the popular Rex Cinema, in Gilesgate Moor. Built by a butcher, George Lamb, it first opened in June 1927 as the Crescent Cinema. With 318 seats it was the smallest cinema venue in Durham. There was no balcony for customers wanting an elevated view and the projectionist had to reach his room via a ladder. In 1941 the cinema had a change of management and was renamed Rex. It showed mainly older films, with Westerns particularly popular and at the time of closure the manageress was Mrs Emily Studholme, a stern figure who had earned a reputation as an 'Iron Lady'. The last film to be shown was *Eagle Squadron*. (*The Northern Echo*, Darlington, 1870–)

— January 25th —

1683: An entry in the diary of Durham resident, Jacob Bee for this date reads:

> A sad cruel murther committed by a boy about eighteen or nineteen years of age, nere Ferryhill, nere Durham, being Thursday, at night. The maner is, by report: When the parents were out of dores a young man, being sone to the house and two daughters was kil'd by this boy with an axe, having knock't them in the head, afterwards cut ther throts, one of them being asleep in the bed, about ten or eleven years of age: the other daughter was to be married at Candlemas. After he had kil'd the sone and the eldest daughter, being above twenty years of age, a little lass, her sister, about the age of eleven yeares being in bed alone, he drag'd her out of bed and kil'd her alsoe. The same Andrew Millns, alias Miles, was hang'd in irons upon a gybett nere Ferryhill upon the 15th day of August, being Wednesday, this year 1683.

(*Northern Echo Memories Supplement*)

———

2013: Captain Andrew Burns of HMS *Bulwark*, County Durham's adopted warship, was presented with a commemorative bell at Durham Town Hall. Capt. Burns received the bell which was taken on board HMS *Bulwark* at the end of a two-day visit to the North East. (*The Northern Echo*, Darlington, 1870–)

~ January 26th ~

1973: On this day a headline in the local press stated, 'Farnley Hey Folk Fight to Save Arcadian Setting.' Residents of Farnley Hey Road in Durham were battling to save one of the city's most picturesque areas from a proposed development of four terraced houses. With support from the city council at a local inquiry held by an inspector, they argued that it would be totally out of character with the current appearance of the site and the whole Arcadian-style backdrop to the cathedral and city would be ruined. The town clerk, Mr D.B. Martin Jones gave an explanation for the city council's refusal to grant permission before the architect of the proposed scheme, Mr Gazzard, asserted that there was an urgent demand for 'economically decent houses particularly in Government-assisted areas.' It was his view that they would not disfigure the view from the cathedral and a landscaping screen of trees would blend the houses into the landscape. Local residents also put forward their views that it would be out of keeping with the area and would increase traffic problems. The inspector, Mrs Christine Mills, then left the meeting to visit the site on Farnley Hey Road. Ultimately, the residents were successful and the terraces were not constructed. (*Durham Advertiser,* 1968–2000)

— January 27th —

1902: A committee meeting at Durham Choristers' School on this day prepared a number of recommendations that were approved by the chapter on February 1st. Arrangements by which choristers were accepted as boarders were clearly defined and it was suggested that fees should be paid half-yearly in advance with help from the Barrington Fund for the sons of clergy with livings in Durham and Northumberland. A list of chargeable extras was to be compiled but these were not to include surplices, sheets or towels. Another matter that received attention was to do with remuneration to be made to a matron, regardless of whether she was the headmaster's wife and it was felt that the selection of choristers should be left to a group composed of the dean, Canon Kynaston, the precentor, the organist and the headteacher. Entries in the Act Book for 1902 to 1904 indicate that a whole series of decisions remained in the hands of the chapter. These included purchasing new desks for the small classroom, providing lockers and a table for boarding pupils, purchasing four large maps, a blackboard and an easel, and filling in a saw pit in the joiners' yard to provide a playground. (Crosby, Brian, *Come on Choristers! A History of the Chorister School, Durham*, Durham: B. Crosby, 1999)

～ January 28th ～

1658: Durham diarist Jacob Bee married Elizabeth Rabbett at St Margaret's church in the Crossgate district of the city on this day. One of only two Grade I listed parish churches in Durham, it dates from the twelfth century and retains much of this original stonework in the interior. (www.stjam.f9.co.uk)

2012: On this date chinese dancers welcomed the Year of the Dragon during celebrations at Durham that also included the annual good luck lettuce catch in the city's marketplace. During this curious episode Durham's deputy mayor, John Wilkinson, caught a lettuce thrown by a lion to ensure good luck for the city over the next year. Colin Wilkes, a member of Durham City Forum which organises the annual event, commented: 'The Chinese New Year lion dance has become one of the highlights of the city calendar and we are very grateful to Ocean's Apart Kung Fu Club for livening up the streets with their colourful, energetic display.' Durham University's Oriental Museum celebrated the New Year with dragon-themed craft activities until the Chinese Lantern Festival (on February 6th) which brought an official end to festivities. Similar festive events took place in Newcastle and Sunderland. (*The Northern Echo*, Darlington, 1870–)

~ January 29th ~

1851: Durham town hall was formally opened on this day when celebrations included a civic banquet. Design work was prepared by P.C. Hardwick of London and according to Nikolaus Pevsner's *Buildings of England*: 'For a Victorian civic building [it is] nicely humble.' Many of its features relate to a medieval hall and these include a hammer-beam oak roof, stained glass windows and painted panels portraying important local events and personalities, and a glass-ceilinged Lantern Room. The Crush Hall, close to the entrance, has items associated with Count Borulawski who was 39in high and died in 1837 aged 98.

During 1555 Bishop Tunstall had ordered construction of a town hall on the west side of the marketplace. This building was extensively rebuilt in 1665 on the orders of Bishop Cosin and further alterations were made in 1752 and 1754 before it was decided, in 1849, to construct a new building. (Clack, P.A.J., *The Book of Durham City*, Buckingham: Barracuda, 1985)

1871: A chapel of ease to St Cuthbert's church was opened at a cost of about £800 in the Framwellgate Moor area of Durham. Constructed in stone with nave, chancel, north porch and bell turret in the Early English style it was set in three quarters of an acre of ground. (Whellan, Francis, *History, Topography, and Directory of the County Palatine of Durham Comprising a General Survey of the County and a History of the City and Diocese of Durham ...*, London: Ballantyne, Hanson and Co., 1894)

— January 30th —

1565: On this day Bishop Pilkington granted a charter which decreed that the City of Durham should be joined with Framwellgate and that government would be vested in an alderman and twenty-four assistant burgesses. They were empowered to publish laws, statutes and ordinances 'for the common benefit'. Before 1565, power was in the hands of a bailiff appointed by the bishop and the charter of 1565 was replaced by a more extensive arrangement issued by Bishop Matthew in 1602. (Whellan, Francis, *History, Topography, and Directory of the County Palatine of Durham Comprising a General Survey of the County and a History of the City and Diocese of Durham...,* London: Ballantyne, Hanson and Co., 1894)

1817: Sir Walter Scott's final long verse narrative *Harold the Dauntless* was published anonymously on this day, in order to determine whether critics and the reading public could detect his style. It drew on Scott's interest in the Viking legends of the Berserkers and he was also said to have been inspired by the view of Durham Cathedral from South Street. A stone tablet on Prebends Bridge is inscribed with the following lines from the poem:

> Grey towers of Durham
> Yet well I love thy mixed and massive piles
> Half church of God, half castle 'gainst the Scot
> And long to roam these venerable aisles
> With records stored of deeds long since forgot.

(www.walterscott.lib.ed.ac.uk/works/poetry/harold.html)

~ January 31st ~

1069: In the early hours of this morning a mob of local people smashed down the gates of Durham and rampaged through the streets to attack Norman troops who had seized the city the previous day. Bodies of Norman soldiers were said to have been scattered along the narrow streets and a number of the occupying force, including their leader Earl Robert Cumin, rushed for a place of refuge in the bishop's palace. The pursuing mob promptly set fire to the timber work of the palace and in the ensuing blaze Cumin and all but two of his troops were killed. As the fire grew in intensity flames threatened the western tower of Durham's stone minster church but local folk are said to have fallen to their knees in prayer. Miraculously the wind changed direction and flames were diverted away from the minster tower. (www.englandsnortheast.co.uk)

2012: On this day restaurants, bars, hotels, cafés and bed and breakfast venues received their 'Taste Durham' quality prizes in the fourth annual awards ceremony held at the Royal County Marriott Hotel in Old Elvet, Durham City. The awards were distributed after assessors from 'Quality in Tourism', acting on behalf of 'Visit England', inspected the businesses. (*The Northern Echo*, Darlington, 1870–)

— February 1st —

1677: On this day it is recorded that:

> At a meeting of the company of drapers and taylors within the citty
> of Durham, It is unanimously agreed by all the freemen of the sayd
> company then present (being 58 in number), that it will be to the
> prejudice, damage and ruin of this citty and corporacon (as they for
> many apparent reasons conceive), if Stockton should be incorporated,
> and therefore the wardens are desired to signify the sence of this
> company to Mr Mayor accordingly, and this corporacon are resolved
> to joyne with the rest of the trades within the city of Durham in
> petitioning the lord Bpp. and in writing to both parliament men
> for the county palatyne of Durham, to prevent the granting of a
> charter, or procuring an act of parliament for incorporating the town
> of Stockton.

Stockton being a town corporate by prescription, it does not appear
what circumstances had given rise to the fears of the good citizens
of Durham. (Richmond, Thomas, *The Local Records of Stockton and
the Neighbourhood; or, A Register of Memorable Events, Chronologically
Arranged, Which Have Occurred in and near Stockton Ward and the North-
Eastern parts of Cleveland*, Stockton: William Robinson, 1868)

2013: On this day an exhibition by artist Paul Belcher entitled
Mortal Engines opened in the Undercroft Restaurant at Durham
Cathedral. The Undercroft Restaurant and adjacent shop
had been opened in November 2012 by Dame Tanni Grey
Thompson. (*Evening Chronicle*, Newcastle upon Tyne, 1885–)

— FEBRUARY 2ND —

1402: Peter Dryng, a local mason, signed a contract on this day to rebuild the walls of the monastic dorter at Durham Cathedral. His terms were almost identical to those of John Middleton who had begun work on September 21st 1398 but then failed to complete his contract with only the southern part of the dormitory complete. Both Middleton and then Dryng were responsible for quarrying, transporting and preparing materials as well as providing scaffolding and tools but did not employ the masons who constructed walls. Work was to be completed by the end of October 1404 and entries in the accounts indicate that this was achieved although Dryng died several months before it was actually finished. (Snape, M.G., 'Documentary evidence for building of Durham Cathedral and its Monastic Buildings' in British Archaeological Association, *Medieval Art and Architecture at Durham Cathedral*, London: BAA, 1980)

1449: On this day Prior Neville licensed the Prior and Convent of Durham to demolish the chapel that served the hospital of St Mary Magdalene and build a new one. The hospital had been completed on land donated by John de Hambledon, at an area known as Southcroft, on the north side of Gilesgate but unfortunately the ground was unstable and by 1448 it was in a ruinous state. (Clack, P.A.J., *The Book of Durham City*, Buckingham: Barracuda, 1985)

— February 3rd —

1646: King Charles I was brought to Durham with an escort of Scottish commissioners on this day. There seems to have been some fear of an attempted rescue, for the Scots wrote to the Earl of Manchester: 'The King came this day from Newcastle to Durham, where he arrived about two o'clock in the afternoon, and the reason we take no long journies is to avoid such inconveniences as might befall us in travelling late in the evening.'

This situation was in stark contrast to an earlier visit to the city in 1633 when he was received by Sir William Belasyse, high-sheriff, and a number of gentlemen of the county. The king visited the cathedral before moving on to the castle where a canopy of state was carried over him by prebendaries. The following Sunday morning the monarch heard a sermon from the bishop at the cathedral along with a congregation made up of nobles, clergy and a choir. After the service Charles I dined at the deanery as a guest of the bishop and during proceedings a valuable cope, property of the church, was presented to the king. (Whellan, Francis, *History, Topography, and Directory of the County Palatine of Durham Comprising a General Survey of the County and a History of the City and Diocese of Durham ... ,* London: Ballantyne, Hanson and Co., 1894)

~ February 4th ~

1594: John Speed (alias Spence) an English Roman Catholic layman was executed at Durham on this day. He had been found guilty of assisting a priest, John Boste, by escorting him from one Catholic house to another. Any sort of assistance to priests had become a capital offence under the Supremacy of the Realm Act of 1585. Eyewitness accounts state that he died 'with constancy, despising the proffers that were made to him to bring him to conform'. Another person found guilty of the same offence was Grace Claxton, wife of William Claxton, of the Waterhouse in the parish of Brancepeth where Boste had been detained. She was reprieved when found to be pregnant.

Speed was one of a group of four known as the 'Durham Martyrs of 1594' which also included John Boste, a priest, who was hanged, drawn and quartered on July 24th; George Swallowell, a convert clergyman, executed at Darlington on July 26th and John Ingram, a priest who was hung, drawn and quartered on July 26th at Gateshead. All four were beatified by Pope Pius XI among the eighty-five martyrs of England and Wales in 1929. John Speed's Feast day is February 4th. (supremacyandsurvival.blogspot.co.uk)

∼ February 5th ∼

1136: On this day King Stephen arrived in Durham to meet David I, King of Scotland during a turbulent episode following the death of Henry I. Stephen had claimed the throne despite Henry's daughter Matilda being the designated heir. She was supported by her husband, Geoffrey Plantagenet, Count of Anjou, and her illegitimate half-brother, Robert of Gloucester, while her maternal uncle, King David I, journeyed south across the border to lend further weight to her claim. On his way to Durham the Scottish chieftain captured Carlisle, Wark, Norham and Newcastle-upon-Tyne but Stephen had hurried northwards with a large force of mercenaries from Flanders and David was forced to parley. When negotiations were completed David was granted Carlisle and Doncaster while Wark, Alnwick, Norham and Newcastle were returned. Inevitably, perhaps, this settlement caused outrage among some members of Stephen's court. These included Ranulf de Gernon, Earl of Chester who was aggrieved at the loss of lands in Cumberland that formerly belonged to his father. In the second Treaty of Durham that was drawn up in 1139 Stephen granted the Earldom of Northumbria to King David's son, Henry. (www.cheshirenow.co.uk/norman_earls_chester.html)

~ February 6th ~

2012: On this day history was made when an ancient order of freemen welcomed its first female members in 700 years. The City of Durham freemen, an all-male organisation since its foundation in the fourteenth century, admitted seventeen women in a ceremony at Durham Town Hall along with two male freemen. Among the women were four sisters and two of their daughters and they joined about 150 Durham freemen who had been admitted either through having served an apprenticeship in Durham or by being related to a freeman. Less than two years earlier the city's freemen had supported proposals to amend admissions criteria to allow equal rights to women. A legal complication delayed progress but during summer 2011 the government approved this change. (*The Northern Echo*, Darlington, 1870–)

2012: An exhibition entitled The Outrageously Modern opened at Durham University's Wolfson Gallery in the Palace Green Library on this date. Items explored magazine culture from the late nineteenth century which launched the careers of writers such as Arthur Conan Doyle and Oscar Wilde. The title was drawn from published Holbrook Jackson's description of the 1880s magazine *The Yellow Book* as being linked 'with all that was bizarre and queer in art and life, with all that was outrageously modern'. (*The Northern Echo*, Darlington, 1870–)

~ February 7th ~

1902: On this day a drill hall that served as the headquarters of 8 Battalion Durham Light Infantry was opened on a site at the bottom of Gilesgate Bank. It was built by Jasper Kell and Sons of North Road, Durham and was demolished during the 1960s. (Richardson, Michael, *Durham: Cathedral City*, Thrupp: Sutton, 1997)

2012: An exhibition celebrating Charles Dickens' links with County Durham opened at Durham County Record Office to coincide with the 200th anniversary of his birth on February 7th. The display of documents, photographs and press cuttings highlighted Dickens' connections with Barnard Castle of Teesdale which he visited in February 1838 while researching *Nicholas Nickleby*. Charles Dickens was accompanied on his fact-finding tour by illustrator Hablot K. Browne, and they claimed to be finding a suitable school for a widowed friend's sons.

Many people held the opinion that the character of Wackford Squeers in *Nicholas Nickleby* was inspired by William Shaw, who was headmaster of Bowes Academy during the 1830s, and that school itself formed the basis for Dickens' portrayal of Dotheboys Hall. Following publication of the book and its exposure of conditions in the 'Yorkshire Schools' most of them were closed down, including Bowes Academy. (www.bbc.co.uk/news/uk-england-tees-16599182)

~ FEBRUARY 8TH ~

1871: On this day it was recorded that:

Considerable excitement was occasioned in Durham by the falling of a portion of the castle. The point at which the accident occurred is situated about thirty yards up the bank from Framwellgate Bridge, and had the appearance of a buttress, curved outwards at the bottom for a few feet, and then rising straight upwards to a height of forty feet. Investigation proved it was no part of the original buildings of the castle, but merely a narrow tower probably erected for some unknown purpose about 150 years ago. About four o'clock this morning some people crossing Framwellgate Bridge heard the sound of masonry rolling down the bank, and this sound was repeated about an hour afterwards. The grand fall did not take place until ten minutes to six o'clock, however, when the whole structure of the tower slid down the side of the bank, severing itself from the general buildings of the castle as cleanly as if it had not been near that ancient structure … An examination of the fallen rubbish showed the masonry of which the tower had been composed to have been of a very decayed nature.

(Fordyce, T. (ed.), *Local Records; or, Historical Register of Remarkable Events which have Occurred in Northumberland and Durham … 1833 to [1875], Being a Continuation of the Work Published by … Mr. John Sykes*, Newcastle upon Tyne: T. Fordyce, 1867–1876)

– February 9th –

1950: On this day a newspaper report gave details of a dramatic episode some four months earlier during which:

> The quiet dawn of a Sunday morning was disturbed at Sherburn Road Ends when a pony race started there on 15 October last year. A crowd of about three hundred who had gathered to see the ponies exercise shouted to their favourites, compared opinions and revved up their cars, vans and lorries to follow the race to its end at Houghton.
>
> The ponies and traps set off and in their wake were eighty or more vehicles, jostling along the road three abreast, jockeying for positions near the front as their drivers and passengers shouted encouragement to their favourites all along the road.
>
> For twenty minutes, along six miles, the noise and disorder continued until the winner ran into Westwick's Corner at Houghton followed by the ensuing sportsmen.
>
> This story unfolded at Durham Magistrates Court when William Schofield of Durham and James Turnbull of Newcastle were fined £2 each and £5 8s 7d costs for obstruction of the highway. A charge of unlawfully playing a game on the highway was dismissed.

(*Durham Chronicle*, 1820–1984)

~ February 10th ~

1900: A gymnasium and laboratory were opened at Durham School by Bishop Westcott. Design work had been completed by W.S. Hicks and the buildings were constructed by Graydon and Sons of North Road, Durham during 1899. Durham School had been founded by Bishop Langley in 1414 and refounded in 1541 by King Henry VIII. During 1844 the school moved from its base on Palace Green to its current location. (Richardson, Michael, *Durham: Cathedral City*, Thrupp: Sutton, 1997)

1924: On this day Max Ferguson was born in Durham before his family moved to London and then Ontario, Canada, where he graduated from the University of Western Ontario with a BA degree in English and French. His career as a highly popular Canadian radio personality and satirist got underway during 1946 when he joined the Canada Broadcasting Corporation (CBC) as a staff announcer at a local station in Halifax, Nova Scotia. As the host of a cowboy music show named *After Breakfast Breakdown* he adopted the voice of an elderly ranch hand and featured a range of raucous and bizarre characters. From 1954 to 1961 he hosted television shows before returning to radio with *The Max Ferguson Show* which featured ethnic music and topical news skits. By the time of his retirement in 1998 he had numerous awards including one for his autobiography, *And Now … Here's Max*. (en.wikipedia.org/wiki/Max_Ferguson)

~ February 11th ~

2013: Mike Barton was confirmed as Durham's new chief constable by the force's Police and Crime Panel (PCP) on this day. He had been temporary chief constable since Jon Stoddart retired in October and was recommended for the long-term appointment by police commissioner Ron Hogg a month earlier. During questioning by PCP members, Mr Barton claimed that austerity cuts meant that chief officers had to challenge the way policing had been carried out in the past. He explained that it was not a cliché to talk of policing in the style of *Dixon of Dock Green*, a highly popular BBC police series that ran from 1955 to 1976 and added: 'It means people want that traditional, safe, known name in every community.' Reinforcing this approach, he said giving power to the people through community policing and greater use of restorative justice would be key.

Mr Barton, aged 56, spent twenty-eight years with Lancashire police force before becoming Durham's assistant chief constable in 2008 and then deputy chief constable in 2009. In these posts he led the force's battle against organised crime with an 'Al Capone style' approach of pursuing criminals for any offence possible. (*The Northern Echo*, Darlington, 1870–)

─ February 12th ─

1927: On this day the large hall at the Barracks, Gilesgate, Durham was 'gaily decorated' for a large gathering of civil and military representatives at the annual dinner of 'B' (Durham) Squadron of Northumberland Hussars Yeomanry: 'There was a large gathering of non-coms and troopers, the company numbering 150. Whilst an excellent repast was being served, Misses Studdy being the caterers, an up-to-date musical programme was provided by Telford's Orchestra from Chester-le-Street.'

Twenty trophies won by the Squadron were on view in a conspicuous place. These included the High Sheriff's Shield, BS Guns Shield, the Yeomanry Aggregate Cup, the Lambton Cup (won by Sergeant Halliday), the Straker Cup (won by S.M. Lee), the cup for the best troop (South Shields) and several other cups won by S.M. Crees.

Following the loyal toast, Squadron Sergeant Major Lee gave 'Our officers' in a brief speech. The chairman, responding, remarked that at their first dinner they had a few friends; that year the number had already increased, and he was going to ask Colonel Bowes to build them a new drill hall for their next gathering. They had reason to be proud of the representative character of that gathering. (*Durham Chronicle*, 1820–1984)

~ February 13th ~

1834: Robert Surtees, a noted historian and writer on aspects of County Durham's heritage, died in Mainsforth on this day. Born in Durham during 1779 he was educated at Kepier School, Houghton-le-Spring and Christ Church, Oxford where he studied law. Moving home to Mainsforth Hall in 1802, he did not pursue a career as a lawyer but devoted resources to collecting materials for his major work *The History of Durham*. In 1807 Robert Surtees married Anne Robinson of Herrington and they entertained guests such as Sir Walter Scott.

During 1816 the first volume of *The History and Antiquities of the County Palatine of Durham* was published and two more volumes appeared later with a final volume published posthumously in 1840. Surtees' work did not include Weardale, Teesdale, Brancepeth or Durham Castle and Cathedral and these aspects were covered by James Raine, the elder, in *The History and Antiquities of North Durham*, 1852.

Robert Surtees was buried in Bishop Middleham Churchyard. A monument was later erected in the church and the Surtees Society was established to continue his work. (en.wikipedia.org/wiki/Robert_Surtees_(antiquarian))

2012: More than 350 people slept overnight in Durham Cathedral to raise in excess of £7,000 for a homelessness charity, 'Moving on Durham'. (*The Northern Echo*, Darlington, 1870–)

— February 14th —

2012: On this day Durham-born Flight Lieutenant Mike Anderson was awarded the Distinguished Flying Cross by the Prince of Wales at Buckingham Palace. It was the second honour to be bestowed on Flt Lt Anderson within two months, following the award of Most Outstanding Airman prize at the Sun Military Awards in December 2011 and related to an incident on January 24th of the same year in Afghanistan. The 27 Squadron Chinook pilot, a former pupil of Belmont School near Durham City, rescued five wounded Afghan children while under fire from Taliban forces in Helmand province. The episode began when four helicopters were rushed to Gereshk but the Allied forces had been lured into an ambush. A gun battle broke out but Flt Lt Anderson managed to land his Chinook during a break in firing and rescued four children. Another youngster was evacuated by supporting US forces but a sixth child had already died. Since joining the RAF in 2003, Mike Anderson had served seven times in Afghanistan, including a tour of duty between September and December 2011. In the early weeks of 2012 he served as a search and rescue pilot at Anglesey off the north-west coast of Wales. (*The Northern Echo*, Darlington, 1870–)

— February 15th —

1908: It was decided today at a meeting that the prospectus for Durham Choristers' School should include an application form, which involved the addition of a third side. Other pages of the prospectus provide an interesting insight into the organisation and day-to-day operation of the school as well as changes from year to year. Further amendments were made in 1911 and 1912 but the number of boys in school still totalled twenty and the routine (timetable) for 1912 indicated that the amount of time devoted to music was at least equal to that spent on schoolwork. Holidays consisted of four weeks in the summer, thirteen days after Easter and another thirteen days starting on the Sunday after Epiphany (January 6th). The equivalent of Speech Day took place in the Chapter House shortly before this winter break. A section in the prospectus under 'Extras' summarised a range of financial and domestic arrangements including 'tuck' which covered expenses incurred by the headmaster, on behalf of the boys, such as clothing and tailor's repairs, boot mending, hair cutting and pocket money. Parents paid for this expenditure on a half-yearly basis. (Crosby, Brian, *Come on Choristers! A History of the Chorister School, Durham*, Durham: B. Crosby, 1999)

— FEBRUARY 16TH —

1951: Under the heading 'A Newsprint Bottleneck' the local newspaper, *Durham Chronicle* reported:

A further five per cent cut in newsprint has been decreed. Two alternatives were open to us – either to reduce the size of our newspapers or to retain the present size and severely cut circulation. We have decided against a further cut in circulation so that our readers will not again be disappointed.

We propose to proceed on the basis of three successive weekly issues at eight pages and one of ten pages until the newsprint position is restored. By doing that all our readers are assured of a copy of this newspaper. We would be glad, however, if readers would place a firm order with their newsagents as the government's limitations on the use of paper prevents us from making the customary allowance for casual sales.

By reducing the size of the newspaper we lose heavily financially because of the exclusion of many advertisements and we therefore ask for the forbearance of all in this difficult period.

(*Durham Chronicle*, 1820–1984)

2013: West End star Ruthie Henshall appeared at Durham's Gala Theatre during her first regional tour. During the show she discussed her appearances on Broadway where she starred in *Les Miserables* and performed a wide range of songs. (www.galadurham.co.uk)

– February 17th –

1753: On this day a violent flood swept away one of the piers of Shincliffe Bridge which resulted in the collapse of the two northern arches. It was repaired during the summer months of 1753 but as the volume of traffic increased it was found to be too narrow and in need of repair. Unstable foundations built on shifting gravel and sand ruled out widening the existing structure and work began on a new bridge during January 1824. It opened in September 1826 with a more direct route into Shincliffe village and was completed at a total cost of £7,056.

Until about AD 1200 there was probably a ford across the River Wear at Shincliffe and the first mention of a bridge appears when land in Upper Elvet was given for its support. It was repaired by the Durham Priory in 1361–62 and John Ogle left 100 silver shillings for its maintenance in March 1372–73. After an inquiry into the bridge's condition and revenues, Bishop Skirlaw (1385–1405) paid, at his own expense, for 'a notable bridge of three arches' and it was this structure that was damaged in 1753. (www.durhamintime.org.uk)

⚊ February 18th ⚊

1512: On this day a fourteen-man jury sitting at Durham Quarter Sessions were told that yeoman Robert Wynke, late of Darlington, Durham, had on January 3rd 1512 stolen a chalice worth 40*s* from Thomas Paull and Henry Lasenby. Robert May and Nicholas Robynson, churchwardens of Marton-in-Cleveland and John Thomson of Darlington, berker, alias Jenkyn Thomson of Darlington, yeoman and William Stapilton of the same, yeoman, came before the jury. Thomson and Stapilton, knowing that Robert Wynke had stolen the chalice, arrested Wynke red handed: and the same day the said John and William allowed Wynke to escape after his arrest and took the chalice to their own use, thereby receiving, aiding and abetting against the bishop's peace.(Fraser, C.M. (ed.), *Durham Quarter Sessions Rolls 1471–1625*, Durham: Surtees Society, 1991)

⚊⚊

1936: The British Union of Fascists, with headquarters at Claypath, Durham arranged a meeting on this day in Durham town hall where Sir Oswald Moseley, leader of the Blackshirts, addressed a large audience. Many people could not get into the building to hear his speech which included comments on the growth of the movement from no branches in 1932 to 500 in February 1936. (The headquarters building, located opposite the United Reform church, became a newsagent's shop.) (Fraser, C.M. (ed.), *Durham Quarter Sessions Rolls 1471–1625*, Durham: Surtees Society, 1991)

— FEBRUARY 19TH —

1737: On this day it was reported that two prisoners were missing from Durham Jail in Saddler Street. The prisoners, John Dodsworth and John Penman had escaped from the jail at about 10 p.m. the previous night after viciously knocking down the under-keeper of the prison. (Simpson, David, *Durham Millennium: A Thousand Years of Durham City*, Darlington: Northern Echo, 1995)

———

2012: Twenty-two couples gathered at St Giles church, Durham to renew their wedding vows in a ceremony conducted by the Bishop of Jarrow on this date. The couples included the Mayor of Durham, Councillor Les Thomson and his wife Lucille, who were married in Bannockburn, Scotland, in 1967 and Dave and Chris Fletcher from the Gilesgate area of Durham, who married at St Giles church in May 2011. After their wedding Mrs Fletcher developed an allergic reaction to the nickel in her white-gold wedding ring and the couple decided on a ceremony to renew their vows with a replacement 18-carat gold ring. Just before that service Mr Fletcher injured his thumb, whilst working at home, and spent the day in an accident and emergency unit but, happily, the attempt to renew their vows went ahead without a problem. (*The Northern Echo*, Darlington, 1870–)

~ February 20th ~

1886: The New Bede Model School opened on this day at the western end of the Bede College site at Bede Bank in the Gilesgate area of Durham. After some forty-seven years of operations the Model School closed its doors for the last time at the end of the summer term in July 1933. The building was renamed 'Carter House' after Miss Phyllis Carter and her father in 1985. (Richardson, Michael, *Durham: The Photographic Collection*, Stroud: Sutton, 2002)

———

2013: On this day new lights were switched on at Durham Cathedral and Castle by Linda Marshall, chairwoman of Durham County Council, during an evening of celebration at the World Heritage Site. The lights were designed by Stainton Lighting Design Services of Thornaby and installed by A.K. Lighting and Signs of West Auckland, County Durham. They replaced a system installed during the 1970s and totalled about 130 lights at the cathedral and 110 at the castle. The replacement lights are low-energy emitting diode lights which are expected to reduce energy consumption by as much as 80 per cent and allow more flexible control. A sound sculpture – *Gabrieli à 2(2)*, a contemporary interpretation of a seventeenth-century sonata written for St Mark's Basilica in Venice was also created inside the cathedral. (*The Northern Echo*, Darlington, 1870–)

— FEBRUARY 21ST —

1836: William Van Mildert, Bishop of Durham, died at Auckland Castle on this day. He was born at Southwark in November 1765 and he studied at the Merchant Taylor's School and Queen's College, Oxford (1784–90).

Following ordination in 1789 he became curate of Witham, Essex and, after lecturing researching and writing on theological topics, he became Regius Professor of Divinity at Oxford in 1819. Appointment as Bishop of Durham in 1826 saw Van Mildert cooperating with Charles Thorp, Archdeacon of Durham, to establish a university at Durham. The Durham University Bill was passed in July 1832 and the first students were admitted in October 1833. Shortly after his death the bishopric lost its palatine status and remaining secular powers and this led to Van Mildert often being credited with the title, 'last of the prince bishops'. (www.dur.ac.uk/library)

2012: On this day a £6.7 million sports complex which extended existing facilities at Durham University's Maiden Castle site was opened by Sports and Olympics Minister, Hugh Robertson. In addition to an extended sports hall which could be used for indoor cricket, it included three dedicated physiotherapy treatment rooms and a multi-purpose dance studio. Sport England contributed £500,000 to the cost of the complex which was available for use by students and members of the public. (*The Northern Echo,* Darlington, 1870–)

— FEBRUARY 22ND —

1936: On this day Lord Londonderry spoke to members of the Conservative League at the Three Tuns Hotel, New Elvet in Durham. He gave details of his recent visit to Germany which included a two hour conversation with Adolf Hitler at a meeting that was also attended by Hess and Ribbentrop. Before this he had met with the German Air Minister, Hermann Göring, and accompanied him on a tour of German aircraft factories and Luftwaffe training facilities. Accompanied by his wife and youngest daughter, the Londonderrys received 'lavish' treatment wherever they went, including attendance at the Winter Olympics as guests of state and social engagements with pro-Nazi German aristocrats, including the Prince of Hesse and the Duke and Duchess of Brunswick. There is a body of opinion that claims the British aristocracy, as a class, was responsible in some way for the policy of appeasement. (Fleming, N.C., *Aristocratic appeasement: Lord Londonderry, Nazi Germany and the promotion of Anglo-German misunderstanding*, Cardiff: Cardiff University, 2007)

1947: The Miner's Memorial at Durham Cathedral was unveiled on this day. Fashioned from Spanish mahogany to designs prepared by Donald McIntyre, it was originally part of a fireplace in Ramside Hall, Carrville on the east side of Durham City and was given by the Pemberton family. (Richardson, Michael, *Durham: The Photographic Collection*, Stroud: Sutton, 2002)

‒ February 23rd ‒

1954: On this day Lady Violet Bonham Carter was welcomed to Durham by the city's mayor and mayoress, Councillor J.R. Kingston and Mrs Kingston, at the Dunelm Hotel. Lady Bonham Carter was a guest speaker at a meeting of the Durham Ladies Lecture Club. (Richardson, Michael, *Memory Lane: Durham City*, Derby: Breedon, 2000)

—

2012: A fire swept through a small sandstone building close to Prebends Bridge on February 23rd. Prebends Cottage is thought to date from about 1771 and was previously a gatehouse for Prebends Bridge which controlled access to the cathedral and castle on Durham's peninsula. At one time it was known as Clarney's Cottage after an early twentieth-century occupant but it is currently owned and rented out by Durham Cathedral and forms a popular setting for photographs of newlyweds.

The fire which was started accidentally in the cottage's bedroom was spotted by three university students who alerted the fire brigade and assisted the only person in the cottage, a man aged about 50, uphill to the public road. Firemen who arrived on the scene went into the burning building to rescue three caged pet rats and although personal possessions, including many musical instruments, were destroyed in the blaze the structure escaped serious damage. (*The Northern Echo*, Darlington, 1870–)

— FEBRUARY 24TH —

1911: A fatal boating accident occurred on this day at a point in the River Wear about 50 yards upstream from the bandstand. Waves were high, but not considered to be dangerous; a strong west wind blew directly upstream as St Chad's graduate crew left their boathouse at about 2.20 p.m. During the journey upstream nothing untoward happened and little, if any, water was shipped. The crew turned just below Ash Tree but they were soon in difficulties. It was unclear whether the cox gave the order to paddle or whether the crew started without instruction, but before ten strokes had been taken a large volume of water lapped into the boat and it was soon submerged in the centre of the river. Crew members, with assistance from other crews, swam and scrambled to the riverbank and it was assumed that the cox, Parsons, had safely reached the racecourse bank. Around 10 minutes had elapsed before it was determined that he was missing and it was more than 2 hours later before his body was recovered. A funeral service was held in the cathedral and he was buried in Elvet Hill churchyard. (Richardson, Michael, *Durham: Cathedral City*, Thrupp: Sutton, 1997)

~ February 25th ~

2012: On this day an exhibition opened at the DLI Museum and Durham Art Gallery which featured the work of one of the most influential artists to come from the north-east region. John Cecil Stephenson was born and brought up in Bishop Auckland, County Durham, and studied at Darlington Technical College before gaining a scholarship to Leeds School of Art. He also attended the Royal College of Art, in London before embarking on a career that saw him widely regarded as one of the leading names in British abstract art. The exhibition was entitled *Pioneer of Abstraction* and showed the route from his early figurative paintings to the geometric images of the thirties. It was composed of forty pieces of work, both painting and drawings, loaned from private and public collections including the British Museum, the Victoria and Albert Museum, the National Galleries of Scotland and the Government Art Collection, as well as the Stephenson family's own collection. (*The Northern Echo*, Darlington, 1870–)

———

2012: On this day crowds gathered on Elvet Bridge in Durham City to see 5,000 plastic ducks tipped into the River Wear at the start of an annual race organised by Durham University Charities Kommittee (DUCK). Several thousand pounds was raised for Water Aid during the race which ended at Kingsgate Bridge. (*The Northern Echo*, Darlington, 1870–)

~ February 26th ~

1966: On this day Private Thomas Griffiths, aged 20, from Shotton Colliery, County Durham died in action while serving with 2nd Platoon of the 1st Battalion of the Durham Light Infantry in Borneo. He was the last DLI soldier to die in action as the 1st Battalion fought against forces from Indonesia in the forests and jungles of Borneo between 1965 and 1966. Their role was to secure 100 miles of border against incursions by Indonesian forces in an area of jungle where a lack of roads meant all supplies had to be airdropped or brought by helicopter. Military operations in Borneo were so controversial that details of the campaign were not disclosed to the House of Commons. It was the regiment's last campaign before it was dissolved in 1968 and amalgamated with others to form the Light Infantry.

The last gallantry award made to a member of the DLI was the Military Cross presented to Major John Arnot for his actions on the same day that Private Griffiths was killed by shrapnel during a mortar bombardment. During the early weeks of 2013 an appeal was launched in support of a new DLI memorial in Durham City. (www.thenorthernecho.co.uk/news/campaigns/dlimemorial)

~ February 27th ~

1830: On this day in a trial at Durham Assizes, William Day, aged 24 and a citizen of Durham, was convicted of bigamy:

> ... with very clear and satisfactory evidence. He was married to a young woman named Ann Greagg, by banns, on the 1st August 1826 at the church of St Luke, Old Street, Shoreditch, London; and on the 15th October last had married a young woman named Jane Coulter (whom he had induced to leave the service of Mr Alderman Lucas to espouce him) at the church of St Sepulchre. The existence of Ann Greagg, and the apprehension of the prisoner in this county, having been proved, the jury without hesitation found him guilty. It was intimated, after the verdict was given, that the prisoner had a third wife living. Mr Justice Parker, after expiating the enormity of the prisoner's conduct, sentenced him to the fullest extent allowed by law ... transportation for seven years. Considerable applause followed the passing of the sentence, which was instantly checked, and strongly censured by the judge.

(www.genuki.bpears.org.uk/Crime1.html)

2013: A press announcement on this day stated that Durham University Museum of Archaeology would leave the Old Fulling Mill on the banks of the River Wear for new exhibition facilities in Palace Green Library early in 2014. An exhibition entitled *Out of the Attic* provided details of the building's history and information about the move to the new premises. (*The Northern Echo*, Darlington, 1870–)

‒ February 28th ‒

1831: On this day Thomas Clarke, aged 19, was executed at Durham after being found guilty of murder at the Spring Assizes. On the evening of August 8th 1830 a 17-year-old servant girl had been brutally murdered at Hallgarth Mill, some 3 miles from Durham. The mill owners, Mr and Mrs Oliver were away visiting friends and had left Mary Ann in the company of fellow servant, Thomas Clarke. The alarm was raised when Clarke arrived at a property in Sherburn in a distressed state. He claimed that a group of six Irishmen had arrived at the mill to ask permission to light their pipes, and had then attacked Mary Ann and then himself. Villagers made their way to the mill where they found Mary Ann's bloodstained body but when police questioned local residents no one had seen or heard any Irishmen in the area. Four men were later arrested at Houghton-le-Spring and questioned about the murder but were able to prove beyond doubt that they had been nowhere near the scene of the crime. Evidence pointed towards Thomas Clarke and his trial for murder began on February 25th 1831. A guilty verdict was returned the following day and a crowd numbering about 15,000 is said to have witnessed his execution. (www.ferryhilllocalhistory.com)

~ February 29th ~

1940: A dramatic chain of events began during the early hours of February 29th 1940 as a lone cyclist, Jesse Smith, made his way home past the Cooperative Store in Wesley Road, Coxhoe, near Durham City. It was a light in the shop window that drew his attention and before it snapped out he caught a fleeting glimpse of a man's face. His first thought was that the premises was being robbed and Smith set off to alert the local policeman, Constable William Ralph Shiell. Within minutes Constable Shiell and a fellow officer, Constable William Stafford, raced to the store where Shiell shone his torch through the front window. He saw nothing but when they made their way to the rear it was immediately obvious that bolts had been removed from the door. While Stafford remained at the back door, Shiell returned to the front where the stillness soon echoed to the sound of breaking glass. Racing around the building to help his colleague, Stafford found that a large plate glass window had been shattered by someone bursting through into the street. He soon spotted figures heading across open ground and then a shot rang out; Shiell lay in the mud with a fatal bullet wound to his stomach. A manhunt began and this tragic episode was concluded on July 11th 1941 when two men were hanged at Durham Jail. (*The Northern Echo*, Darlington, 1870–)

~ March 1st ~

2012: Durham World Heritage Site Visitor Centre won a City of Durham Trust Architectural Award for 2011 on this day. Based in a former nineteenth-century almshouse building at No. 7 Owengate, the project was described as 'a restoration incorporating a new build that brought back vitality and interest to the historic core of the city'. It was praised for the careful refurbishment of the almshouse, which combined old and new elements using simplicity of line and detail. (www.durhamworldheritagesite.com)

2013: On this day Durham-based organisers of an appeal to raise funds for a Durham Light Infantry (DLI) memorial announced that a collection of silverware and cutlery formerly used on the tables of DLI officer's mess was to be auctioned. Items ranged from solid silver punch bowls to meat skewers, posy vases, sets of knives and forks and rose bowls, most items coming from the Third and Fourth Battalion of DLI and 68th Regiment of Foot. Some of the tableware would have been used during campaigns. When the DLI was disbanded in 1968 much of its silver went to Light Infantry Regiments and some went to freedom towns (where military units had been granted the freedom to parade through the town) of the region. (*The Advertiser*, Durham: 2000–)

— March 2nd —

2009: On this day Durham University Chancellor Bill Bryson was made an honorary freeman of Durham. He was proposed by Carol Woods, Deputy Leader of the City Council for his services to arts and tourism, education and his international commitment to, and support of, the City of Durham. Sir Bobby Robson and the sculptor Fenwick Lawson also received this honour at a civic reception in Durham Town Hall and, upon receiving the award, Bill Bryson was fulsome in his praise of the city and its world-class university. He commented, 'The real quality that sets Durham apart in my view, that no other city has in such abundance, is sincere, welcoming, consistent and boundless friendliness. You are really the most wonderful people in the world here. It is that above all else that makes me always glad to be here and very, very proud to be part of this city.' His special day in Durham was almost spoiled by a 'wardrobe malfunction' as he left London wearing trousers and a jacket from different suits but his wife Cynthia retrieved the situation by bringing the correct trousers on a later train. Bill Bryson was the 22nd person and the first American to receive the honour. (www.palatinate.org.uk)

~ MARCH 3RD ~

1195: Hugh de Puiset (or Pudsey), Bishop of Durham, died on this day after holding office for some forty-two years. He was probably born in 1125 and was elected Bishop of Durham in spite of opposition from Henry Murdac, Archbishop of York. He was consecrated on December 20th 1153 by Pope Anastasius II and enthroned at Durham on May 2nd 1154. As Bishop of Durham, Puiset was granted mineral rights in Weardale and it was probably the silver extracted from lead ore in that area that assisted the bishops in setting up their own mint. Well-known for his lavish lifestyle, he was not highly regarded as a scholar although he did serve as a patron to Roger of Hoveden, a medieval chronicler who began writing in about 1169. Hugh de Puiset oversaw completion of a number of building projects including the New Bridge, now named Elvet Bridge in Durham, the rebuilding of Norham Castle and construction of the first bridge over the Tweed at Berwick in conjunction with the King of Scots. Work at Durham Cathedral included the building of the Galilee Chapel and constructing a shrine to contain the bones of Bede and it was on Puiset's orders that a record of revenues and resources was compiled in the Boldon Book of 1183. (Stephens, L. and S. Lee (eds), *Dictionary of National Biography*, London: Smith, Elder and Co., 1885–1900)

‒ MARCH 4TH ‒

1836: During 1831 the Ecclesiastical Commissioners were established in order to investigate and report on the revenues and patronage of the Church of England. Following their first report, issued in March 1835, which deprived the Bishop of Durham of his status as a Prince Palatine and reduced his annual income to £7,000, a second report, produced on March 4th 1836 made major changes to cathedral chapters. It signalled the end of old sinecure prebendaries such as that held by Francis Egerton, the 9th and last Earl of Bridgewater, who had been appointed to the Fourth Stall by his brother in 1780. He lived in Paris until his death in 1829 surrounded by cats and dogs dressed as ladies and gentlemen. In future the Durham Chapter was to consist of a dean and six canons, two of whom had to be professors in the university. All other titles were abolished and instead of holding separate estates each post holder was to be paid a fixed salary. Canons would receive £1,000 each year and the dean twice as much. When a vacancy arose the dean would become warden of the university with an additional annual payment of £1,000. (Stranks, C.J., *This Sumptuous Church: The Story of Durham Cathedral*, London: SPCK, 1993)

~ March 5th ~

2012: On this day local news outlets carried reports of a bright light, lasting about 30 seconds, that had blazed a trail across the north-east sky over the previous weekend. A series of eyewitness reports had been received by Durham police who were able to confirm that there had not been any reports of aircraft in difficulties and a spokeswoman suggested that the sightings related to an asteroid or similar object burning out. Scientists at Kielder Observatory report the sightings as 'a huge fireball' travelling in from north to south across Northumberland and they rated it at magnitude -9. (A brightness of magnitude -6 is required for it to be seen in daylight and, according to the International Meteor Organisation, only one in 12,000 reaches magnitude -8.) Dr David Whitehouse, an author and astronomer, commented that the object sighted was probably about the size of a fist and, in all likelihood, was the debris of a planet that never properly formed. He speculated that it was 'a chunk of rock' that had probably originated from somewhere between Mars and Jupiter and had been in space for millions of years. (*The Northern Echo*, Darlington, 1870–)

– MARCH 6TH –

1860: On this day a meeting of the Special Chapter took place 'to consider Mr Scott's designs for the termination of the Central Tower and it was agreed that the work should be to complete the tower to the same architectural features which it possessed when the cement was placed upon it'. Sir Gilbert Scott had plans for an open crown on flying buttresses supported by great pinnacles, but the chapter restricted him to heightening the pierced battlements and the little square pinnacles surmounting the corner buttresses. (Pocock, Douglas (ed.), *St. Cuthbert and Durham Cathedral: A Celebration*, (Durham: City of Durham Trust, 1995)

———

1940: On this day Durham's riverside ice-skating rink opened on a site close to the River Wear at Freeman's Place. The venture was largely the work of John 'Icy' Smith who had built factories to produce ice for commercial and household purposes in Barnard Castle and Darlington. As demand increased, Smith established a factory on Durham's Framwellgate waterside and the ice rink was constructed on a nearby site with 7 miles of pipework to ensure that the huge pad of ice remained cold. The rink was enclosed within a huge marquee which blew into the river several times before it was totally destroyed in 1944. (www.ihjuk.co.uk/halloffame/jSmith.html)

MARCH 7TH

1938: Sir Paul Douglas Nicholson, Lord Lieutenant of County Durham from 1997 to March 7th 2013, was born on this day at Brancepeth near Durham City. After attending Harrow School he was commissioned during National Service in the Coldstream Guards and then continued his education at Clare College, Cambridge. As a prominent amateur rider during his youth he twice won the Liverpool Foxhunter steeplechase in 1963 and 1965 and later served as President of the Coaching Club (1990–97.) Qualification as a chartered accountant led to Paul Nicholson joining Vaux Breweries in 1965 and between 1976 and 1999 he was chairman of the Vaux Group. Other posts that he held include chairmanship of the Tyne and Wear Development Corporation (1987–98) and the inaugural presidency of the North East Chamber of Commerce in 1995. He was knighted in 1993 for 'Services to Industry and the Public in Northeast England'. (en.wikipedia.org/wiki/Paul_Nicholson_(businessman))

1952: On this day representatives from seventeen northern rowing clubs held a meeting in the Royal County Hotel, Durham and agreed to formally constitute the new Division 7 of Group III of the Amateur Rowing Association. This arrangement represented the first grouping of north-east clubs and later became the Northern Rowing Council. (www.nerowing.com/darctimeline.html)

— MARCH 8TH —

2013: On this day Sue Snowdon replaced Sir Paul Nicholson as Lord Lieutenant of County Durham in a ceremony that saw her become the first female recipient of the post. She is also said to be the thirtieth Lord Lieutenant of County Durham, who are appointed by the Crown to keep the monarchy informed of issues affecting the area, arrange royal visits and promote honours. Mrs Snowdon spent her early working life as a primary school teacher and overcame serious health problems to become a magistrate and one of the founders of a flourishing food festival. After becoming involved in the Butterwick Hospice, based in Bishop Auckland, she became the charity's fundraiser manager and played a leading role in organising the Wear Valley Food Festival which saw attendance figures climb from 6,000 in the first year (2001) to 30,000 in 2012. Mrs Snowdon sees the promotion of County Durham as a priority in her new role and her first official duty as Lord Lieutenant was to deliver a speech for International Women's Day at County Hall in Durham in which she outlined her beliefs for the county. She will serve as Lord Lieutenant until her 75th birthday on April 1st 2026. (*The Northern Echo*, Darlington, 1870–)

— March 9th —

1863: John Gully, prize fighter, horse racer and politician died at Durham on this day. His remarkable life began at Wick, near Bath, where he was born into the family of an innkeeper on August 21st 1783. Soon afterwards his father became a butcher in Bath and John Gully inherited the business after his father's death.

In 1805 the business failed and Gully was imprisoned for debts. Here he was visited by a popular prize fighter, Henry Pearce, and an unofficial contest was arranged between them within the prison walls. This allowed Gully to pay off his debts and another bout against Pearce was staged on October 8th 1805. It lasted twenty-eight rounds and continued for 1 hour and 17 minutes but ended in defeat for Gully. He had more success in 1807 with two victories over Bob Gregson, the Lancashire giant, for two guineas a side.

Following his retirement from boxing in 1808, John Gully became landlord of London's Plough Tavern and ventured large amounts of cash in horse racing. After initial losses he enjoyed considerable financial success and purchased Ackworth Park, near Pontefract. Between 1832 and 1837 Gully was MP for Pontefract and shortly before his death he purchased the Wingate Grange estate and collieries near Durham City. (en.wikipedia.org/wiki/John_Gully)

~ MARCH 10TH ~

1555: Statutes of Durham Cathedral for this date relating to the renewal of the Cathedral Foundation after the Dissolution of the Priory state that: 'There shall be eight poor men to be nourished out of the goods of the church, men oppressed with poverty and distressed by want, or crippled and mutilated in warfare, or worn out with old age or in some other way reduced to weakness and want.' The statutes also indicated that these men should assist the sub-sacrists with the lighting and extinguishing of lights, ringing of the bells and any other duties that the dean required. In recent times the bedesmen have been primarily concerned with looking after the western end of the cathedral and helping vergers in its day-to-day running by preparing for services and providing information for visitors. (Nixon, Philip and Dennis Dunlop, *Exploring Durham History,* Derby: Breedon Books, 1998)

———

1863: A stonework inscription below a headless statue of *Albert the Good* in Wharton Park near Durham railway station explains the stone base and a nearby oak tree were set at this location on March 10th 1863 by William Lloyd Wharton, chairman of the North Eastern Railway Company who lived at nearby Dryburn Hall. It was in commemoration of the marriage of Prince Albert Edward to Princess Alexandra of Denmark. (Woodhouse, Robert, *County Durham: Strange but True*, Stroud: Sutton Publishing, 2004)

– MARCH 11TH –

2002: Durham Clayport Library was officially opened on this day by BBC North East News presenter Carol Malia, county councillor Alan Cox and library manager June Garland as part of a £30 million Millennium City development at the bottom of Claypath. The first group of visitors through the door was made up of twenty of the former South Street library's most frequent users and they were greeted by colourful entertainers specially brought in for the occasion. In addition to making the first selection from a stock of over 18,000 books and an online catalogue of the county's 800,000 stock holdings the guests also received a commemorative certificate of library memorabilia. After the opening ceremony, the Palatinate Ensemble String Quartet provided musical entertainment at the library while St Margaret's Primary School choir sang in the children's area. Covering two floors, the library includes a technology area fitted out with twenty-two computers, digital media equipment and a sound and vision library. It also incorporates a designated children's area and teen area complete with a Playstation 2 while the first floor level is dedicated to answering queries with a dozen computers, local studies collections and sixty study spaces. (*The Advertiser,* Durham: 2000–)

~ MARCH 12TH ~

1792: Durham's Globe Theatre was opened on this day in Silver Street behind the Shakespeare public house. Entertainment took the form of an occasional prelude called *Apollo's Holiday* written by the theatre manager James Cawdell, a new comedy *Wild Oats* and a farce entitled *The Spoiled Child*. The foundation stone for the theatre had been laid with due ceremony on July 6th 1791. On that occasion members of the local Masonic order were prominent in the procession that left Granby Lodge in Old Elvet and wound its way around the city's marketplace before arriving at the prepared site. Following a musical item, the Grand Secretary of the Masonic Order read aloud details from an engraved plate that was then deposited within the foundation stone and after the stone and plaque had been secured Revd Edward Parker delivered a speech in honour of Masonry. Another piece of music was then played before the procession resumed its route along the Bailey to the 'Queen's Head' where 'a most elegant entertainment' was served up. After dinner a collection was made amounting to £3 10*s* 0*d* for workmen and prisoners. Each debtor received 2*s* 6*d* and each felon 6*d*. (The theatre was demolished in the 1960s.) (www.durhamfreemasons.org)

~ MARCH 13TH ~

2013: On this day a first-year Durham University physics student was celebrating after her project to study laser welding in space was selected by a panel of experts at the European Space Agency in the Netherlands. Ioana Ciuca and fellow students from the Polytechnic University of Bucharest, in Romania had taken up their studies at Durham after opting for the best teaching on cosmology in Europe. Their success followed a week-long training course at the German Aerospace Centre and it means that their project will be put into action on the Rexus (Rocket borne Experiments for University Students) during 2014. Development of the International Space Station has made it essential to discover how the properties of materials can change in microgravity, and the group of Romanian students is particularly interested in assessing how the welding of strong, lightweight materials such as titanium alloys changes if they are welded in free fall rather than under the Earth's gravity. A spokesman from Durham University's Centre for Advanced Instrumentation – part of the Department of Physics – commented that it was an outstanding achievement as most Rexus projects were submitted by postgraduate and postdoctoral students. (*The Northern Echo*, Darlington, 1870–)

~ MARCH 14TH ~

2012: On this day a granite sculpture depicting a four-lobed Willmore torus – a symmetric Willmore surface – was unveiled in honour of Professor Tom Willmore on Durham University's Science Site. During the Second World War he made crucial innovations that helped barrage balloons to remain tethered to Arctic convoys supplying Russia and his techniques were also adopted in a major Allied air raid on German industrial targets in the Ruhr valley which disrupted electric and telephone systems. After the war, the Kent-born mathematician turned down an Air Ministry job to devote himself to further studies and during 1946 he began a lectureship at Durham University. Promotion followed and he went on to become head of the department of mathematical sciences and dean of sciences. Though Tom Willmore died in 2005 aged 85 his work is studied across the world where Willmore Surfaces and Willmore Conjecture have become important mathematical concepts. (*The Northern Echo*, Darlington, 1870–)

2012: An unusual outdoor exhibition that mixed fashion and science was held on Palace Green at Durham on this date. Pairs of denim jeans were arranged in rows to show that everyday clothing can be used to purify the air that people breathe. Known as catalytic clothing, the jeans contain 'photocatalysts' within the denim to break down pollutants in the air. The exhibition was organised by Durham University's Science Learning Centre North East. (*The Northern Echo*, Darlington, 1870–)

~ March 15th ~

1944: On this day the Ceremony of the Honouring of Durham Light Infantry took place in Durham City. This gave the DLI the 'right to march through the streets of the ancient city on all ceremonial occasions with bayonets fixed, colours flying and bands playing'. This gathering was probably the first occasion that the city council had held an outdoor meeting and it was attended by thousands of members of the public as well as the mayors of Durham, Stockton, Hartlepool, Sunderland, Gateshead, South Shields, Darlington and Jarrow. Alderman F.W. Goodyear, leader of the Durham City Council said:

> Of all the brave men who are fighting and dying for England, none are braver or are doing better work than the men and lads who have gone from this county. Never dreaming of being anything else but being civilians, they have made wonderful soldiers in the time of country's need. Their deeds are a shining example to all who serve, their record is one of which this county and the nation is rightly proud.

After receiving the honour, and following the word of command, the units fixed bayonets and simultaneously uncased the colours before a general salute saw the regimental band leading the parade through the city to the marketplace where the mayor took the salute. (www.thenorthernecho.co.uk/history/memories)

— MARCH 16TH —

1865: The last public execution took place at Durham Jail on this date when Matthew Atkinson was hanged by Thomas Askern for the murder of his wife at Spen, near Winlaton. The execution produced unexpected drama for, when Askern drew back the bolt and Atkinson plunged downwards, the rope snapped. He was removed from beneath the scaffold and a replacement rope was found so that he could be hanged again after a delay of about 10 minutes. Thomas Askern was the hangman for Yorkshire and had carried out all five of the public executions at Durham between 1859 and 1865 but he was not chosen again by the Sheriff of County Durham. His place was taken by William Calcraft. (www.capitalpunishmentuk.org)

— MARCH 17TH —

1911: On this day there was culinary advice under the heading 'The Logic of Sweets':

> If the perusal of these lines will induce our enterprising housewives to make the 'sweet' course dainty and attractive and at the same time economical a good object will have been achieved. So frequently is the orthodox pie or pudding momentous and distasteful that no apology is needed for suggesting simple variants. For this we must get back to what logicians call 'first principles'. We do not believe the familiar taunt that women are illogical creatures. It is a libel on the fair sex. Every woman knows that among the most popular of all sweets are the Christmas pudding, mince pie and Eccles cakes. Nor is the penny bun to be despised. All of these derive their savouriness from the little Greek currant which is the chief flavouring agent of the best confections. More than that it is very nutritious. Currants have a natural sweetness derived from the rays of the sun and they are full of grape sugar the finest form of concentrated food. Here we have a delicious fruit. Nature's own nutritive sweet. The logical conclusion is to use it. There are countless ways of using currants, all of which are worth trying.

(*Durham County Advertiser*, 1855–1968)

— MARCH 18TH —

1929: Durham's second city centre cinema, 'The Palladium' opened on a site in Claypath on March 18th with a showing of *Garden of Allah* featuring Rex Ingram and Alice Terry. Its proprietors were Messrs Holliday, Thompson, Gibson and Drummond who also opened 'The Majestic' on the outskirts of Durham in 1938. Mr Holliday, chairman of the directors was a Durham City alderman and nephew of John Holliday who had opened a theatre at Framwellgate in 1884. The new cinema opened for both 'film and theatrical' purposes, but in practice it only operated as a cinema. Seating was arranged in stalls and circle levels and it was the first cinema in Durham to operate on Sundays when one evening performance was allowed after the programme had been approved by both the Chief Constable and the Bishop of Durham. The cinema was damaged by fire on January 16th 1934 but was refurbished and reopened less than two months later, on March 5th, with a showing of *It's a Boy* starring Leslie Henson. Further restyling in late 1967 was followed by a reopening with *The Bible – In The Beginning* but, following closure in 1976, it operated as a bingo hall until 1982 when it became a church. It then stood empty from 2004. (Williams, David, *Cinema in a Cathedral City: Cinema Exhibition in Durham City and its Environs 1896–2003*, Wakefield: Mercia Cinema Society, 2004)

— MARCH 19TH —

1921: On this day a war memorial was unveiled at St Oswald's Churchyard, Church Street, Durham by Mrs Roberts of Hollingside House and dedicated by the Bishop of Durham H.H. Henson. The Calvary memorial stood 20ft high with a gabled top section on a slender octagonal column. Plaques on the four faces of a pedestal were inscribed with the full names of ninety men lost during the First World War and the wording 'INRI / To the glory of God / and in honour of / all the parishioners who served / and in grateful remembrance / of those who gave their lives / for the cause of righteousness / and peace in the Great War / 1914–18. R.I.P.' Mrs Roberts, who unveiled the memorial, had lost two sons, Gerard Chipchase Roberts and Frederick John Roberts, during the war years. The memorial cost £300 which was raised by public subscription and fund raising events, such as a sale of work in the Church Institute that contributed £230. (www.newmp.org.uk)

1960: Dr Graeme Forster, managing director of Metaltech Ltd, was born at Durham on this day. After attending Durham Johnston School (1971–78) he gained a BSc degree (1983) from the University of Northumbria and PhD in 1989. He won a series of award for his work in industry and his leisure pursuits include racehorse ownership and managing Northern League soccer teams. (www.metaltech.co.uk)

~ March 20th ~

2012: A new banner in honour of St Cuthbert was raised over his grave in the cathedral shrine in celebration of his feast day. The £35,000 banner of St Cuthbert had been commissioned by John and Lyn Cuthbert of the Northumbrian Association and had been designed and fashioned by dedicated, highly skilled Northumbrian artisans. It was paraded to Durham Cathedral by pilgrims retracing the journey of monks carrying Cuthbert's coffin during the tenth century. More than 100 people walked from Chester-le-Street to Durham where they collected the red banner at the town hall for the final procession up to the cathedral. They were met at the north door by the Very Revd Michael Sadgrove, Dean of Durham and Canon Kennedy, Vice Dean. Chris Kilkenny, the Northumbrian Association's historian, spoke about the creation of the banner before it was formally received and carried to the Shrine of St Cuthbert. The Rt Revd Mark Bryant, Bishop of Jarrow, dedicated and blessed the banner at a St Cuthbert's festival evensong in the cathedral during the evening. The original banner included sacred cloth raised on a spear at the Battle of Neville's Cross in 1346 and it hung in the cathedral until the sixteenth century. (*The Northern Echo*, Darlington, 1870–)

— March 21st —

1870: Charles Hodgson Fowler was proposed for Fellowship of the RIBA on this date and his sponsors on this occasion were George Gilbert Scott, E. Welby Pugin and Robert Johnson. The proposal was approved by the council seven days later and he was elected FRIBA on 16th May. Aged 30, Hodgson Fowler had already designed seven new churches, all of which, apart from one at Sykehouse in Yorkshire, were in County Durham. It seems that it was not until the 1880s that he designed any other complete church outside Durham county for after moving to Durham in 1864 he devoted most of the early 1870s to restoration work at Durham Cathedral. During the late 1870s Hodgson Fowler prepared designs for an increasing number of alterations and restoration projects in more southerly areas of the country. (Wickstead, John, C., *Hodgson Fowler (1840–1910): Durham Architect and his Churches*, Durham: Durham County Local History Society, 2001)

1936: On this day Thomas William Hutchinson, aged 14, played in a schoolboys' rugby international match for England against Wales at Cardiff Arms Park in front of a crowd numbering 30,000. Appearing at right centre three quarter, he was the only representative from Durham County. He died on active service in the Second World War and his name appears on the New Brancepeth War Memorial. (Richardson, Michael, *Durham: Cathedral City*, Thrupp: Sutton, 1997)

— MARCH 22ND —

1869: John Dolan, aged 37, was executed at Durham Jail after being found guilty of murder at Durham Assizes just over three weeks earlier on February 27th. The offence was committed on December 9th 1868 in Sunderland where Dolan and Hugh John Ward shared lodgings with Dolan's girlfriend, Catherine Keehan. During the previous day Dolan had gone out drinking and returned at 1.40 a.m. while Ward was still out (also drinking). He sent Keehan to fetch more beer and when Ward returned he spoke to her before retiring to his room. Dolan sat for a while quietly drinking his beer and then suddenly leapt at the unfortunate woman. As he tried to drag her into the bedroom she screamed for help and Ward raced from his room. The two men began to fight on the stairs as Keehan rushed out to alert the police. When they returned to the house in Union Street the disturbance seemed to have ended and the police officers left. Within a very short time the two men began to fight again and Keehan fled to alert the policemen. When they entered the house Dolan had dealt Ward a fatal blow with a shoemaker's knife and he was taken into custody. (www.genuki.org.uk)

— MARCH 23RD —

1967: On this day Her Majesty Queen Elizabeth II visited Durham to make the annual distribution of Maundy money at the cathedral. (The Queen's Maundy money is made up of British silver coins given to deserving elderly people in recognition of their service to the church or community and it takes place on Maundy Thursday. The number of men and women receiving Maundy money corresponds with the age of the sovereign during that year.) For the ceremony the queen was escorted from Durham Castle to the cathedral by Bishop Ian Ramsay and Sir James Duff, Lord Lieutenant of County Durham. She also attended a private sherry party at the deanery, where Dean Wild entertained residents of the college, before joining 100 invited guests and the Bishop of Durham for lunch in the Great Hall of the Castle. This was the first time that the distribution of Maundy money had taken place in Durham. (Richardson, Michael, *Memory Lane: Durham City*, Derby: Breedon, 2000)

2012: On this day about 900 youngsters took part in the Durham County School Games at Durham University's Maiden Castle sports ground and the Freeman's Quay Leisure Centre, Durham City, as part of the county council's Olympic Legacy programme – Join In. (*The Northern Echo*, Darlington, 1870–)

MARCH 24TH

1873: On this day Mary Ann Cotton was executed at Durham Jail after being found guilty of the murder of her stepson, Charles Cotton. During her lifetime, twenty-one people who were either relatives or close acquaintances of hers had died through probable arsenic poisoning. Born in 1832 in Murton, Mary became an apprentice dressmaker at the age of 16 and some four years later married William Mowbray. After moving to Devon they had five children but, by the time the Mowbray family moved back to the North East, four of the children had died. The couple lived at a number of addresses before settling in Sunderland and during this time she had three more children. Before long these children and William Mowbray had also died; Mary claimed £35 as insurance payments. This pattern of bereavements continued, for whilst working as a nurse at Sunderland Infirmary she met and married George Ward who died after fourteen months. Less than a month later she went to work as a housekeeper for James Robinson, whose 10-month-old son was dead within a week. More of Robinson's children died before Mary left his household and married Frederick Cotton. It was not until 1872 that post-mortem examinations revealed arsenic in the bodies of her victims and she was found guilty of murder on March 8th 1873. (www.dur.ac.uk)

— MARCH 25TH —

1668: On this day Henry Grice, a London merchant, bequeathed the rents of a number of properties for the purchase of bread that was to be distributed to the poor of Brancepeth, near Durham after Sunday evening services. (Merrington, J.P. and M.P. Merrington, *Brancepeth 900: The Story of Brancepeth and its Rectors 1085–1985*, Durham, 1985)

———

1918: Private Thomas Young (January 28th 1895–October 15th 1966) a soldier in the 9th Battalion of the Durham Light Infantry received the Victoria Cross for his actions which began on this day. The citation explains:

> During the period 25th – 31st March 1918 at Bucquoy, France, Pte Young, a stretcher bearer, worked unceasingly evacuating the wounded from seemingly impossible places. On nine different occasions he went out in front of British lines in broad daylight, under heavy rifle, machine gun and shell fire and brought back wounded to safety. Those too badly wounded to be moved before dressing, he dressed under fire and then carried them back unaided. He saved nine lives in this manner.

A memorial to Pte Young has been erected in his home village of High Spen which also displays the name of William Dobson, Coldstream Guards, a VC holder from the same village. (en.wikipedia.org/wiki/Thomas_Young_(VC))

~ March 26th ~

1355: On this day Bishop Hatfield visited the Durham convent and issued a list of findings. These reflect the good character and conduct of the monks because virtually the only fault recorded was that discipline was a little too severe. Among his instructions were a directive that a competent doctor should be available to tend brethren and that infirm monks should receive appropriate care with light meals backed up with daily visits by the cellarer. In addition, monks were to have an appropriate time for recreation and contact with friends. (www.british-history.ac.uk)

2012: The Honourable Henry Francis Cecil Vane of Selaby Hall, Gainford, took the oath to become the latest high sheriff of County Durham. Aged 53, the son and heir to Lord Barnard is also a distant descendant of a former high sheriff from the period when the post holder was a parliamentary appointment. Sir George Vane was the county's high sheriff during the English Civil War at a time when the monarchy was temporarily abolished. During the 2012 ceremony at Durham County Court the new high sheriff was informed that it was an entirely different role that he was about to undertake in what was a largely ceremonial post. (*The Northern Echo*, Darlington, 1870–)

— MARCH 27TH —

1934: On this day Durham's best-known cinema opened on the site of the old Miners' Hall in North Road, which had been vacated in 1915. A distinctive tower and green copper dome ensured that this building was the most imposing along the whole street frontage. Durham's mayor, James Fowler, performed the opening ceremony of the 'Regal' which included a ballroom; it clearly intended to be recognised as the city's foremost picture house.

During almost sixty years of operations as a cinema there were several changes of ownership with each one bringing a different name. Between 1947 and 1972 it was known as 'The Esoldo' until 1979 when it traded as 'The Classic' and then it became 'The Cannon' in 1979. After more than a decade the cinema closed again, in 1990, only to reopen during the following year as 'The Robins'. In spite of a sustained campaign to save the cinema, final closure came during 2003 which left Durham without a dedicated cinema. The Gala is now a base for live drama, comedy and cinema. (Williams, David, *Cinema in a Cathedral City: Cinema Exhibition in Durham City and its Environs 1896–2003*, Wakefield: Mercia Cinema Society, 2004)

1678: Sir Ralph Cole was elected as first Member of Parliament for Durham City on this day, and then re-elected a year later. He died on August 9th 1704 and was buried at Brancepeth. (www.historyofparliamentonline.org)

MARCH 28TH

1424: On this day a ransom treaty was agreed at Durham to facilitate the release of James, King of Scotland. He had been taken prisoner by English privateers during a voyage to France on March 22nd 1406, at the age of 12, and spent the following eighteen years as a prisoner of King Henry IV. His release also saw the exchange of English hostages and it brought the hope of more peaceful times for the borders area. (en.wikipedia.org/wiki/George_II,_Earl_of_March)

1838: Durham-born playwright Thomas Morton died on this day after spending much of his life at Pangbourne-on-Thames. Following the death of his father, his uncle Maddison, a stockbroker, paid for Thomas Morton's education at Soho Square School. It was here that he gained a strong interest in the theatre and, though he entered Lincoln's Inn on July 2nd 1784, he was not called to the bar. Instead he turned to writing theatrical works and his first drama *Columbus, or A World Discovered* was performed at Covent Garden on December 1st 1792. In total he wrote about twenty-five plays and a number of them enjoyed considerable popularity. A keen follower of cricket, Thomas Morton was made an honorary member of the Garrick Club on May 8th 1837. (Stephens, L. and S. Lee (eds), *Dictionary of National Biography*, London: Smith, Elder and Co., 1885–1900)

~ March 29th ~

2004: On this day Durham Gala Theatre was the venue for the official opening ceremony of the 45th International Session of the European Youth Parliament. The event, which was supported by Barclays and facilitated by the North East Assembly, saw the arrival of more than 250 young people from twenty-eight European countries for the opening of the North East 2004 Session. It represented the first time that such an event had been held in the region and the opening ceremony included live music and song from the Durham County Youth Choir. The Lord Lieutenant of County Durham, Sir Paul Nicholson delivered a keynote speech welcoming the delegates to Durham and the Gala Theatre and he was followed by the North East Assembly's Lead Member on Europe, Councillor Michael Davy who added a further welcome on behalf of the region. The final speech of the opening ceremony was made by the Session President, Ms Turkuler Isiksel, aged 22 from Istanbul. She pointed out that the European Youth Parliament usually took its participants to flashy capitals such as Vienna, Rome or Brussels and it was rare for organisers to introduce delegates to the genuine buzzing region of a host country and not just its showcase capital. (*Evening Chronicle*, Newcastle upon Tyne, 1885–)

~ March 30th ~

1606: An entry in the parish registers of St Mary-le-Bow church, Durham records that 'Roger Lumley, Gent. one that dyed in the jayle, bur. 30 March 1606'.

The 'jayle' (jail) in question was located within the city's Great North Gate. Originally constructed around 1072, it was extensively rebuilt during the early fifteenth century on the orders of Bishop Langley, to accommodate the city jail. It became known locally as 'Gaol Gates' and during 1774 the prison reformer, John Howard described conditions after a fact-finding visit:

> The men at night are put into dungeons. One is seven feet square and has three prisoners while another, the 'Great Hole' has only a little window. In this I saw six prisoners, most of them transports, chained to the floor. They had been in that situation for many weeks and were very sick.

During 1820 Bishop Barrington provided funds for construction of a new prison and the Great North Gate, which had become an obstruction to traffic, was demolished. (www.englandsnortheast.co.uk)

2012: On this day a press statement announced that 'Durham City Vision' a regeneration group with the mission of helping Durham to lose its 'beautiful but boring' image had been abandoned just halfway through its planned sixteen-year programme. (*The Northern Echo*, Darlington, 1870–)

— MARCH 31ST —

1311: Richard Kellaw, a monk at Durham, was universally elected as Bishop of Durham and consecrated in this post at York on May 30th 1311. From among his own brethren at Durham, he chose a seneschal (steward), a chancellor and a confessor without displaying the pomp and ceremony of his contemporaries. Bishop Kellaw is said to have dealt in an even-handed manner with any episodes of mutiny or disorder within his diocese. His term of office was predominantly defined by continued raids from Scottish forces.

During 1312 Robert Bruce was at the head of a powerful army that burned Hexham and Corbridge before reducing the outskirts of Durham to ashes. He also sent Sir James Douglas, with a considerable force, to Hartlepool, where he 'carried off much spoil and many prisoners of both sexes'. There was a similar campaign by Scottish forces after the Battle of Bannockburn in 1314 and during the following two years Hartlepool was again plundered. This resulted in local residents taking valuable possessions with them on to ships in the harbour. Bishop Kellaw died on October 9th 1316. During the nineteenth century a grave that was identified as his final resting place was excavated in Durham Cathedral. (Richmond, Thomas, *The Local Records of Stockton and the Neighbourhood; or, A Register of Memorable Events, Chronologically Arranged, Which Have Occurred in and near Stockton Ward and the North-Eastern Parts of Cleveland*, Stockton: William Robinson, 1868)

~ April 1st ~

1333: King Edward III arrived in Durham on his march northwards and lodged in the priory on this date. A few days after, Queen Philippa came from Knaresborough to meet him and being unacquainted with the peculiar customs of the church of Durham, went through the abbey gates to the priory, and after supping with the king retired to rest. This alarmed the monks, one of whom went to the king, and told him that Cuthbert could not bear the presence of a woman. Unwilling to give any offence to the church, Edward immediately ordered the queen to rise. She returned through the gate by which she had entered wearing only her undergarments, and went to the castle where she passed the night. (Whellan, Francis, *History, Topography, and Directory of the County Palatine of Durham Comprising a General Survey of the County and a History of the City and Diocese of Durham* ... , London: Ballantyne, Hanson and Co., 1894)

1628: On this day Richard Hutchinson, organist at Durham, was threatened with expulsion unless his behaviour improved. Specific reference was made in the Act Book to his haunting of alehouses and a brawl, but the situation did not improve and a month later he was partially deprived of his office. (Crosby, Brian, *Come on Choristers! A History of the Chorister School, Durham*, Durham: B. Crosby, 1999)

~ APRIL 2ND ~

1866: A dietary table for Durham County Jail, as approved by the Justices assembled at the General Quarter Sessions of the Peace on this day and subject to the approval of the Secretary of State, itemised meals that were to be provided for prisoners. Prisoners were categorised into six different classes depending on their length of confinement and there were slight variations in most classes for males and females.

Class 1 prisoners, both male and female (confined for a term not exceeding fourteen days) were to be given 1 pint of oatmeal gruel for breakfast and supper with 1 pound of bread for dinner. Each category of prisoner received 1 pint of oatmeal gruel for breakfast and those in Class 2–6 were also given 1 pint of soup per week. Class 3 prisoners – those confined for any term exceeding one month and not more than three months, and prisoners on remand – were also given 1 pound of potatoes, but there was also a ruling that boys under 14 years of age should only receive 6 ounces of bread at each meal. (win1089.vs.easily.co.uk/pete/badrick/durhamprishistory6.htm)

~ April 3rd ~

1967: On this day a ceremony to mark the formal opening of the Millburngate Bridge at Durham was led by the chairman of Durham County Council, Councillor S.C. Docking. The bridge was constructed with a balanced cantilever, concrete beams and two concrete piers using designs prepared by the Durham County Council Engineer and Surveyor, Mr H.B. Cotton and County Architect, Mr G.W. Jelson. The contractors were Holst and Co. Ltd and the total cost amounted to £340,000. It was built as an integral part of a new road traffic scheme in Durham and links the A690/A691 on the west bank of the river with the A690 and A181 on the east. Before its construction traffic passing through Durham crossed the old Framwellgate and Elvet Bridges in the city centre. The other element of the road scheme is the New Elvet Bridge which opened eight years later and the Millburngate shopping centre, adjacent to the bridge, is part of the overall plan. Beneath the bridge is one of only two weirs at Durham – the other being at the Old Fulling Mill. Marking the line of an early ford it incorporates a salmon leap and fish counter for monitoring sea trout and salmon. (www.bridgesonthetyne.co.uk/milburn.html)

~ April 4th ~

1821: On this day the foundation stone of a new subscription library was laid on the site of the old jail in the City of Durham, with Dr Fenwick delivering a suitable address to the company assembled. (Sykes, John, *Local records; or, Historical register of Northumberland and Durham, Newcastle-upon-Tyne, and Berwick-upon-Tweed*, Stockton on Tees: Patrick and Shotton, 1973)

2012: Durham County Council launched a new service for visitors to the area in the form of the Visitor Information Network. The council had faced wide criticism after closing offices in Durham City and Barnard Castle but this innovative system was intended to deal with enquiries from an anticipated influx of visitors during the Easter holiday. The Visitor Information Network included a Visitor Contact Centre for telephone, text and email inquiries, accommodation booking and ticket sales. Face to face, telephone or computer access to information was to be available at sixteen locations including Durham World Heritage Site Visitor Centre, Durham Indoor Market, Durham Gala Theatre and the Durham Dales Centre. In addition, a total of sixteen tourist information boards throughout the county have been renovated and eighty leaflet racks put in place. (*The Northern Echo*, Darlington, 1870–)

~ April 5th ~

2012: On this day a gang of professional thieves made a hole in the wall of Durham University's Oriental Museum before breaking through to steal items from the Malcolm MacDonald Gallery. Well-equipped burglars began their slick operation at about 10.40 p.m. and after about 40 minutes they had created an opening measuring about 2ft by 3ft. The gang then removed an eighteenth-century jade bowl and Dehua porcelain figurine which were on display in separate cabinets at the museum on Elvet Hill. The bowl was fashioned in 1769 and has a Chinese poem painted on the inside while the figurine of seven fairies in a boat measures about 30cm in height. Both items are from the Qing Dynasty, China's last imperial dynasty, which ended about a century ago. The raid was specifically timed for the beginning of the Easter weekend holiday so that few students would be in the area surrounding the museum and museum staff reported the suspects had been observed during a visit on March 29th, which may well have been a reconnaissance mission. The initial police operation, immediately after the raid, involved up to 120 officers and cost around £70,000. The items were safely recovered at a location some 2 miles from the museum. (*The Northern Echo*, Darlington, 1870–)

~ April 6th ~

1828: On the evening of this day (Sunday) the ancient chapel at the west end of Durham cathedral, called the Galilee, was opened for the first time for evening lectures. Divine service was performed by Revd P. George, one of the minor canons, assisted by Mr Stimpson, one of the choristers, as clerk. Reverend W.N. Darnell then delivered an excellent lecture.

The name of the Galilee Chapel is probably derived from the fact that it was the final stage in the procession from the high altar which represents Christ's return to Galilee. It is also known as the Lady Chapel because Bishop Pudsey (1153–1195) began work on a Lady Chapel at the east end of the cathedral only for cracks to appear in the walls. This was interpreted as an indication that St Cuthbert did not want a Lady Chapel so close to his tomb and the bishop ordered craftsmen to build at the west end. The narrowness of the site resulted in the considerable width, of almost 15 metres, compared with its length and by the time of Cardinal Langley in the early fifteenth century it was almost ruinous. He ordered reroofing and strengthening of foundations and, as recently as 1973 and 1993, windows have been added in honour of St Bede and the Virgin Mary. (www.dur.ac.uk/r.c.widdison/tour)

~ April 7th ~

1610: St Oswald's church vestry book for this date includes payments for wine to be used for the celebration of Holy Communion at Fenkeley (Finchale) Priory. Located on Church Street in Durham City, the mother church of St Oswald is surrounded by an attractive churchyard facing towards the south side of the cathedral. Much of the church fabric, including the tower, dates from the early fifteenth century but the aisles and much of the chancel had to be rebuilt in 1834 after subsidence resulting from coal workings. Apart from some impressive woodwork, perhaps the most striking feature of St Oswald's is the tower staircase which is fashioned from medieval grave covers with about a dozen of them displaying carvings made up of crosses, swords, a horn, a battleaxe, a book and a spade. Finchale Priory, which is located in a scenic bend of the River Wear about 3 miles north of Durham City, once formed part of St Oswald's benefice (church living) and it became a tradition for the church's choir to make an annual pilgrimage there on Ascension Day in order to sing the Ascension Day Eucharist. (Richardson, Michael, *Memory Lane: Durham City*, Derby: Breedon, 2000)

~ APRIL 8TH ~

1843: On this day the Durham Spring Assizes concluded, after continuing for the very unusual period of a fortnight. There were ninety-seven prisoners in the calendar, besides upwards of forty civil cases, and some of the latter were left undecided. (Richmond, Thomas, *The Local Records of Stockton and the Neighbourhood; or, a Register of Memorable Events, Chronologically Arranged, Which Have Occurred in and near Stockton Ward and the North-Eastern Parts of Cleveland*, Stockton: William Robinson, 1868)

———

1942: Canon Arthur Michael Ramsay married Miss Joan Hamilton at Durham Cathedral Galilee Chapel on April 8th. The ceremony was conducted by Rt Revd Leslie Owen Bishop of Jarrow with Revd Eric Abbott (later Dean of Westminster Abbey) as best man. Canon Ramsay was Bishop of Durham 1952–56 (and escorted Queen Elizabeth at her coronation in June 1953) and then served as Archbishop of York (1956–61) and Archbishop of Canterbury (1961–69). During a cathedral sermon following his retirement he referred to himself and the congregations as 'we who love Durham'. Michael Ramsay died in 1988. (Richardson, Michael, *Memory Lane: Durham City*, Derby: Breedon, 2000)

———

1948: On this day HRH Duke of Gloucester KG unveiled the Forces memorial window at Durham Cathedral. It was completed at a cost of £2,000 to designs by Hugh Easton. Below the window are three plaques, each with a rope-carved border commemorating the three services. (www.newmp.org.uk)

~ April 9th ~

1940: A significant archaeological discovery was made on this day at a Roman villa site at Old Durham, some 400 metres south of Old Durham Farm. Quarrying operations were underway nearby and when a small test pit was excavated by workers they uncovered masonry and then half of a Roman tile. Further careful investigation soon revealed that the quarrymen had unearthed the lining of a small Roman bathhouse complete with a hypocaust system. Excavations continued at different times between 1941 and 1943, with much of the voluntary labour supplied by students from St John's College, Durham and from Durham School. Other items uncovered included examples of Samian Ware and several Neolithic flints which indicated a native British homestead which had become romanised. Further excavations close to this site in 1948 and 1951 uncovered circular walled and paved areas which could have storage areas for stacks of corn. (Proud, Keith, *Durham City*, Chichester: Phillimore, 2003)

2013: A County Durham Archaeology Day was held at County Hall in Durham City. It featured lectures about recent discoveries in the region and updated material relating to current research methods. The range of locations covered included an Iron Age site at Great Chilton as well as the Second World War prisoner-of-war camp at Harperley. (*The Northern Echo*, Darlington, 1870–)

~ April 10th ~

1950: On this day a memorial grandstand was opened at Hollow Drift, home of Durham City Rugby Football Club, by E. Watts Moses, an old Dunelmian and President of the RFC. It was dedicated by Canon Thurlow, Rector of St Margaret's church. The brick-built stand was planned by Mr H. Elliott, a member of the club and his company Messrs Dixon Elliott carried out construction work. Costs totalled £1,500 and the club received an anonymous loan of £500 which was to become a gift if the remaining £1,000 was raised during the following year (and this happened). Opened during the club's 78th year, the ceremony took place 'in a gale accompanied by snow, rain and sleet' and a memorial plaque displayed the inscription:

> This stand was erected to the memory of those playing members of the Durham City Rugby Football Club who gave their lives for their King and Country in two World Wars and this plaque is set to declare their glory in a place which they all loved.

Lists of servicemen lost in action totalled nineteen during the First World War and thirteen in the war years 1939–45. (www.newmp.org.uk)

⁓ April 11th ⁓

1778: Prebends Bridge, across the River Wear below Durham's South Bailey, was opened to the public on this day after several years of construction work. The design was completed by George Nicholson, architect to the dean and chapter and the building costs of £4,316 were met by the prebends (or canons) of the cathedral. An earlier footbridge, built some 150 yards upstream in 1574 and shown on John Speed's map of 1611, was swept away during the 'Great Flood of 1771'. It forms part of the estate of Durham Cathedral and is a Grade I listed structure. Although it is wide enough to accommodate vehicles, Prebends Bridge is mainly used as a footbridge as it now only leads to riverside pathways and a closed road barrier at the entrance to the South Bailey. Along with Framwellgate and Elvet, Prebends is one of three stone arch bridges in the central sector of Durham and deterioration in the stonework has resulted in restoration work in 1955–56 and 2011–12. A nearby sandstone property, Prebends Cottage, also known as Bett's or Clarney's Cottage, dates from about 1771 and in earlier times it served as the gatehouse for Prebends Bridge. (www.transportheritage.com)

~ April 12th ~

1909: Durham's first branch of the Cooperative Society's stores opened on this day at Neville's Cross. Design work was completed by local architect, George Ord, and construction of the building was carried out by the company of Durham-based George Gradon. A feature of the opening ceremony was a convoy made up of two motor vehicles and several trolleys and carts. Complete with colourful decorations, they travelled in procession from Durham marketplace to Neville's Cross, and following the official events committee members and invited guests were entertained with afternoon tea at the adjacent Neville's Cross Hotel. (The Cooperative Society Store has since been demolished.) (Richardson, Michael, *Memory Lane: Durham City*, Derby: Breedon, 2000)

1938: On this day the Silver Link footbridge that connects Gilesgate in Durham with Pelaw Wood on the other side of the River Wear was officially opened. Design work was completed by Mr J.W. Green, city surveyor and engineer, incorporating features that were to be found in the bridge above the Zambesi Falls. Construction work was carried out by the Cleveland Bridge and Engineering Company of Darlington. A civic party that crossed the newly opened bridge included the mayor, Councillor W.E. Bradley and Alderman J.T.E. Dickeson, chairman of the parks committee. (fopw.wordpress.com/history)

~ APRIL 13TH ~

1498: On this day John Ellys of Brancepeth, near Durham 'being minded to fight against the Turks and enemies of Christ, was summoned by the Prior of Durham to the Cathedral where, standing near the shrine of St Cuthbert, the sign of the cross was made by the Prior upon his breast. At his earnest request his right breast was branded with a cross.' (Merrington, J.P. and M.P. Merrington, *Brancepeth 900: The Story of Brancepeth and its Rectors 1085–1985*, Durham, 1985)

1603: King James I rested at Durham on April 13th 'on his progress to take possession of his English crown. He was received by the magistrates, and afterwards entertained in the castle by the bishop, who attended him with a hundred gentlemen in tawny livery coats. His Majesty was pleased to signalise his visit by the liberation of all the prisoners "except for treason, murther and papistrie."' (Whellan, Francis, *History, Topography, and Directory of the County Palatine of Durham Comprising a General Survey of the County and a History of the City and Diocese of Durham* ... , London: Ballantyne, Hanson and Co., 1894)

1896: An explosion at Brancepeth Colliery in the late hours of this day resulted in the death of twenty miners. The colliery was one of the longest in County Durham, owned by Messrs Straker and Love and employing between 400–500 workers. Fortunately, only about seventy were below ground when coal dust was ignited by shot firing. (www.englandsnortheast.co.uk)

⁓ April 14th ⁓

1499: On this day the Prior of Durham granted his licence to John Ellys, of the parish of Brancepeth, John Blenkinsop, parish of Chester-le-Street and William Brown, parish of Morpeth, to lead the lives of hermits. (Sykes, John, *Local records; or, Historical register of Northumberland and Durham, Newcastle-upon-Tyne, and Berwick-upon-Tweed*, Stockton on Tees: Patrick and Shotton, 1973)

1873: Durham Races were staged for the first time on an area beside the Wear which is still known as 'The Racecourse' and a local newspaper, the *Durham County Advertiser* described the scene:

> The arrivals by train were vast: the number who came by road in conveyances or on foot was unpredictably large. An influx of so many thousands upset the city's characteristic quietude. From an early hour until late at night the streets presented an animated spectacle. Between eleven and two o'clock the flow of men and women down Elvet Bridge was something appalling and it became a question whether the grounds would be sufficient to accommodate all.

Race goers included a large number of members of the nobility whose carriages filled two nearby fields and 'some thousands of miners, the handsome wages of which they are now in receipt contributed in no small degree to their enjoyment both during and after the races'. (*Durham County Advertiser*, 1855–1968)

— APRIL 15TH —

1844: Durham Gilesgate railway station was opened to the north of the city on this date, but it lost its passenger services on April 1st 1857 when the present Durham station became operational. The freight yard and goods terminus at the Gilesgate site remained in use until complete closure on November 7th 1866, by which time it had been handling only one daily goods train from Tyne Yard. (Hoole, Ken, *A Regional History of the Railways of Great Britain: Vol. 4, the North East*, Newton Abbot: David and Charles, 1974)

1871: The Right Honourable John Robert Davison, MP for Durham City died on this date whilst visiting a friend at Sudbury in Suffolk. Born on April 7th 1826 at Durham, he was educated at the city's grammar school and at the University of Durham from where he graduated in 1849 with a BA degree. In the same year Davison was called to the bar at the Middle Temple and went on the Northern Circuit. During 1866 he was made a Queen's Counsel and two years later he was elected as Liberal MP for Durham, holding the seat until his death. (www.halhed.com)

1987: On this day phase two of Durham's Millburngate Shopping Centre was officially opened. (Simpson, David, *Durham Millennium: A Thousand Years of Durham City*, Darlington: Northern Echo, 1995)

– April 16th –

2013: Local newpapers reported that a selection of twelfth-century recipes had been discovered when a Latin manuscript was re-examined by Professor Faith Wallis, of McGill University, Canada. Written in the Priory of Durham Cathedral in about 1140, the food recipes were hidden among instructions for medical ointments and cures and predate the previous oldest examples by about 150 years. Many of the recipes were for sauces that would be served with mutton, chicken, duck, pork and beef and another was for a chicken dish 'Hen in winter' which indicates the use of older birds during the winter months. The sauces include several Mediterranean flavours and involve ingredients such as parsley, sage, pepper, garlic and coriander. The manuscript also describes one recipe as originating from central France. Experts pointed out that this discovery indicates the extent to which international travel and exchange of ideas was taking place during the medieval period. A group of postgraduate students were hoping to recreate some of the recipes at a workshop session later in the month led by food historian Caroline Yeldham. (*Durham Times*, Durham: Newsquest, 2007–)

— APRIL 17TH —

1905: On this day Revd George Sydney Ellam, curate to the rector of St Margaret's church in Crossgates, Durham since 1894 was appointed vicar of Satley in west Durham. Unfortunately, he did not hold this post for long for just a few weeks later, on May 13th, he was fatally injured in a motorcycle accident at Neville's Cross. Local newspapers reported that 'Mr Ellam was much liked by all classes, but especially among the poorer members of the congregation. His death caused a painful sensation throughout Durham City.' A road in Neville's Cross, Ellam Avenue is named after him and altar rails at St Margaret's and the Chancel at St John's churches are dedicated in his memory. (www.thenorthernecho.co.uk/archive)

———

2012: On this day Durham University announced that Europe's oldest book, the seventh-century St Cuthbert's Gospel, was to go on display in the city after a £9 million fundraising campaign. The first display was anticipated in July 2013 in Durham's Palace Green Library where the Lindisfarne Gospels was also exhibited on a three-month-long loan from the British Library. (www.dur.ac.uk/news)

~ April 18th ~

1556: Cases dealt with by the Durham Quarter Sessions at Durham on this day reflect the nature of feuding and outbreaks of riotous behaviour prevalent at the time in the area between the rivers Tweed and Tees. Several of the incidents involved groups of malefactors who 'illegally and riotously disseised' (wrongfully disposed) other individuals of either property or land holdings. Other cases were straightforward accusations of robbery such as the one involving a group of men who 'on 12 November 1555 with force and arms broke riotously into the house of George Archer and Robert Archer at Bradbury and found and carried away 20 wainloads of hay worth £10 and 100 quarters of threshed oats, beans and peas worth together £40 belonging to George and Robert Archer and consumed the same with their livestock'.

Another case followed an episode on April 11th 1556 when bailiffs 'wished to distrain (seize for non-payment of rent) to the amount of £8 ... 6 oxen according to the law and custom of England to impound them' only for a group of husbandmen 'with force and arms riotously to recover the same to their damage and against the peace'. (Fraser, C.M. (ed.), *Durham Quarter Sessions Rolls 1471–1625*, Durham: Surtees Society, 1991)

~ April 19th ~

1617: King James I entered Durham on this day as he journeyed northwards to Scotland. One of His Majesty's footmen, Master Heaburne, took up position beside the mayor and aldermen of the city at Elvet Bridge. On the king's arrival the mayor delivered a loyal speech and surrendered the staff and mace to the monarch before presenting, on behalf of the citizens of Durham, a silver gilt bowl with a cover. After delivering his speech, the mayor was instructed by Master Heaburne to remount his horse and ride ahead of His Majesty. After just a few yards another stop was made while an apprentice recited some verses to the king. The procession then resumed its route with the staff and mace carried at the head of the party on the way to Durham Cathedral. Two days later, on Easter Monday, King James rode south to watch a horse race on Woodham Moor (close to the modern township of Newton Aycliffe) and after returning to Durham for the night the royal party resumed their journey to Scotland on April 22nd, St George's Day with a visit to Newcastle on the route. (Richmond, Thomas, *The Local Records of Stockton and the Neighbourhood; or, A Register of Memorable Events, Chronologically Arranged, Which Have Occurred in and near Stockton Ward and the North-Eastern Parts of Cleveland*, Stockton: William Robinson, 1868)

~ April 20th ~

1945: Gerald Neil Steinberg, known as Gerry Steinberg, was born in Durham City on this day and was educated locally before gaining a Teacher's Certificate at Sheffield College of Education and a Diploma of Education of Backward Children (Special Educational Needs) at Newcastle Polytechnic. His career in teaching began at Hexham Camp School in 1966 and he then moved to Elemore Hall, in County Durham, three years later. Between 1975 and 1987 Gerry Steinberg was a member of staff and then head teacher at Whitworth House Special School in Spennymoor. A developing involvement in political work after he joined the Labour party in 1969 saw him become election agent for Durham MP, Dr Mark Hughes, during 1973 and he was elected to Durham City Council two years later. In June 1987 Steinberg became a Member of Parliament for Durham City and he held this post until standing down in 2005. During his later career he was a member of a number of Parliamentary Committees including the Education and Skills Select Committee and the Public Accounts Committee. He was admitted as an honorary freeman of the City of Durham at a specially convened meeting of Durham City Council on December 8th 2005. (en.wikipedia.org/wiki/Gerry_Steinberg)

~ April 21st ~

2012: More than 150 people attended an event in Durham Town Hall on this day which was held as part of a consultation process linked to a £2.2 million Heritage Lottery Fund bid for improvements to the city's Wharton Park. During the summer of 2011 Heritage Lottery Funding amounting to £44,000 had been successfully secured and full public participation was arranged in readiness for the second stage funding bid. There has been a park on this sloping site since July 1858 when William Lloyd Wharton gave use of the land to the city and it soon became popular with local folk. The Durham Miners' Association held the first Gala in Wharton Park on August 12th 1871 and large crowds were also drawn to royal events such as celebrations for the coronation of George V in 1911. The Labour party had a long tradition of Women's Gala Days in the park dating from 1925 until 1980 and brass band concerts were often organised by the Durham County Brass Band League. During 1990 a considerable investment in the park was made when £100,000 was spent on the bandstand, arched entrances and the conservatory. The spectacular settings continued when a beacon was lit at 10.00 p.m. on Monday, June 4th for celebrations surrounding HM Queen's Diamond Jubilee. (www.durham.gov.uk)

~ April 22nd ~

1612: Needy residents of Brancepeth parish benefitted from the will of Hercules Brabant which carried this date and stated that 'a yearly rent of 20*s* out of his lands at Redworth should be given to the vicar and churchwardens of Staindrop to be distributed to them and their successors to 20 of the most aged and impotent poor people of that parish'. He also gave two sums of 20*s* to the two parishes of Brancepeth and Heighington and 'directed that if the £3, or any part thereof should not be regularly paid, for every month's non-payment be charged the said land with the payment of 10*s* for the same uses'. (Mackenzie, Eneas and Metcalf Ross, *An historical, topographical and descriptive view of the County Palatinate of Durham ...* Newcastle upon Tyne: Mackenzie and Dent, 1834)

1891: Sir Harold Jeffreys was born at Fatfield on this day and after studying at Durham University he moved to St John's College Cambridge where he became a fellow in 1914. After teaching mathematics and geophysics he finally became the Plumian Professor of Astronomy. In addition to a knighthood in 1953, Harold Jeffreys received several other honours and awards which reflect his wide variety of scientific contributions. He died in Fatfield on March 18th 1989. (www.e-education.psu.edu)

~ APRIL 23RD ~

1699: An entry in the diary of Jacob Bee for this date records 'upon St George's Day there fell haile in and about Durham that was estemated to be, by report, five inches about, some reports seven, and some four but I am sure they were three inches and more.'

Since Jacob Bee's day scientists have explained how hailstones are formed when liquid below freezing collects around a solid object such as a particle of dust or another hailstone. A hailstone falls to the earth when it is too heavy for an updraft to keep it up and extremely large hailstones are formed when a hailstone bounces up and down between updrafts. Owing to the fact that hailstones are of different sizes they do not fall at the same speed. Usually, the larger the hailstone then the faster it will fall. Another contributory factor is wind which can slow or accelerate the velocity while a third and lesser consideration is the shape of the hailstone because different shapes create differing amounts of air resistance. During the Middle Ages people used to ring church bells and fired cannons in an attempt to prevent hail which could cause damage to crops. (www.hypertextbook.com)

‒ April 24th ‒

2012: Information published on this day in the *Complete University Guide 2013* named Durham University as the country's fifth best university. This was the same position as the previous year and made it the North East's foremost higher education institution (with twenty-seven out of the thirty-four subjects offered featuring in the top ten category). This announcement followed a best-ever rating in *The Sunday Times University Guide* which placed Durham as the UK's third best university. It was also ranked among the world's top 100 universities and included in the top fifteen globally for employer reputation in terms of the quality and demand for its graduates. Durham University was founded in 1832, making it England's third oldest higher education institution after Oxford and Cambridge, and it now operates from two sites, one in Durham City and the other, the Queen's Campus, at Stockton-on-Tees. On Tyneside, Newcastle University climbed one place from 24th place in the previous year to 23rd and had sixteen departments in the top ten nationally while Northumbria University moved up from 60th place to 54th. Sunderland University also improved from its previous 91st placing to 89th. *(Sunderland Echo,* Sunderland: Northeast Press, 1997‒)

— APRIL 25TH —

1633: The Brancepeth estate which had been held by Edward Ditchfield was conveyed on this date to Lady Anne Middleton, Abraham Crossells and John Jones. (Merrington, J.P. and M.P. Merrington, *Brancepeth 900: The Story of Brancepeth and its Rectors 1085–1985,* Durham, 1985)

2012: Plans were announced today for a mass bike ride, the Etape Pennines, that was to take place on a 78-mile route through County Durham later in the year. Described as cycling's equivalent of the Great North Run, it would follow roads along parts of Weardale and Teesdale with several steep inclines involving a total ascent of 5,407ft. Even before the official launch the event had attracted interest from about 2,000 cyclists, including eleven from overseas and the final total was expected to reach in the region of 3,000. The event was expected to raise thousands of pounds for Marie Curie Cancer Care, its official charity, as well as a number of other good causes. Heading the official launch was Rob Hayles, who gained a silver medal in the pursuit event at the 2000 Sydney Olympics. The Pennines ride, which passes through some of County Durham's most scenic areas, was planned after the success, over five years, of Etape Caledonia which has benefited the Perthshire economy by around £2 million each year. (*The Northern Echo,* Darlington, 1870–)

~ April 26th ~

1939: Michael Heaviside, VC holder, died on this day. Born on October 28th at No. 4 Station Lane, Gilesgate in Durham City, he served as a private with the Royal Army Medical Corps during the Boer War and after returning to his home area where he worked as a miner at Craghead, he joined the 4th Durham Light Infantry as a reservist. Following the outbreak of the First World War, Michael Heaviside was transferred to 15 DLI and it was his actions at Fontaine-lès-Croisilles, in France on May 6th 1917 that led to his awarding of the Victoria Cross. The citation records that under heavy fire he took food and water to a wounded comrade who was only yards away from enemy lines. He was presented with his VC in a ceremony at Buckingham Palace on July 21st 1917 and in the late 1940s a road on a recent housing development in Gilesgate was named Heaviside's Place in his honour. (www.dlisouthshields.org.uk)

2012: A 15ft-high sculpture of a coal miner was unveiled at Low Burnhall near Durham, where the National Trust charity have planted 64,500 trees since purchasing the site in 2008. Fashioned from various types of wood it is the work of artists Ruth Thompson and Anna Turnbull. (*The Northern Echo,* Darlington, 1870–)

~ APRIL 27TH ~

1834: A meeting was held on this day at the Queen's Head Inn, Durham by a group of friends of Robert Surtees who had died some two months earlier. John Ralph Fenwick, MD was in the chair as it was agreed to establish a literary society to be called 'The Surtees Society' and, in accordance with his taste and pursuits, to have for its object the publication of unedited manuscripts illustrative of the intellectual, the moral, the religious and the social condition of those parts of England and Scotland, included on the east between the Humber and the Firth of Forth, and on the west between the Mersey and the Clyde, a region which at one period constituted the ancient Kingdom of Northumberland. A leading figure in the Society for a number of years was James Raine (1791–1858) librarian to the Dean and Chapter of Durham, who served as the Society's secretary and also the editor of fifteen of its first twenty-four volumes. The Surtees Society is typical of many national and local learned societies that were established during the nineteenth century to produce texts, books and articles relating to aspects of religious and secular history. (reed.dur.ac.uk/xtf/view?docId=ead/rls/susall.xml)

~ April 28th ~

1871: Mr Wharton (James Lloyd Wharton) was this day elected Member of Parliament for the City of Durham in the place of the Right Hon. John Robert Davidson, deceased. Contrary to general expectation, the result of the poll was to be declared at 5 p.m. and at that time there were between 4,000 and 5,000 spectators assembled in front of the town hall. They were noisy, good humoured, and exceedingly demonstrative; the scene presented by the waving ribbons, the floating streamers and the constant movements of the gaily dressed throng, was of the most animated and attractive character. Most of the windows, too, were graced by groups of ladies; and, therefore, as the two candidates marched from the committee rooms, they were not only greeted by the cheers of their friends below, but were flattered and encouraged by the smiles of their graceful admirers above. The Mayor (Mr Ald. Ward) announced that numbers received for Mr Wharton were 814 and for Mr Thompson 776. This showed a majority of thirty-eight for the former gentleman, and he therefore declared him duly elected to serve in Parliament for the City of Durham. (Fordyce, William, *The History and Antiquities of the County Palatine of Durham ...,* Newcastle upon Tyne: T. Fordyce, 1850)

~ April 29th ~

1639: An entry from the journal of John Ashton, 'Privy Chamber-man Extraordinary' records:

The next day being Monday, I caine to Durham, the bishop's sea of that diocesse, where he hath a goodly auncient castle for his habitation which was now taken up for the king, who came that same night to towne. The towne is pleasantly seated and environed with the river Weere, especially that part where the castle, cathedral and prebends' houses stand, which resembles a horse shooe, being separated from the rest of the towne (as it were) within the river, save onely one space to goe to those buildings like the distance betweene the two ends of the horse shooe. In this towne are much gentry, it being the London (as it were) of those north parts, which extend as farre as Barwick [i.e. Berwick]. The cathedral church is very lardge and by some sequalled to Yorke, but more out of affeccion than truth, there being noe comparison, this coming farre short of Yorke for beauty and state, the two vast(i.e too vast) pillars it hath serving better for perpetuity than comeliness in architect.

(www.archive.org)

122

~ APRIL 30TH ~

1948: Details of the Durham College's Rag Week were announced in press columns on this day with a range of events to appeal to all age groups and interests. Following the opening day procession from Palace Green on the Saturday, highlights included an informal tea dance on Wednesday afternoon and a full-scale ball in the town hall two days later with dancing until midnight to Norman Richardson's band. The current Rag Mag also gave details of a 'spicy revue entitled *Sugar and Spice*' which was being performed in the Assembly Rooms, North Bailey. In the twenty scenes which make up the revue, there were eight new song and dance numbers especially written for the show, with topical sketches and plenty of comedy. For those with more of a sporting interest, a Rag Week darts competition was taking place daily. Above all, the emphasis was placed on fundraising for charities, with collectors wandering through city streets all day during the procession and '… the only protection which persons and shops will have from this invasion will be provided by an immunity badge costing 2/6 or 10/6 for shops'. Rag Mags 'will also be on sale for whoever insists on some immediate return for his outlay'. (*Durham Chronicle*, 1820–1984)

~ May 1st ~

1895: Durham Swimming Club began its tradition of opening each new season with a 7 a.m. May Day swim in the River Wear on the 1st May. The club claims to be the second oldest in the country having been formed in 1861, a year after the one at Brighton, when Mr Wilkinson, landlord of the Royal Tent pub at the rear of Saddler Street, organised a meeting in his bar. Swimming was becoming popular throughout the country and it received a boost in Durham with the opening of the Baths and Washhouses in Elvet 1855. William Lloyd Wharton of Dryburn Hall, chairman of the North Eastern Railway, agreed to become the club's first president and John Henderson, who became Durham's MP in 1864, was one of the early subscribers. (www.thenorthernecho.co.uk/history)

2012: On this date Durham World Heritage Visitor Centre in Durham City was announced as the winner of this year's Royal Institute of Chartered Surveyors Award for best Tourism and Leisure Project in the north east of England. Based in former Durham University Almshouses, it opened in June 2011 and has made a significant contribution to tourism in the area. It is also used by schools and Durham University as offices. (www.durhamworldheritagesite.com)

~ MAY 2ND ~

1649: Durham Castle was sold on this day to the Lord Mayor of London, Sir Thomas Andrewes, for the sum of £1,267 10*d*. Andrewes had built up considerable wealth during the 1620s and '30s by trading with the New England colonies as a member of the guild of the Leathersellers' Company from premises at the White Lion, Fish Street Hill, London. As a devout Puritan, he provided large sums of money to support parliament's campaign against King Charles I and he was heavily involved in administering the finances of their armed forces between 1642–45. Sir Thomas Andrewes was a commissioner at the trial of Charles I in January 1649 at Westminster Hall and although he did not sign the death warrant he was present at the king's execution on January 30th 1649. During 1650 some 3,000 Scottish soldiers were held captive at Durham Castle following their defeat at the Battle of Dunbar. Many of them died in appalling conditions and others were transported as slaves to New England. The castle reportedly suffered considerable damage at this time. Sir Thomas Andrewes' highly successful business dealings continued through the 1650s. (www.winthropsociety.com/settlers/founders.htm)

— MAY 3RD —

1919: Following a prayer by the city on this day, King George V granted 'the privilege of bearing within the confines of the said city a sword ornamented with the royal arms which should be borne before the mayor erect and sheathed and that the bearer of the sword might be attired in an appropriate cap or hat to which no special name or significance should be attributed.' In fact, two swords are displayed in the guildhall, which is incorporated within Durham town hall. One is the old civic sword which dates from 1895 while the current one was presented to the city by the Earl of Durham in 1913 to commemorate his election as mayor. This fine two-handed sword displays the royal standard, with the coat of arms on the hilt. Above this are the city coat of arms, the county coat of arms and the coat of arms of the Earl of Durham. The scabbard is fashioned from purple velvet, the colour of the old palatine of Durham. Along with the chains of office, the mace, robes, hats, city seal, armorial bearings and civic plate, the swords represent important symbols for the Charter Trust and the Mayor of Durham City. (www.durham.gov.uk)

‒ May 4th ‒

1964: The passenger service from Durham to Sunderland via Penshaw was closed on this day after operating (for passengers) since March 9th 1840. The line's most impressive feature was the Victoria Viaduct which spans the river Wear and which was chosen in preference to an iron bridge proposed by John Green, a Newcastle-based architect. Constructed between 1836 and 1838 to designs by James Walker, this magnificent masonry bridge was based on the patterns of Trajan's Bridge at Alcantara in Spain where spans of 98ft carry the roadway at a height of 170ft. Building work was supervised by the famous north-eastern engineer, T.E. Harrison, with free stone from Penshaw Quarries supplemented by Aberdeen granite in the quoins of the large arches. The total length of the bridge is 811ft and the track was about 120ft above the river level. The main arch was claimed to be the largest in Europe at the time of its construction and the viaduct's name was chosen because the last stone was laid on the day of Queen Victoria's coronation. As the line originally carried the LNER, it formed part of the first rail link between the rivers Thames and Tyne. (Emett, Charlie, *Durham Railways*, Stroud: The History Press, 2009)

~ MAY 5TH ~

1913: 'The Globe', Durham City's first purpose-built cinema, was opened on a site at the northern end of North Road where a timber house had previously stood. Spreading along the street frontage it soon became popular for twice-nightly performances at 7 p.m. and 9 p.m. and, at about the time of the outbreak of war in 1914, a glass canopy was added to its facade in order to display the times of shows. 'The Globe' closed in August 1957 and was then used as a furniture shop. Part of the building remains at the upper end of Castle Chare.

Moving pictures were first shown in Durham City during the 1890s at theatres such as the 'People's Palace of Varieties' in Court Lane. Another important venue for moving pictures was the Assembly Rooms in the city's North Bailey. Early films featured factual subject such as King Edward VIII's coronation and Queen Victoria's funeral procession and the first movie drama was probably *The Great Train Robbery*, but during the early days short films were of secondary importance to dramatic performances or music-hall entertainers. (*Durham Times*, Durham: Newsquest, 2007–)

— MAY 6TH —

1935: A beacon was constructed on Shincliffe Bank Top by members of local scout troops as part of the celebrations that marked King George V's Jubilee. A range of events had been arranged by the parish council during the day and the culmination of the festivities was the lighting of the beacon at 10.00 p.m. A series of beacons were lit across the mainland of England including twenty-nine in parts of County Durham. (Richardson, Michael, *Durham: Cathedral City*, Thrupp: Sutton, 1997)

———

2009: Ten little girls aged between 9 and 12 became the first females to join the world-famous Durham Choristers for an inaugural rehearsal at the cathedral on this day. They were pupils at the Chorister School in Durham City whose previous students include the former Prime Minister Tony Blair, and in addition to their academic studies they would receive voice training and take part in an intensive rehearsal schedule. Until this moment, however, membership of the cathedral choir had been an exclusively male preserve. Originally only monks were eligible to join the choir but laymen and boys were first admitted in the 16th century. The new arrangement meant that girls would alternate with boys who currently sang the choir's soprano line in cathedral services from October 2012. (www.dailymail.co.uk/news)

~ MAY 7TH ~

1557: Cases heard by officials and jurors at the Durham Quarter Sessions on this day for the most part involved the use of force and violence in the pursuit of theft. Some episodes were carried out by individuals such as Christopher Burden who 'with force and arms broke and entered the close of Richard Laxe at Ferryhill and stole a web of linen cloth worth 7*s*' or Andrew Joplynge, a wheelwright from the Edmundbyers area, who 'with force and arms attacked Lionel Snawe and Christopher Vasey so that their lives were despaired of, and stole an axe worth 12*d*.' Another incident at Haughtenfield involved a group of men from the Darlington area 'who with force and arms assembled unlawfully and riotously attacked Thomas Hereson so that his life was despaired of' and in a different case five men from the Stanhope area were charged under the statutes against disseising (wrongful dispossession) after they 'with force and arms entered the free tenement of Lancelot Trotter at Eastgate in Weardale and expelled him.' (Fraser, C.M. (ed.), *Durham Quarter Sessions Rolls 1471–1625*, Durham: Surtees Society, 1991)

~ MAY 8TH ~

1903: An inquest was held on this day in the mayor's chamber at Durham town hall where the coroner and a jury deliberated over the ownership of 25 gold sovereigns. The coins had been unearthed by three local boys, Frank Elvin, Fred Brown and Norman Modral in Pelaw Wood, where they had been buried beneath a layer of leaf mould close to a tree with the markings 'R.G.H.' and within a heart-shaped edging. After due consideration the jury declared that the boys were the rightful owners of the coins. (*Durham Chronicle*, 1820–1984)

2002: HM Queen Elizabeth II and Prince Philip, Duke of Edinburgh, visited County Durham during the second day of her golden jubilee tour of the North East. The morning was spent in coastal villages such as Easington which had previously been the setting for thriving coal mines before the royal party travelled to Durham City for lunch in the Great Hall of Durham Castle. On their arrival in Durham they were met by the Lord Lieutenant of County Durham, Sir Paul Nicholson and scores of dignitaries including the naturalist Dr David Bellamy and University Chancellor Sir Peter Ustinov. (www.news.bbc.co.uk)

~ May 9th ~

2013: As workmen continued to clear debris, caused by landslips, from the channel of the River Wear at Durham, concerns were raised about a possible threat posed by a series of landslips to the regatta scheduled for June 8th and 9th. On Christmas Eve 2012 part of a vicarage garden in Church Street disappeared into the river and, as landslips continued during the early weeks of 2013, access to the riverbank via Pelaw Woods was restricted in the interests of public safety. Remedial work was also scheduled on the opposite bank at Maiden Castle where damage and collapse has occurred in recent years. At the beginning of May 2013 Durham County Council ordered an investigation into the problem. A full geotechnical survey lasting several months would attempt to determine why hillsides close to the river were continuing to move and to formulate long-term solutions. In the meantime Environmental Agency staff continued to clear the river of rubbish (which last year included a dentist's chair) while council workers tidied riverbanks. Their combined efforts formed part of this year's 'Litter Free Durham Big Spring Clean Campaign'. (*The Northern Echo*, Darlington, 1870–)

— MAY 10TH —

1967: Brancepeth Castle was awarded Grade I listed building status by English Heritage on this date. A series of buildings have covered this site since the Bulmer family were based here in the Norman period. Alterations and rebuilding work was carried out by the Neville family in the late fourteenth century but in 1569 their involvement in the Rising of the North led to its confiscation by the Crown. Since that time the Brancepeth estate has had a number of owners including Robert Carr, 1st Earl of Somerset; Ralph Cole of Newcastle and Sir Henry Belasyse and in 1796 it was purchased by the Russell family. Between 1818 and 1821 the castle was extensively remodelled for Matthew Russell by Scottish architect John Paterson who added a gatehouse with two massive round towers extending from the north-east corner of the curtain wall. Further alterations were made in the mid-nineteenth century by Anthony Salvin for William Russell. During the First World War the castle was used for convalescence by Newcastle General Hospital and it then became the regimental headquarters of the Durham Light Infantry. Since 1978 it has been privately owned by the Dobson family. (www.britishlistedbuildings.co.uk)

~ MAY 11TH ~

1762: On this day a ruling was announced in the House of Commons by 88 votes to 72 that the result of the parliamentary election at Durham in December of the previous year should be overturned. The by-election was between two Whig candidates Major General John Lambton and Major Ralph Gowland and it was characterised by the use of 215 so-called 'mushrooms' (non-resident voters) to gain a majority of 23 for Gowland. This tactic of using non-resident voters was a popular method of 'maximising the vote' at that time and in the case of the Durham election most of them had become honorary freemen after the writ for the election had been issued. If their votes were invalid then Major General Lambton would have gained a victory by 192 and the House of Commons ruling was that he should replace Major Gowland as the Member of Parliament. A direct result of this episode was the passing of the so-called 'Durham Act' or Freemen (Admission) Act of 1763 which prevented any honorary freeman from exercising his vote within twelve months of his election. Contemporary reports describe a celebratory mood in Durham when Major General Lambton entered the city as the new Member of Parliament. (www.dur.ac.uk)

— MAY 12TH —

1541: On this day, almost seventeen months after the closure of the Benedictine monastery, King Henry VIII refounded Durham as the Cathedral church of Christ and the Virgin Mary with a dean and twelve prebendaries (major canons) along with twelve other minor canons. The last prior of the monastery, Hugh Whitehead, became dean and other members of the old establishment who were not appointed as prebendaries were given positions in various churches around the bishoprick of Durham. Unlike their monastic predecessors, all secular clergy at Durham were allowed to marry and have children. They had to ensure that the poor were cared for, and the roads and bridges repaired 'to the glory of God and the happiness of our subjects', as well as fulfilling a lengthy list of financial obligations linked to the former monastery. The dean occupied the hall of the former priors at the east end of the college and within the cathedral church a stone screen across its width on the west side of the crossing was removed. Other changes included whitewashing the walls to cover pictures painted on them. (Lomas, Richard, *An Encyclopaedia of North-East England*, Edinburgh: Birlinn, 2009)

— MAY 13TH —

1927: Cases dealt with at Durham Magistrates' Court included a charge against William Smith, aged 20, of Frederick Street North, Meadowfield who denied driving a motor bus to the danger of the public on the Durham to Brandon road. Superintendent Foster said the defendant, at a blind corner, cut through a narrow opening and Sgt Smith, who was a passenger on a United bus, stated that without any warning the defendant cut in between two buses. It was a regular habit, he added, for these young lads to see who could get first to the next stopping place. A fine of £1 was imposed and the chairman said the magistrates intended to make representations against small weak boys being allowed to drive these buses.

In other cases – For having been drunk in charge of a horse and cart at Carrville, Samuel Dorn (41) of Middle Rainton, was fined 15s. For riding a bicycle on the footpath, John Stranger (32) of Brandon Colliery was fined 5s and for playing football on the highway, six men from Quarrington Hill were fined 5s each. (*Durham Chronicle*, 1820–1984)

― MAY 14TH ―

1922: A wall-mounted First World War memorial was unveiled on this day at St Nicholas' church in Durham marketplace. The ceremony was performed by Col John Ridley Ritson OBE, TD, DL of Sniperly Hall and the memorial was dedicated by the Rt Revd Bishop of Jarrow. Design work on the memorial was prepared by a parishioner, Mr W.G. Footitt and a local company, John Lowes and Son of Gilesgate carried out the work. Colonel Ritson, a member of the firm of Messrs Ritson and Sons, colliery owners, had seen military service in the South African War before travelling to France with 50th Northumbrian Division in the early stages of the First World War. In 1915 he was wounded and taken prisoner during the second Battle of Ypres. (*Durham County Advertiser*, 1855–1968)

2012: Three more women became freemen of Durham City in a ceremony held in Durham Town Hall. Until recent times membership was based on medieval craft guilds and was entirely the preserve of men but since women were first admitted their numbers have risen to seventeen. The three latest freemen were sisters Theresa Ford and Irene Bryden along with Revd Pat Billsborrow. (*The Northern Echo*, Darlington, 1870–)

～ MAY 15TH ～

1657: Letters patent were issued by the Privy Council on this day to found a college in the cathedral precincts at Durham and to endow it with church lands. This educational establishment was to comprise of a provost, two senior fellows or preachers and twelve other fellows who included four professors, four tutors and four schoolmasters. It was also stated that there were to be twenty-four scholars, twelve exhibitioners and eighteen pupils in the free school attached to the college. (Stranks, C.J., *This Sumptuous Church: The Story of Durham Cathedral,* London: SPCK, 1993)

———

1984: The incoming mayoress of Durham, Mrs Gladys Shuker, wore a replacement chain of office for the first time on this day at the annual meeting of Durham County Council. A chain for the mayoress had been presented in 1901 by the immediate ex-mayoress, Lady Anne Lambton, but it was stolen in 1983 and never recovered. The replacement was specially fashioned by John M. Sweeney of Newcastle during 1983–84. Other chains of office include one for the mayor which was presented to the city in 1870 and another for the deputy mayor while a deputy mayoress' badge was also presented by the immediate past mayor, Gordon McIntyre in 1953. (www.durham.gov.uk)

― May 16th ―

1882: A highly unusual case was concluded on this day when William Marwood hanged 37-year-old Thomas Fury for stabbing to death a prostitute named Maria Fitzsimmons. The crime had been carried out in Sunderland more than thirteen years previously on February 19th 1869 and in modern parlance would be termed a 'cold case'.

It was during 1879 that the whole episode began to unravel when Henry Charles Cort was convicted of robbery and attempted murder and was sent to Pentonville to serve a fifteen-year sentence. For whatever motive, Cort made a written statement in which he identified himself as Thomas Fury and confessed that he had stabbed Maria when she attempted to rob him. At the opening of his trial in Durham before Mr Justice Watkin Williams he initially pleaded guilty but on the judge's advice he subsequently withdrew this plea. The actual trial lasted just one day with the case for his defence being that if he had killed Maria then he was only guilty of manslaughter. This move was rejected by the jury and he was convicted of murder. Less than three weeks later, showing no sign of fear, he was hanged in the yard of Durham Jail. (www.capitalpunishmentuk.org)

― MAY 17TH ―

1827: An investigation of the vault containing St Cuthbert's body was examined on this day under the direction of Durham Cathedral's librarian, Revd James Raine. Also present at the time were prebendaries, Dr Darnell and Dr Gilby and a number of cathedral officials and workmen. It was established that the vault contained three coffins with a large slab of Frosterley marble acting as a cover following the last investigation in 1542. The two earlier coffins were believed to date from 1104 and the seventh century. The innermost of these three nesting coffins was richly carved and within it were the skeletal remains of St Cuthbert clothed in a fine set of robes. A number of items were also discovered including an ivory comb, silver altar and purse as well as a pectoral cross. Fashioned from gold, the cross was inset with garnets and a length of silk cord twisted with gold was found on the breast bone. Legend suggests that the actual body of St Cuthbert was removed from this location before the arrival of King Henry VIII's commissioners and reburied in a secret location that was known only to twelve monks. (Stranks, C.J., *This Sumptuous Church: The Story of Durham Cathedral,* London: SPCK, 1993)

— MAY 18TH —

1997: The inaugural Northumbrian University Boat Race took place on this date on the River Tyne at Newcastle and involved the boat clubs of Durham and Newcastle universities. Four races form the main rowing event: Men's senior eights for the Clasper Trophy, Women's senior eights for the Chambers Trophy, Freshmen for the Renforth Trophy and Freshmen for the Taylor Trophy, while an additional race for junior rowers is held before the main university events over the main course. On most occasions a team from the Tyne Rowing Club represents Newcastle while rowers from Durham Schools, such as Durham School and St Leonard's, competed for Durham. Bad weather caused the cancellation of the event in 2000 and 2003 and Newcastle won the overall title for the first time in 2009. On most occasions a range of local entertainment accompanies the races and in other years the setting has included events such as a parade of tall ships, a University Sailing Contest and a University Canoe Water Polo Event. Presentations take place after completion of races in Baltic Square on the south side of the river. (en.wikipedia.org/wiki/Northumbrian_University_Boat_Race)

~ May 19th ~

1826: William Stephen Gilly was installed as prebend of the ninth stall of Durham Cathedral on this day. Although the ninth stall was the poorest of twelve stalls of Durham Cathedral, providing only £312 annually, Gilly also received £1,491 each year as his share of the chapter income and a house with a free supply of coal at No. 9 The College. Some two months later he was inducted as Perpetual Curate of St Margaret's church, Durham which at that time is said to 'abound in mean houses divided into squalid tenements' while the church itself attracted 'vagrants and loose and suspicious characters who passed along the Great North Road'. Gilly is reported to have worked hard to improve living conditions for the poorer classes in Durham City as well as campaigning for the abolition of slavery. (Gilly, W.S. and Hugh Norwood, *The Peasantry of the Border: An Appeal on their Behalf … with an Account of the Eventful Life of Canon Gilly …*, Aylesbury: Square Edge Books, 2001)

2012: After thirty-two years as conductor of the Durham Choral Society, Richard Briers retired at the end of a concert in Durham Cathedral. The first half consisted for the most part of sacred music by Handel, Mozart, Bach and Vaughan Williams while the second half was Sir Edward Elgar's *The Music Makers*. (*The Northern Echo*, Darlington, 1870–)

– MAY 20TH –

1966: Front page headlines in local press reports for this day highlighted the dangers posed by a section of the A1 road near Durham. Agitation for action to end the 'A1 terror' had increased during the previous week when Durham Central Education Executive again called for an 'on the spot' investigation into hazards facing pedestrians on the Neville's Cross-Whitesmocks stretch of the route. Mr Charles F. Grey, MP for Durham, who was giving full support to the campaign, had agreed to lead a deputation to the Minister of Transport, Mrs Barbara Castle, to seek a reversal of her recent decision that neither a footbridge nor a subway was justified along that stretch of trunk road. Durham County Police had also indicated its grave concern and stated the view that a footbridge would represent the only complete answer, that the speed limit should be dropped to 30mph and that the provision of light-controlled pedestrian crossings should be considered. Local residents had also voiced their fears for elderly pedestrians and schoolchildren attempting to cross this busy highway and now *Durham County Advertiser* newspaper was calling on Durham County Council and Durham City Council to take a leading role in the campaign. (*Durham County Advertiser*, 1855–1968)

— May 21st —

1170: On this day St Godric died at Finchale Priory where he had been based for some sixty years. Born in about 1070 in the parish of Walpole, Norfolk, he soon began to travel widely in this country and then mainland Europe as he developed considerable skills as a sailor. His deep religious convictions led Godric to visit shrines and religious sites including pilgrimages to Jerusalem and Rome in 1102 and it soon became clear to him that he had to live his life in near solitude as a hermit, to pray and study the scriptures. After basing himself at Finchale, Godric became a true hermit. He fasted regularly and worked through the night to clear land near a chapel that he had built to the memory of St John the Baptist As his reputation spread pilgrims arrived in search of Godric's healing powers and to hear his teachings, and senior churchmen corresponded with him. But, as illness took hold, he was confined to bed for almost a decade before his death. Cared for by monks from Durham, Godric was initially buried in the nearby city before his remains were removed to a permanent grave at Finchale. (*The Northern Echo*, Darlington, 1870–)

~ MAY 22ND ~

1960: A Mark 1 Hawker Hurricane was proudly displayed on Palace Green during a ceremony to mark the consecration and laying up of the standard of 607 County of Durham Squadron at Durham Cathedral. The standard was hung over the squadron's war memorial in the south transept which commemorated the weekend fliers and ground crews who had fought alongside regular RAF air crews during the Second World War. Formed on March 17th 1930 as a light bomber unit, 607 Squadron was re-designated as a fighter squadron in 1937. After returning from France in May 1940, five sections of the squadron were scrambled from their home base at RAF Usworth in their Hawker Hurricanes. They were tasked with intercepting two formations of German bombers heading towards the Northumberland coast and in the half-hour battle that followed six enemy aircraft were shot down and six others were badly damaged. During the rest of the war 607 Squadron saw service in West Sussex and Kent, Scotland and overseas in India and Burma. Along with many others, 607 Squadron was disbanded on July 31st 1945 only to be reformed in May 1946 when the RAF Auxiliary Air Force was set up. The final disbandment was in March 1957. (*The Northern Echo*, Darlington, 1870–)

~ MAY 23RD ~

2012: Professor John Rogister of Durham City was invested with the insignia of a Grand Officer of the National Order of Merit at a ceremony that took place at the French Embassy in London. The honour, which is the equivalent of a knighthood, was awarded in recognition of his contribution as a historian of France. Professor Rogister joined the staff at Durham University as a lecturer in modern history in 1967, gained promotion to senior lecturer in 1982 and retired in 2001. He was also a visiting chair at the Universities of Paris-X (Nanterre), Montpellier–III and Lyons–2 and on three occasions he was invited to deliver a series of guest lectures at the College de France in Paris. He continues as an associate director of studies at the Ecole Pratique des Hautes Etudes, a research department at the Sorbonne where he had lectured during the late 1980s. During the investiture ceremony H.E. Monsieur Barnard Emie, the French Ambassador, referred to the importance of Professor Rogister's book, *Louis XV and the Parlement of Paris* and his contribution as founding editor of the journal *Parliaments, Estates and Representation*. (www.e-mailstrategies.com/ebulletins/showissue.php3?page=/526/14666/35625&rec=0)

~ MAY 24TH ~

1893: Following its establishment just over five years earlier on University land at Pinkerknowle, Durham City Golf Club extended the initial layout of six holes to the full nine holes on this day. This development followed the employment of the club's first professional, David Brown, in May 1889 and the first greenkeeper in 1892. Membership now totalled ninety with annual subscriptions fixed at one guinea. Another important landmark was reached in February 1894 when it was decided to permit ladies to join the club 'under such regulations to be determined by the Committee'. (www.durhamcitygolfclub.co.uk)

———

1913: Considerable excitement spread throughout the Durham area on this day when Lieutenant Waldron made an unscheduled landing on the city's racecourse in his bi-plane. An army airman, he was heading northwards to Montrose in Scotland and two days later he was able to continue his journey. After stopping at Berwick upon Tweed to take on fuel, Lieutenant Waldron completed the section from Durham to Melrose in five and a half hours. (Richardson, Michael, *Memory Lane: Durham City*, Derby: Breedon, 2000)

———

1947: Councillor Frederick Foster, Mayor of Durham, died on this day after just seven months in office. Born in Bishop Auckland, he served as a policeman in South Africa before returning to his home area where he became Superintendent of Durham Division in 1922. (Richardson, Michael, *Memory Lane: Durham City*, Derby: Breedon, 2000)

— MAY 25TH —

1922: A memorial cross was erected in grounds to the south of Bede College on this day. Standing around 14ft high and set on a square pedestal it is inscribed in three columns with eighty-six surnames and initials along with the year in which they entered the college. The front panel has the wording: 'In loving and proud memory of those sons of Bede who in the Great War where so many of their brothers served and suffered gave their lives for their King and Country. Lest we forget.' Total cost amounted to £1,000 and it was set within a paved area that included seats and steps along the slope. (www.newmp.org.uk)

2012: On this day a new mayor, Councillor John Wilkinson, began his term of office in Durham City after his appointment by the City of Durham Charter Trust. Following the ceremony at Durham town hall, Councillor Wilkinson, a retired teacher and representative for Deerness ward, mingled among shoppers in the marketplace to distribute the 'Mayor's Shilling', a traditional gift to the poor and needy. The two charities supported during his year of office were 'Heel and Toe' which assists children with cerebral palsy and 'Blind Life In Durham'. (*Sunderland Echo*, Sunderland: Northeast Press, 1997–)

~ May 26th ~

1429: The wooden spire of the central tower within the abbey at Durham was struck by lightning on this day. The blaze was first discovered at about 7 a.m. and burned fiercely for the rest of the morning. Prior Wessington wrote a detailed account of the immediate events surrounding the fire and expressed his relief that none of the dozen or so men who worked among the burning timbers and molten lead were injured. Initial repair work cost £233 6s 8d but twenty-six years later a complete rebuild was needed. A shortage of funds meant that this thorough renovation was not completed until about 1490. (Stranks, C.J., *This Sumptuous Church: The Story of Durham Cathedral*, London: SPCK, 1993)

1938: On this day Robert Hoolhouse, aged 21, was hanged in Durham Jail after being convicted of the murder of Margaret Dobson, a farmer's wife, some four months previously. Her body was found in a shallow ditch near her home at Wolviston. She had been raped, strangled and stabbed twice with a penknife. Much of the case against Hoolhouse was based on bloodstains discovered on his clothes and although his defence lawyer argued that he had been convicted entirely on circumstantial evidence the jury returned a guilty verdict. (*North Eastern Gazette*, Middlesbrough 1936–1940)

~ MAY 27TH ~

1949: A parade of vehicles belonging to Durham County Fire Service took place at The Sands, riverside land on the northern edge of Durham City and more than 200 members of Durham Fire Brigade gathered for a visit by HM Inspector of Fire Services, Mr P.P. Booth. Trophies rewarding efficiency were presented by the Chairman of Durham County Council, Alderman J.W. Foster and numbered among thirteen appliances that featured in the event, there were four from Durham City. (Richardson, Michael, *Memory Lane: Durham City*, Derby: Breedon, 2000)

1960: HM Queen Elizabeth II and HRH Prince Philip the Duke of Edinburgh visited a number of locations in Durham City on this day. The royal car had entered the outskirts of the city through the Sherburn Road estate where hundreds of local residents lined the route and after an appearance on the balcony at Durham town hall the royal visitors had lunch at the castle. The queen was presented with a silver St Cuthbert's pectoral cross which had been made by the late W.A. Bramwell, a Durham City silversmith. During a short visit to the cathedral the royal guests were accompanied by the Earl of Scarborough, Chancellor of Durham University. (Richardson, Michael, *Memory Lane: Durham City*, Derby: Breedon, 2000)

— MAY 28TH —

1851: Gustavus Hamilton Russell celebrated his twenty-first birthday on this day with a lavish party at the family home of Brancepeth Castle. Two fattened oxen were roasted and then distributed among workers on the estate while an impressive dinner was prepared for long serving retainers of the family in the great hall of the castle. During the evening a ball was staged for 200 sons and daughters of the estate farmers. Celebrations continued in the Russell almshouses at Cornsay where a dinner was staged by the tradesmen of Durham. A congratulatory address was sent by the Corporation of Durham City and in reply Gustavus Russell stated, 'To find that my family stands on high in the estimation of the City of Durham affords me sincere pleasure, and it will by my earnest endeavour to realise its expectations.' (Merrington, J.P. and M.P. Merrington, *Brancepeth 900: The Story of Brancepeth and its Rectors 1085–1985*, Durham, 1985)

～ May 29th ～

1828: A ceremony involving choristers at Durham Cathedral was restarted on this day, after it had lapsed in 1811, and continues on the same day each year. At the end of divine service the choristers make their way to the top of the middle tower where they sing anthems. The origins of this curious choral performance date back to the Battle of Neville's Cross on October 17th 1346 when Scottish and English armies clashed on a narrow moorland ridge just west of Durham City. The English troops had already chosen the best ground before Scottish forces assembled and after an even opening phase the Scots were outmanoeuvred and began to retreat. As Scottish losses mounted, their king was captured and imprisoned. During the following year English forces were able to press home their advantage, by occupying most of Scotland south of the rivers Forth and Clyde. One curious aspect of the annual ceremony is that the singing only takes place on three sides of the tower. The fourth side remains unused after a chorister was fatally injured when he fell from this high point. (www.english-heritage.org.uk)

~ MAY 30TH ~

1814: A silver goblet celebrating the efforts of a Durham citizen known as 'the patriotic tailor' has the following inscription: 'Presented on the 30 May, 1814, by a number of respectable inhabitants of the City of Durham to William Robinson as a mark of respect for his endeavours to procure and disseminate amongst them the earliest accounts of the late most glorious events and for his loyal conduct on every other occasion.' When news of Napoleon's downfall reached Durham on June 28th 1815, thirteen days after the Battle of Waterloo, William Robinson paid for the coach to be covered with flags, ribbons and laurel branches before riding on top, with a white banner, to spread the great news at towns and villages along the route to Newcastle. A few months later, when surviving members of the Black Watch Regiment passed through Durham, he organised a public subscription for their benefit. From his home in Millburngate, William Robinson organised the first circulating library in Durham for the benefit of fellow citizens and assembled a fascinating collection of military items. Following his death in 1837 the inscribed goblet was held by family descendants until it was handed over to Durham City. (*North Magazine: A Magazine for Durham, Northumberland and North Yorkshire*, York, 1971–)

1834: A general meeting of the Surtees Society was held on this day at which a report from a committee was considered in order to establish the rules of the society. It was agreed that there should be a patron of the society with the Lord Bishop of Durham filling that post and that the Warden of the University of Durham would serve initially as president while five members of the council could form a quorum to deal with business. In addition, the annual membership subscription was set at one guinea which included a free copy of a society publication that would carry 'the armorial bearings of the University of Durham in conjunction with the armorial bearings of Mr Surtees'. (Whellan, Francis, *History, Topography, and Directory of the County Palatine of Durham Comprising a General Survey of the County and a History of the City and Diocese of Durham* ... , London: Ballantyne, Hanson and Co., 1894)

2012: On this day the Rt Revd Justin Welby, Bishop of Durham, welcomed a new apprentice joiner, Peter Bennett, to his cathedral. This took place under the 'Foundation for Jobs' campaign which aimed to find 1,000 apprenticeships and internships by January 2013. In his post, which was sponsored by the City of Durham freemen, Peter Bennett would work alongside experienced joiners to produce a variety of pieces for use within the cathedral. (*The Northern Echo*, Darlington, 1870–)

∼ JUNE 1ST ∼

1837: The University of Durham was granted a royal charter by King William IV on this day and the first degrees were conferred one week later. Archdeacon Thorp's initial prospectus had stated that the period of education at Durham was to cover four years and although this arrangement was changed at a later date the initial intake of students graduated after completing four years of study. During July 1833 Thorp published *Preliminary Arrangements* which included a list of many of the staff and a complete list of both staff and students in the first calendar. During 1834 and 1835 the university's set of statutes were prepared and approved. The new institution was to be governed by the dean and chapter, with the bishop acting as Visitor while the affairs of the university were to be overseen by the warden, a senate and a convocation. The senate was composed of a small numbers of university academics and the Convocation initially consisted of members of the university who held higher degrees such as a Doctorate or Master's degree from Oxford, Cambridge or Dublin. Their numbers would be increased by holders of Durham higher degrees once these had been awarded. (Brickstock, R.J., *Durham Castle: Fortress, Palace, College,* Google Books, 2007, http://books.google.co.uk)

— JUNE 2ND —

1627: An entry in the Durham Cathedral Treasurer's Book on this day states: 'Mr Todd is appointed to bring in the Song books which he hath provided for the Quire [choir], And he to have paid by the treasurer for his paines ten pounds as moneyes come in …'

Two years later in 1629 an entry states: 'It is also agreed that Songe Bookes of the common and ordinarie services of the quire being now torne and decaied shall be new and fairely prickt out againe by Mr Todd and Toby Brookinge into fortie Quires of paper alreadie provided for that purpose and that they shall be rewarded and paid for their paines by the treasurers for the tyme being according to that agreement which Mr Cosin shall make with them for the same.' (Crosby, Brian, 'Durham Cathedral's liturgical music manuscripts, *ca. 1620–ca. 1640*', *Durham University Journal v. 66*, 1974, pp. 40–51)

1921: Brancepeth village First World War Memorial was unveiled by Lieutenant Colonel Hugh Bowes TD, DL, at 4 p.m. on this day. Sited on the north side of the church, it was designed by W.H. Wood and fashioned by masons from the estate using stone given by Viscount Boyne. It was dedicated by Ven. P.A. Derry, Archdeacon of Auckland. (Richardson, Michael, *Memory Lane: Durham City*, Derby: Breedon, 2000)

⁓ JUNE 3RD ⁓

1633: King Charles I left Durham Cathedral at 10 a.m. at the end of a visit that began on June 1st when he arrived with an escort provided by the high sheriff, William Belasyse. He had been met at the north door of the cathedral by the dean, Dr Hunt, with a carpet laid specially for the royal visit. After making his entry the king knelt 'on a faldstool with a costly cover, provided with cushions of purple velvet and began to say the Lord's Prayer in a low voice, while a canopy of silk and gold, supported on eight gilded staves, was held over him by eight Prebendaries of the church.' Further prayers and anthems were followed by a visit to St Cuthbert's tomb and the next day morning prayers in the cathedral were followed by a banquet. Before he left on June 3rd the king sent a letter to the dean and chapter with comment about things he had observed during this visit including 'certain meane tenements' in the churchyard which he considered 'most unfitting for that place' with instructions that after his departure tenements and their occupants should be removed. (Dufferwiel, Martin, *Durham: A Thousand Years of History and Legend*, Edinburgh: Mainstream, 1996)

— JUNE 4TH —

1948: Arrangements were announced on this day for the annual gala of County Labour Women at Durham. Mr Hugh Dalton was to make one of his first public engagements since his appointment as Chancellor of the Duchy of Lancaster and other chief speakers attending would include Mr Emanuel Shinwell, Secretary of State for War and Miss Mary E. Sutherland, Chief Women's Officer of the Labour Party. Ten bands would feature at the event along with 150 banners as thousands of women passed in procession through the central area of the city from Elvet Station to Wharton Park between 1.30 p.m. and 2.15 p.m. Most of the counties MPs were also expected to attend 'To enable this vast concourse of people to have an uninterrupted passage through the streets, traffic is to be diverted for an hour from 1.15 at the Salutation Corner (Framwellgate Moor), Sherburn Road Ends and the New Inn … In the event of rain, the Miners' Hall will be substituted for Wharton Park.' (*Durham Chronicle*, 1820–1984)

1948: Hetton Union Street Methodist church organ 'reopened' after renovation and improvements by a former choirmaster, Mr W. Strachan. New stops had been added and the small organ keyboard 'is now on pneumatic action'. (*Durham Chronicle*, 1820–1984)

— JUNE 5TH —

1253: The new high altar in Durham Cathedral was dedicated to St Mary the Virgin by Clement, Bishop of Dunblane who issued an indulgence to all who visited it with devotion and prayers. Eleven days later the first five altars in the row of nine which were eventually to stand against the eastern wall of the new extension were consecrated by the Bishop of Whithorn who also granted an indulgence. It seems likely that these five altars were the central section of the nine although they may have been the five at the northern end. After this time work slowed with only five altars standing in March 1257 when the Bishop of Brecin offered an indulgence and the last indulgence in its favour was granted in March 1279. (Snape, M.G., 'Documentary Evidence for Building of Durham Cathedral and its Monastic Buildings' in British Archaeological Association, *Medieval Art and Architecture at Durham Cathedral*, London: BAA, 1980)

1822: Stephen Kemble, actor, comedian and theatre owner died on this day at Durham City. He had moved to Durham in retirement after managing theatres at Glasgow, Edinburgh and Newcastle and became a close friend of the little Count Joseph Boruwlaski. (Proud, Keith, *Durham City*, Chichester: Phillimore, 2003)

~ JUNE 6TH ~

1459: An Indulgence published in London on this day recorded details of a fire in Durham Cathedral on 25th March 1459. It carried the names of three diocesans of the Northern Province, William Booth, Archbishop of York; his brother Laurence Booth, Bishop of Durham and William Percy, Bishop of Carlisle who each granted forty days remission of penance to all who within the next seven years should help in any way to repair the damage. The true extent of the fire has remained difficult to determine as medieval accounts tend to exaggerate such disastrous episodes and in this instance reports stated that 'the nave, tower, aisles and other buildings ... the bells and some great and costly goods were ... utterly consumed and turned to embers.' It seems certain that the central tower was badly damaged but there was no evidence on stonework to suggest that the nave and aisles were completely gutted. (Snape, M.G., 'Durham Cathedral: an "unknown" fire', *Transactions of the Architectural and Archaeological Society for Durham and Northumberland*, 1974, pp. 71–74)

1878: Durham-based Charles Hodgson Fowler was elected a Fellow of the Society of Antiquaries of London and thereafter signed his drawings and plans as 'C. Hodgson Fowler F.S.A.' He had moved to Durham in 1864 as clerk of works to Durham Cathedral and remained in the city for the rest of his life. (Wickstead, John, C., *Hodgson Fowler (1840–1910): Durham Architect and his Churches*, Durham: Durham County Local History Society, 2001)

⏤ June 7th ⏤

1957: Patrick Joseph McAloon (known as Paddy McAloon) was born this day in Durham and became a highly successful songwriter and member of the band Prefab Sprout. The group was formed in Newcastle in 1978 and enjoyed considerable success during the 1980s and early 1990s highlighted by a Top Ten hit in the UK Singles Chart with *The King of Rock 'n' Roll*. Apart from songs for his own band, Paddy McAloon has written material for artistes including Kylie Minogue, Wendy Mathews and Jimmy Nail. In September 2009 Prefab Sprout released their latest album *Let's Change The World With Music*, featuring the lead single *Let There Be Music*. (en.wikipedia.org/wiki/Paddy_McAloon)

⏤⸱⏤

2012: Durham Flower Club celebrated fifty years of existence with a golden anniversary cake at its meeting at Sherburn Community Hall. Guests included Councillor John Wilkinson, Mayor of Durham and Cynthia Wilkinson, the mayoress. A demonstration entitled *A Thread of Gold Running Through* was arranged by national demonstrator Janet Hayton. (*The Northern Echo*, Darlington, 1870–)

∼ JUNE 8TH ∼

2012: A group of Durham University students claimed a new record for the world's longest netball match that ended on this day after a 72 hour marathon challenge. Twenty-three members of the university's netball squad were confident of receiving official confirmation from Guinness World Record officials. They passed the previous best time of 61 hours, set by a Canadian club, at 1.00 a.m. but continued for a further 11 hours in the hope of retaining the title for as long as possible. The players who were selected from three University teams during nine months of preparations spent up to four hours on court before taking a break and then returning to action. Many tried to sleep on the floor and those who suffered injuries were treated and bandaged before returning to the action. The final score was 3,560 – 3,414 and the event raised around £10,000 for Help for Heroes, Sport in Action Zambia and club funds. (*The Northern Echo*, Darlington, 1870–)

2012: Multimillion pound plans were announced for a scheme that would see offices and leisure facilities on the Freeman's Reach site in Durham City. A business consortium intended to invest £27 million on the development which would create up to 800 jobs. (*The Northern Echo*, Darlington, 1870–)

~ JUNE 9TH ~

2012: Organisers cancelled the 179th Durham Regatta which was scheduled for this day and the following day. Although the race programme had previously been curtailed by bad weather, it was the first occasion on which the country's second oldest regatta, predating Henley, had been cancelled. The cancellation at daybreak followed a series of heavy downpours that caused dangerously high river levels around Durham City. Thousands of rowers were expected to compete and many from around the country and overseas were already in Durham before the decision was made. An innovative feature would have been a modern recreation of an 1815 parade of boats in honour of the victory at Waterloo. Day two was cancelled at 6.30 a.m. on the Sunday (10th) and organisers were counting losses amounting to several thousand pounds. (*Durham Times*, Durham: Newsquest, 2007–)

2012: Police officers led by Durham's chief constable, Jon Stoddart, took part in a cycling tour of all twelve principal police stations in the force area in the lead up to his retirement later in the year. During the 121 mile circuit which began at Aykley Heads, Durham City, riders experienced several types of weather conditions in their efforts to raise funds for Durham Agency Against Crime and the Women *v.* Cancer charity. (*The Northern Echo*, Darlington, 1870–)

~ JUNE 10TH ~

2011: It was announced that Professor Rosemary Cramp, one of this country's leading experts on archaeology, had been made a Dame Commander of the Order of the British Empire. This latest honour followed her CBE which was awarded in the 1987 New Year's Honours List. Her interest in archaeology began on her father's farm in Leicestershire and, when she was just aged 12, she unearthed the remains of a Roman villa. After graduating from St Ann's College, Oxford, in 1950, she spent time on the staff as a lecturer and then joined the staff of Durham University's department of archaeology in 1955, where she took a particular interest in the Anglo Saxon and later medieval periods. In 1966 Rosemary Cramp was promoted to senior lecturer and five years later she became Durham's first female professor. During the next thirty-five years she played a leading role in expanding the archaeology department and lectured widely in Britain and abroad. She has also played a leading part in the campaign to achieve World Heritage Status for Monkwearmouth and Jarrow. On her retirement in 1990 she became a professor emeritus and set up the Rosemary Cramp Fund to provide small grants for students and staff. (www.palatinate.org.uk)

⌐ June 11th ⌐

1112: St Giles church on Gilesgate in Durham City was founded by Ranulph Flambard, Bishop of Durham (1099–1128) and dedicated by him on this day (St Barnabas' Day). The north wall of the nave has two narrow round-headed windows and is part of the original church while the chancel dates from about 1190. The tower was added during the thirteenth century and an upper storey was completed on the orders of Cardinal Langley in the early fifteenth century and houses two bells. The original portion of the church served as a chapel to a nearby hospital which was destroyed by fire in 1144 when William Cumin made an illegal attempt to take over the bishopric. The hospital was rebuilt some ten years later at Kepier on the orders of Bishop Pudsey. In the sanctuary of St Giles church there is a remarkable wooden figure of a thin man in armour gazing calmly upwards. With a thin, long, bearded face, his head is resting on a scroll enclosing two skulls. It is a memorial of John Heath who died in 1591 and, along with Bernard Gilpin, founded the Kepier School at Houghton-le-Spring. (Proud, Keith, *Durham City*, Chichester: Phillimore, 2003)

⁓ June 12th ⁓

1663: On this date the Chapter of Durham gave a detailed reply to a series of questions posed by Bishop Cosin. He had been appointed in 1661 and within the diocese he attempted to enforce universal compliance with the Church of England. At this point in time the chapter had spent £4,306 3s 1d on the cathedral and £3,616 7s 3d on the repair of houses and chancels of churches. It had also given the king a gift of £1,000 in addition to amounts given to him by individuals. Other amounts included £566 13s 4d to old choirmen and the poor and £400 for the redemption of captives, so that the overall total amounted to £13,259 3s 8d. Future work included rebuilding the minor canons' houses, additional work in the choir, repairing turrets and pavements and installing a new font and pulpit. The estimated cost for these works was around £3,000. It was also clear that there were not as many services as in previous times and although the chapter had made considerable progress Bishop Cosin was not satisfied. Further visitations took place during 1665 and then 1668 with more thorough checks into what had been completed. (Stranks, C.J., *This Sumptuous Church: The Story of Durham Cathedral*, London: SPCK, 1993)

~ JUNE 13TH ~

1808: Fear of invasion by French forces during the early stages of the nineteenth century led to increased activity by local volunteer forces and on this day the Durham Volunteers, commanded by Lieutenant Colonel Shipperdson, marched from Durham City to Stockton-on-Tees where they were brigaded with the Stockton volunteers. During their stay they were inspected by Colonel Seddon 'who was pleased to express in a very unfeigned manner, that he had not for some time seen either militia or any other corps who could exceed them in discipline. In the evening there was a concert of vocal and instrumental music, conducted by Mr Friend, and patronised by the officers of the two corps, which was followed by a ball, when the room was thronged by all the beauty and fashion of the surrounding neighbourhood.' On June 24th the Durham Volunteers returned home. (Richmond, Thomas, *The Local Records of Stockton and the Neighbourhood; or, a Register of Memorable Events, Chronologically Arranged, Which Have Occurred in and near Stockton Ward and the North-Eastern Parts of Cleveland*, Stockton: William Robinson, 1868)

1934: George Chandos Cradock, who had played a major role in developing music in the Durham area, died on this day. Soon after moving to Durham in 1905 he founded the Durham Amateur Operatic Society and for twenty years he was choir master at St Nicholas' church. After retiring as tenor soloist at Durham Cathedral in 1931 he was musical instructor for the Workers' Educational Association. (*Teesdale Mercury*, Barnard Castle: Teesdale Mercury, 1855)

~ JUNE 14TH ~

1913: A second chapel was dedicated on this day at St Hild's College, Durham almost exactly a year after the foundation stone had been laid by Mr J.W. Hills DCL, MP. St Hild's College had been established in 1858 as a teacher training college for women and after the granting of a supplemental charter in 1895 women were allowed to receive degrees from Durham University. Accordingly, in 1898 graduates from St Hild's College were the first three female graduates from Durham. The College of the Venerable Bede had opened in 1839 as a training college for males and in 1975 the two colleges combined and subsequently became a University Council controlled college four years later. At this point they no longer specialised in education and each college had its own chapel. The Hild Chapel has been adapted as the Joachim Room for staging college functions but on St Hild's Day the service is held in the old chapel. Although extensions have been added to the original St Hild's College buildings and a £2.9 million renovation was carried out during 2003, original names such as 'New Dorm', 'Upper Precincts' and 'Lawrence Wing' have been retained. (www.dur.ac.uk/hild-bede)

― JUNE 15TH ―

1812: On this day, 'The freemen of Durham, in consequence of several encroachments, perambulated the boundaries of that city, a custom which had been neglected since the inclosure of the adjacent moors. The procession set out from the town hall at 10 o'clock the grassmen on horseback, attended by the banners of the various trades, the city waits (music), drums, beadle etc.' (Fordyce, T. (ed.), *Local Records; or, Historical Register of Remarkable Events which have Occurred in Northumberland and Durham … 1833 to [1875], Being a Continuation of the Work Published by … Mr. John Sykes,* Newcastle upon Tyne: T. Fordyce, 1867–1876)

―――

1829: 'A young man named William Taylor, apprentice to Mr John Forsyth, of Durham, slater, having been sent to assist in making certain repairs in the roof of the cathedral, fell from a height of 78 feet upon the flags, in the Chapel of the Nine Altars and, wonderful to relate, received only trifling injury.' (Fordyce, T. (ed.), *Local Records; or, Historical Register of Remarkable Events which have Occurred in Northumberland and Durham … 1833 to [1875], Being a Continuation of the Work Published by … Mr. John Sykes,* Newcastle upon Tyne: T. Fordyce, 1867–1876)

— June 16th —

2012: Thousands of people lined the streets of towns in County Durham as the Olympic torch was carried on a southerly route from Tyneside to Durham City on this day. Steadily falling rain failed to dampen the spirits of onlookers as the flame moved through the city's narrow streets to the Racecourse where a huge crowd of spectators followed its progress on a huge screen. Entertainment at this spacious venue included indie rockers Little Comets and former *Britain's Got Talent* contestants Twist and Pulse. The torch was carried on the final leg of the relay by Durham-born television presenter, Matt Baker, who lit a cauldron that burned all night. Moments after he had ignited the cauldron at the Racecourse the skies brightened and a rainbow appeared in the sky. After an overnight stay in the city the torch left Durham during an event in the marketplace when England and Durham cricketer, Paul Collingwood, carried the flame on the first leg of the relay shortly before 8.45 a.m. (*The Northern Echo*, Darlington, 1870–)

1954: Lady Reading, Director of the Women's Voluntary Service (WVS) was accompanied during her visit to Durham today by the mayor, Councillor E. Blyth. During her visit she addressed local representatives on the subject of 'Civil Defence'. (Richardson, Michael, *Memory Lane: Durham City*, Derby: Breedon, 2000)

~ JUNE 17TH ~

1966: A press report on this day stated that Ald. Norman Richardson, the former Mayor of Durham who made the city tourist-conscious and was largely responsible for the launching of the Publicity and Tourist Development Committee, had told the city's traders that Durham was 'on the spring-board and ready to jump.' But this optimism was tempered by the realisation that the Tourist Development Committee badly needed re-energising by a transfusion of new members from outside organisations, bringing with them new ideas and fresh enthusiasm. Earnings from tourism were increasing year by year and Ald. Richardson said it was right that Durham, steeped in history, should share in this prosperity, but he was sad to think that so long was being taken in doing something about it. He said it was twelve months since he asked for a Tourist Information Office, which many cities had, to be set up in the marketplace. Critics pointed out that there was a serious shortage of hotel accommodation but he felt this would improve if there was a proved demand. This influx of visitors to Durham would pose a challenge which must be met by continually 'trimming up' the city to make it as attractive as possible. (*Durham County Advertiser*, 1855–1968)

~ June 18th ~

1679: Elizabeth, wife of Cuthbert Coulson, was buried on this day and an affidavit was issued two days later. (The affidavit, a written declaration on oath, was to certify that burial had taken place in a woollen shroud, in accordance with an Act of Parliament from the reign of Charles II to encourage woollen output.) (*St. Mary le Bow, Durham, Burial Register, 1687–1801*, Durham Record Office: P/Du.MB 2)

1834: At 6 p.m. the different boats upon the River Wear proceeded in grand procession from the Prebends Bridge up the river to Old Durham, accompanied by a band of music, which played the greater part of the way. The rowers in the boats were all dressed in their different uniforms and each boat had a small flag flying from its stern. The boats afterwards came back to the Prebends Bridge and each took in some ladies and proceeded up the water again towards Old Durham. The rowing on the water terminated a little after 9 p.m.; after which a quantity of fireworks were set off from a platform, erected for that purpose at the water side near the Banks mill. On the following day a similar exhibition took place. (Richardson, M.A., *The Local Historian's Table Book, of Remarkable Occurrences, Historical Facts, Traditions, Legendary and Descriptive Ballads, &c., &c., Connected with the Counties of Newcastle-upon-Tyne, Northumberland and Durham*, Newcastle upon Tyne: M.A. Richardson, 1841–1846)

— June 19th —

1636: Jacob Bee was baptised at the chapel of St Margaret's, Framwellgate, on this day and grew up in Durham to spend his working life there as a skinner and glover. Over about twenty-five years he compiled entries in a diary which include many references to weather conditions: May 31st 1682, 'Betwixt 11 and 12 at night, was a very fearfull thunder with flashes of fire, very tirrible'; August 15th 1682, 'A blazing stare appeared'; November 20th 1682, 'Being Munday this yeare and a great wind which blew one half of the west end of a window in Abby church'; December 20th 1689, 'A figure of a comet appeared about three quarters of an hour after four at night, the first appearance was in the form of a half-moon, very firie, and afterwards did change itself to a firye sword and run westward.' (thediaryjunction.blogspot.co.uk)

1921: A war memorial plaque was dedicated in the chapel of Hatfield College, Durham during a service led by Revd Canon J.T. Fowler, former vice principal and chaplain of the college. Fashioned from oak, it had three panels with the names of twenty-six former students who had been killed in action below the inscription: 'In memory of members of this college who in the years 1914–18 laid down their lives in the Great War.' (www.newmp.org.uk)

— JUNE 20TH —

1959: During a ceremony on this day, Professor J.B. Kemp, Mr and Mrs D.R. Nicholls and Deaconess Freda Buckley laid foundation stones of the Gilesgate Baptist church in Durham. (Richardson, Michael, *Memory Lane: Durham City*, Derby: Breedon, 2000)

—————

2011: Durham World Heritage Site Visitor Centre opened at No. 7 Owengate in a former almshouse that had been constructed during the 1830s. It replaced a seventeenth-century almshouse property on Palace Green which was needed for educational purposes and the eight long-term occupants were transferred to the Owengate building. Here the same internal arrangement provided four rooms on each of the two floors along with a communal area on the ground floor. Foundation inscriptions on this newer building refer to both John Cosin, the bishop who established the Palace Green property some 200 years earlier and Edward Maltby, the bishop in the 1830s. The exposed position in Owengate has led to deterioration of external features and probably accounts for the removal of chimneys which would have been linked to five internal fireplaces. The internal layout provides an ideal venue for providing permanent displays as well as for staging temporary exhibitions and events. (www.durhamworldheritagesite.com)

– June 21st –

1675: The first election of representatives for County Durham took place on this day. It followed legislation during 1673 which empowered the freeholders of Durham to elect two knights for the county, and the mayor, aldermen and freemen of the City of Durham to elect two burgesses to represent them in Parliament. At the election the candidates were John Tempest, Esq., Thomas Vane Esq. of Raby Castle and Sir Thomas Clavering, Bart. of Axwell. The two former were elected. Mr Vane died of smallpox two days after his election and was succeeded by his younger brother, Christopher Vane Esq. The election of members for the city was delayed by technical difficulties until 1678. Sir Ralph Cole, Bart of Brancepeth Castle and John Parkhurst, Esq. of Catesby, Northamptonshire were returned. (Whellan, Francis, *History, Topography, and Directory of the County Palatine of Durham Comprising a General Survey of the County and a History of the City and Diocese of Durham* … , London: Ballantyne, Hanson and Co., 1894)

———

1836: Legislation for separating the Palatinate Jurisdiction of the County Palatine of Durham from the Bishoprick of Durham became law on this date. Doubts about the construction of this Act led to the enactment of the Durham County Palatine Act of 1858. (Townsend, George Henry, *The Manual of Dates: A Dictionary of Reference to all the Most Important Events in the History of Mankind to be Found in Authentic Records,* London: Frederick Warne, 1874)

~ JUNE 22ND ~

1897: Public celebrations marking the sixtieth anniversary of Queen Victoria's accession to the throne were held throughout the country on this day. The actual date of accession was two days earlier and this was marked by a family service at St George's Chapel. On Tuesday June 22nd, Queen Victoria telegraphed a message to all the countries of the Empire before leaving Buckingham Palace for St Paul's Cathedral in a large procession that was greeted by cheering crowds along the whole route. In Durham the city was full of flags and shields portraying the queen amid masses of floral bunting. All children were presented with a bag of cakes and a commemorative mug and the local newspaper *Durham County Advertiser* devoted two full pages to coverage of both local and national celebrations. As darkness fell the River Wear was a blaze of light as an illuminated boat procession travelled from Prebends Bridge to the racecourse and bonfires were lit around the city, with a huge blaze on the old pit heap known locally as 'The Duff Heap' which marked the site of Kepier Colliery beside Sunderland Road. (Richardson, Michael, *Durham: Cathedral City*, Thrupp: Sutton, 1997)

ᵔ JUNE 23RD ᵔ

1903: Lord Roberts of Kandahar, a cousin of Captain Roberts of Hollingside, visited Durham on this day to receive an honorary degree from the university. Frederick Sleigh Roberts was one of the most successful commanders of the armed forces during the nineteenth century. He served in India during the Indian Rebellion (or Mutiny) of 1857 and took part in an expedition to Abyssinia as well as the Second Anglo-Afghan War before leading British forces to success in the Second Boer War. Down the years he received a series of honours and awards including the Victoria Cross for his actions on January 2nd 1858 at Khudaganj and on February 23rd 1892 he was created Baron Roberts of Kandahar in Afghanistan and of the City of Waterford. While he was in Durham he inspected members of the Church Lads' Brigades who then marched from Palace Green through the city towards Elvet Bridge. (Richardson, Michael, *Memory Lane: Durham City*, Derby: Breedon, 2000)

1911: Celebrations were held in Durham on this day following the coronation of King George V the day before. (George had become king on the death of Edward VII on May 6th 1910.) Londoners staged a Festival of Empire while in Durham flags and bunting were hung in the marketplace and a great bonfire was lit on Gilesgate Moor. (Simpson, David, *Durham Millennium: A Thousand Years of Durham City*, Darlington: Northern Echo, 1995)

~ JUNE 24TH ~

1987: The Bounds Wall with Racket Ball Courts structure at Ushaw College received listed building status Grade II* on this day. Dating from 1850 it was the work of Joseph Hansom and represents an impressive mid-nineteenth-century games area in its original form. Few, if any, other such multiple games facilities have survived from that era and its importance is increased by the adjacent group of college buildings. Ushaw College was built as a Roman Catholic School and seminary between 1804 and 1808 as one of the replacement institutions of the English College at Douai in northern France. At that time it was known as St Cuthbert's College and it continued to expand during the nineteenth century. The area of playing fields located immediately to the east of the main building and known as The Bounds was set up as part of the original foundation. Construction of a new library building during 1851 encroached on this area and The Bounds was relocated further to the east. It was designed as an integrated games complex incorporating ball places and racquet houses along with two courts for the game of cat. Cat is an ancient game, a precursor to baseball and rounders played by two sides of seven players, believed to have been adopted at the English College at Douai. (Pevsner, Nikolaus, *County Durham*, Harmondsworth: Penguin, 1983)

~ JUNE 25TH ~

2013: An audience at Durham's City Theatre enjoyed a production of *Private Lives* by Noel Coward staged by the Durham Dramatic Society. This amateur group, based in Durham, was formed in 1929 and flourished during the Second World War (1939–45) after the Voluntary Entertainment Service was set up in November 1939. Many of the productions were the work of Margaret Marshall who was responsible for organising a total of 934 shows (variety and plays); 228 of these were three-act plays and almost all were performed by Durham Dramatic Society. They included more than 100 performances of *Gaslight*, a real favourite with troop audiences, with Margaret Marshall playing the role of Mrs Manningham. In more recent years *Gaslight* has again featured in productions by Durham Dramatic Society, most notably in April 2001 when Liz Cooke played Mrs Manningham, Mike Smith the evil husband and Ian Woodhouse the retired Detective Rough. In 1950 the Society began to use the old Civic Restaurant in Back Silver Street for rehearsals and storage and from 1968 plays were staged in the Assembly Rooms in Saddler Street. The City Theatre, one of the country's smallest with only 71 seats, was opened in 1986 using the former British Restaurant building in Fowler's Yard. (www.durham-city-theatre.co.uk)

— June 26th —

2012: World-renowned opera star, Sir Thomas Allen was officially installed as Chancellor of Durham University at a morning ceremony in Durham Cathedral. Originally from Seaham Harbour, Sir Thomas received the Durham University chancellor's robes and cap and took an oath of office during the ceremony. His appointment as the twelfth chancellor in the university's 180 year history was announced in October 2011 and he received the robes from his predecessor as chancellor, travel writer Bill Bryson. One of his first duties as chancellor saw Sir Thomas, who is said to have inspired Lee Hall to write *Billy Elliot*, confer honorary doctorates of letters on Philip Pullman, author of the highly successful trilogy *His Dark Materials* and David Inshaw who is well known for his painting *The Badminton Game* which is on display at the Tate Gallery. Their certificates were presented during congregation ceremonies at the beginning of a week that saw thousands of students graduate. Professor Chris Higgins, vice-chancellor of Durham University, congratulated Sir Thomas on his installation and referred to him as 'a truly inspirational person and an excellent role model.' For his part, Sir Thomas said that he was both 'hugely humbled and immensely proud.' (*The Northern Echo*, Darlington, 1870–)

— JUNE 27TH —

2012: News reports speculated on the reasons for a clock bell starting to chime again for the first time in decades. Located on the roof of Durham Crown Court, the bell had been chiming again for over a week but with an increasing gap of about 30 seconds between chimes, so that it was now taking 5 or 6 minutes to complete the noon signal. Staff based at the Crown Court were perplexed by the unscheduled resumption of the chimes and offered any number of reasons including an Act of God, a bolt of lightning during a thunderstorm and even beyond the grave activity of an executed murderer. (*The Northern Echo,* Darlington, 1870–)

———

2012: Two well-known BBC personalities were awarded honorary degrees at a ceremony in Durham Cathedral. Biddy Baxter, editor of *Blue Peter* from 1965 to 1988 who graduated from Durham with a degree in Social Studies in 1955, was awarded an honorary Doctorate of Letters as University vice-chancellor Professor Chris Higgins took the opportunity to sport his *Blue Peter* badge. Jeremy Vine, radio and television presenter, who graduated with a degree in English Language in 1986, was awarded an honorary Doctorate of Civil Law. (*The Northern Echo,* Darlington, 1870–)

~ JUNE 28TH ~

1750: Edward Chandler, Archbishop of Durham by his will dated on June 28th 1750, demised the sum of £2,666 13s 4d in 2 ¾ per cent stocks, the interest to be applied in the relief of six poor widows in the diocese. (Whellan, Francis, *History, Topography, and Directory of the County Palatine of Durham Comprising a General Survey of the County and a History of the City and Diocese of Durham* ... , London: Ballantyne, Hanson and Co., 1894)

1839: A railway station was opened at Shincliffe at the western terminus of a line from Sunderland that had been started by Sunderland Dock Company in 1831. Initially this line ended at Sherburn House Station, near Sherburn Hospital, with plans to extend it to Old Elvet. Opposition from local landowners meant that the proposal was abandoned and instead the line was taken to Shincliffe. Approaching the village from the east, the line crossed Shincliffe's main street near the Railway Tavern, a nineteenth-century hostelry that closed in the early years of the twentieth century. Shincliffe town station was opposite the site of the inn on the north side of the railway line. From Shincliffe a wagonway crossed the river by a bridge to reach Houghall Colliery and continued through a tunnel below Houghall Wood to link with a pit near Croxdale. (*Durham Times*, Durham: Newsquest, 2007–)

— JUNE 29TH —

1919: Today local newspapers reported on the fate of captured German field guns following unofficial festivities in Durham marketplace to mark the signing of the Treaty of Versailles. In December 1918 four guns had been handed to the city as war trophies by the Northumberland Fusiliers and when news of developments at Versailles reached the departing customers of city centre public houses, demobbed soldiers and sailors seized the guns and dragged them round the marketplace whilst singing patriotic songs. Some members of the volatile crowd then proposed heaving them into the river and the guns were pulled down Walkergate. However, matters did not go according to plan as the first gun crashed through the doors of the Palace Cinema to the considerable annoyance of patrons inside the building. Before long they were back on track, where a sewer pipe presented a temporary obstruction before the guns were heaved into the River Wear. (*Durham County Advertiser*, 1855–1968)

2012: Gary Fildes, director of Kielder Observatory, the only dark-sky public observatory in Europe, received an honorary Master of Science degree from Durham University. A lifelong interest in astronomy prompted him to raise funds to build the observatory which opened in 2008. (*The Northern Echo*, Darlington, 1870–)

– June 30th –

1927: The Kerr Memorial Arch at Durham School was officially opened on the annual Speech Day. It bears the inscription: 'In grateful memory of Graham Campbell Kerr, a loyal son of the school, born 1872, s.n. 1886–1890. Assistant Master 1895–1901. Governor of the Red Sea Province, Sudan, 1909. Died August 18th 1913.' The arch is at the front entrance to the school and has Grade II listed status. Durham School was founded by Bishop Langley in 1414 and refounded by King Henry VIII during 1541, before moving from buildings on Palace Green to the present site adjacent to Quarryheads Lane in 1844. (en.wikipedia.org/wiki/Durham_School)

2012: An exhibition *Restoration: Bishop Cosin, His Library and the Changing Face of Durham* opened in the Dunelm Gallery at Palace Green Library on this day. The exhibition marked completion of a £350,000 conservation project at the library and celebrated the work of Bishop John Cosin who was responsible for the construction of several of the city's best-known buildings. As a close ally of Charles I he was exiled during the English Civil War but after the restoration of the monarchy he was appointed to the influential post of Bishop of Durham by Charles II. (*The Northern Echo,* Darlington, 1870–)

~ JULY 1ST ~

1639: James Hull bequeathed to Thomas Hull 'all that seat house in Brancepeth and garth, one little Close, bounding on ye King's High Street, west and south; on Cowper's Loaning, north and in late occupation of Nic Cocky (Curate of Brancepeth).' The bequest was confirmed by Rector Cosin. (Merrington, J.P. and M.P. Merrington, *Brancepeth 900: The Story of Brancepeth and its Rectors 1085–1985*, Durham, 1985)

———

2013: An exhibition of the Lindisfarne Gospels opened in a building on Palace Green close to Durham Cathedral. It was a symbolic moment for the city, the county and the whole region as for the first time since the Reformation the Gospels were reunited with St Cuthbert, the holy man who inspired the sacred text and whose shrine is located within the nearby walls of Durham Cathedral alongside the Venerable Bede. The exhibition formed the centrepiece of a range of activities and events that had taken place in the region during the run up to the Gospel's return and which reflected the journeys of St Cuthbert and his monks from the Scottish Borders southwards into Yorkshire. During their stay in Durham, the Gospels were within a temperature and humidity controlled environment, with pages of the book turned just once, halfway through the three month exhibition. (*The Northern Echo*, Darlington, 1870–)

– JULY 2ND –

1983: High Speed Train power car No. 43153 was named 'University of Durham' in a ceremony at Durham Station on this day. The power car had arrived empty from Heaton Traction Maintenance Depot and after the unveiling of the name plaque by the Chancellor of Durham University, Dame Margot Fonteyn de Arias, the HST went immediately into revenue-earning service by forming a special train to Leeds. Dame Margot was presented with a model of the power car as a memento of the occasion. An entry in the catalogue of *Railwayana Auctions* in May 2009 listed the 'Nameplate University of Durham with integral Badge, Ex HST Class 43 Number 43153 built by BREL Crewe and introduced to traffic in 1981. Named at Durham Station on July 2nd 1983 by Dame Margot Fonteyn-de-Arias, Chancellor of the University. This cast Newton plate was removed in June 1991 and replaced with a reflective style plate with separate Badge. Currently running unnamed for Great Western. Alloy construction measuring 42¼' x 9' face has red ground, shield a white ground and red cross, rear badge ex loco. A small photograph of Dame Margot unveiling the plate accompanies. Hammer Price £1,800.' (Allen, David H., *Diesels in the North-East*, Poole: Oxford Publishing, 1984)

~ July 3rd ~

1875: Founded in 1871, the Durham Miners' Gala drew huge crowds in succeeding years and on July 3rd 1875 the LNER Railway Company withdrew all trains from Bishop Auckland, Lanchester and Newcastle to Durham. The company claimed that its railways could not cope with the huge number of passengers travelling to the gala, but it is possible that the real reason was politically motivated. (www.englandsnortheast.co.uk)

———

2012: On this day news reports indicated that a potential English national anthem had been rediscovered and rerecorded to celebrate the Queen's diamond jubilee. The song entitled 'England' was written by Hubert Parry during 1918 making use of words from John of Gaunt's monologue in Shakespeare's play *Richard II*. Parry died in the same year and the anthem was largely forgotten until it was rediscovered by Professor Jeremy Dibble of Durham University. He arranged a recording on a CD to be released later in 2012 to celebrate the diamond jubilee. It also included a recording of *Jerusalem* which Professor Dibble claimed was the first for nearly a century to be performed as it was originally conceived. (*The Northern Echo*, Darlington, 1870–)

~ July 4th ~

1891: The annual demonstration of the miners in the county of Durham was held on Durham Racecourse. The speakers were Messrs S. Storey, Atherley Jones, T. Burt and W.R. Cremer MPs in addition to the agents and leading members of the Miners' Executive. The amount of the Miners' Fund was stated as £52,260. (*Monthly Chronicle of North-Country Lore and Legend, Part LIV, August,* London: W. Scott, 1891)

1942: St Catherine's church, New Brancepeth was destroyed by fire on this day after two youths broke into the vestry and lit candles. The flames then ignited fabric and the blaze spread through the building. The only item to be salvaged was the bell which had originally come from a shipwreck. During the fire the vicar tried to retrieve some items from the church and received injuries that needed hospital treatment. St Catherine's congregation moved into the church hall and transformed it into the fine place of worship that is still in use. The church building destroyed in the fire had been built on land provided by Lord Boyne. Costs incurred in constructing the Gothic-style stone church amounted to £2,000 and there was seating for 252 worshippers. It had been consecrated by Bishop Westcott on September 11th 1890. (www.brandonparish.org.uk)

~ July 5th ~

1593: On this day the Catholic priest John Boste was apprehended in the house of William Claxton, in the village of Waterhouses a few miles west of Durham City. He had been betrayed by a man named Ecclesfield or Eglesfield and Boste was taken in chains to the Tower of London for interrogation by Queen Elizabeth herself. Although he was subject to periods of torture on the rack, he refused to renounce his Catholic beliefs and was moved back to Durham to appear at the July Assizes. The verdict was delivered – 'guilty as charged' and John Boste was sentenced to be hung, drawn and quartered. The gallows in Durham were located opposite the present County Hall at Dryburn and it was here on July 24th 1594 that the Catholic priest was martyred. It was a particularly gruesome episode for, after climbing a ladder to the gallows, a noose was placed around his neck and the ladder was removed. The priest fell only a short distance and was left hanging and kicking until the rope was cut. He landed on his feet and very much alive until the executioner carried out a series of barbaric mutilations. John Boste was canonised by Pope Paul VI in 1970. (*The Northern Echo*, Darlington, 1870–)

‒ July 6th ‒

1926: Local press outlets reported an accident at drift mine workings in Kepier Wood in which John Smith, aged 25 from the Claypath district of Durham City, had been trapped by a fall of stone. Coal mining in County Durham had reached a peak in 1923 when 170,000 miners were employed and, along with a fall of stone, the other hazard was gas explosion. The problem of roof safety had been addressed as early as 1728 when the use of pillars to support roofs was first recorded. Coal tubs were drawn by steel ropes along a waggonway that was linked to Grange Colliery and passed underneath the arches of the Brasside–Belmont viaduct. (Richardson, Michael, *Durham: The Photographic Collection*, Stroud: Sutton, 2002)

1962: Honorary degrees were conferred on several eminent personalities in a ceremony at Durham Castle on this day. Best known of these was Charles Spencer Chaplin, popularly known as Charlie Chaplin, who was awarded a D. Litt (Doctor of Letters) degree. Born in London in April 1889 he carved out a spectacular career as vocalist, actor and filmmaker. Other recipients were Earl Grey DCL, the Earl of Scarborough, chancellor of the University and Dr Benjamin Spock DSc. (Richardson, Michael, *Memory Lane: Durham City*, Derby: Breedon, 2000)

~ JULY 7TH ~

1917: Second Lieutenant Frederick Youens of the 13th Battalion, the Durham Light Infantry was seriously injured during a night patrol and had to return to friendly trenches to have his injuries dressed on this day. While he was there German forces staged a brief but fierce bombardment that was soon followed by an attack on the front line involving about fifty enemy troops. Although he was only half-dressed, Youens immediately rushed forward to help and reorganised a Lewis Gun team that had been disrupted by the enemy's fire. A grenade was lobbed towards them but Frederick Youens picked it up and hurled it back towards the attacking force. Seconds afterwards another bomb landed nearby and as Youens attempted to retrieve and return it the bomb exploded. He suffered fatal injuries. Reporting on the awarding of the Victoria Cross to Frederick Youens, the London Gazette stated, 'There can be little doubt that the prompt and gallant action of Second Lieutenant Frederick Youens saved several of his men's lives and that by his energy and resource the raid was completely repulsed.' Second Lieutenant Frederick Youens VC is buried in Railway Dugouts Burial Ground. (imtheboy.wordpress.com)

~ JULY 8TH ~

1674: Dennis Granville, Archdeacon of Durham and prebendary of the first stall, was making his way through the cloisters of Durham Cathedral after a funeral attended by many of the area's leading figures when county bailiffs arrested him for debt. They paid no attention to his claim that his status as one of the king's chaplains meant that he could not be arrested and the undersherriff declined to intervene on his behalf. Granville was then imprisoned 'with many aggravating circumstances' and this prompted him to appeal to the king. The order came for the undersherriff and the creditor, whose claim had led to Granville's arrest, to be prosecuted but they were then excused after claiming that they were unaware of his role as a king's chaplain. Dennis Granville had married Bishop Cosin's daughter, Anne, in 1660 and constantly pestered his father-in-law to hand over Anne's dowry. Cosin refused to do this as he was convinced that any such payment would immediately be passed to Granville's creditors and this resulted in endless acrimonious correspondence between the two men. (Stranks, C.J., *This Sumptuous Church: The Story of Durham Cathedral,* London: SPCK, 1993)

— JULY 9TH —

1283: Anthony Bek, Archdeacon of Durham, was elected bishop on this day and consecrated on January 9th in the following year. During his term of office he played an important role in the major events of King Edward I's reign and under Bishop Bek the palatine power 'reached the high meridian of its greatness' and the court of Durham displayed all the appendages of royalty. Surrounded by his officers of state, or marching at the head of his troops, in peace or in war, he appeared as the military chief of a powerful and independent franchise. Nobles addressed the palatine sovereign kneeling, and instead of menial servants, knights waited in his presence-chamber and at his table bareheaded and standing. He founded the collegiates of Chester and Lanchester, erected towers at Gainford and Coniscliffe, and added to the buildings of Auckland and Barnard Castles. He died on March 3rd 1310 at his manor house of Eltham, and was the first prelate of Durham who was buried within the cathedral. (Whellan, Francis, *History, Topography, and Directory of the County Palatine of Durham Comprising a General Survey of the County and a History of the City and Diocese of Durham* ... , London: Ballantyne, Hanson and Co., 1894)

1950: A Durham Light Infantry Memorial Garden was dedicated in the cathedral precincts at a service conducted by the Bishop of Durham. Brigadier J.A. Churchill laid the wreath. (www.durhamrecordoffice.org.uk)

~ July 10th ~

1771: On this day a new theatre opened in Durham City with a production of *The West Indian* and other entertainment to a very genteel audience, who expressed the greatest satisfaction at the elegance of the playhouse and of the performance in general. *The West Indian* had been produced in London earlier in the same year with opening scenes that depict a lavish reception being prepared for a planter coming to England as if it was the lord mayor who was expected. A servant in the early scenes of the play comments, 'He's very rich and that's sufficient. They say he has rum and sugar enough belonging to him to make all the water in the Thames into punch.' The sugar planter ranked among the biggest capitalists of this era when the slave trade was at its peak. (Sykes, John, *Local Records: or, Historical Register of Remarkable Events Which Have Occurred in Northumberland and Durham, Newcastle upon Tyne, and Berwick upon Tweed from the Earliest Period of Authentic Record, to the Present Time* ..., Newcastle, 1833)

1968: On this day the Durham Light Infantry was disbanded and became part of a newly created regiment, the Light Infantry, which also incorporated the King's Own Yorkshire Light Infantry, the King's Shropshire Light Infantry and the Somerset and Cornwall Light Infantry. (www.lightinfantry.co.uk/history.html)

~ July 11th ~

1474: John Raynoldson, of Cocken, and John Ferry, of the same place, did penance in Durham Cathedral on this day, for violating the Liberties of St Cuthbert. Each walked bareheaded, covered with a linen shirt, and carrying in his hand a lighted candle of the weight of half a pound. John Robynson, of the same place, performed a similar penance in Finchale Abbey. In the same year Lionel Claxton, gentleman, did penance in the chapel of Bearpark, for a like reason. (Sykes, John, *Local Records: or Historical Register of Remarkable Events Which Have Occurred Exclusively in the Counties of Durham and Northumberland, Town and County of Newcastle upon Tyne and Berwick upon Tweed; with an Obituary of Persons of Talent, Eccentricity, and Longevity*, Newcastle: T. Fordyce, 1866)

1823: James Brown, widely known as the 'Durham Poet', died in the Old Elvet district of Durham. Born in Scotland he spent many years in Newcastle plying his trade as a tailor but when his first wife died he married an elderly lady 'not devoid of eccentricities' who had property in Durham. Brown's pamphlets such as *Poetry, Scriptural Hieroglyphics* and *A Sublime Epistle, Poetic and Politic* produced during an electoral campaign showed bizarre features, but he thrived on apparent compliments from unlikely admirers such as the Emperor of Morocco, Emperor of Russia and the King of England, while the actual writers became highly amused. In 1820 he produced a collection of doggerel poetry with a portrait showing him sounding a trumpet to alarm sinners. (Simpson, David, *Durham Millennium: A Thousand Years of Durham City*, Darlington: Northern Echo, 1995)

⁓ July 12th ⁓

1759: Richard, Earl of Scarborough, Richard Trevor, Bishop of Durham and the Honourable James Lumley were presented with the freedom of the city by the corporation of Durham. The honour was conferred in recognition of their efforts in promoting the navigation of the River Wear. During this same year parliament approved plans for improvement of the river channel and a scheme was proposed to alter the course of the Wear to make it navigable between Durham and Sunderland. The increasing size of ships made such a project impractical and Sunderland had also developed into the north east's main port so in reality, little if any work was carried out. (Simpson, David, *Durham Millennium: A Thousand Years of Durham City*, Darlington: Northern Echo, 1995)

2012: A service was held in Durham Cathedral on this day to pay tribute to volunteers who support vicars in their ministry. The Church of England's Durham diocese commissions Authorised Pastoral Assistants (APAs) for five years at a time to work alongside clergy when dealing with people at vulnerable periods of their lives, including sickness or depression. During the service some APAs were recommissioned while others were commissioned for the first time. (*The Northern Echo*, Darlington, 1870–)

— JULY 13TH —

2007: Today 274 young people from schools across north east England commemorated the bicentenary of the abolition of the slave trade (1807) by recreating the slave ship, *Brookes*, on Palace Green between Durham's castle and cathedral. Lying on a full-size outline of the ship's hold, the young people took up space that would have been occupied by 248 slaves during the transatlantic Middle Passage. In 1788 parliament had attempted to regulate the slave trade by stipulating the number of Africans that a ship could transport across the Atlantic. Illustrations show the slave ship *Brookes* carrying 454 Africans as its regulated number but on earlier crossings it had transported as many as 609. This innovative exercise had been prepared by staff from Durham University Library Heritage Collections to enable pupils to learn more about the slave trade. At 11.30 a.m. Education Outreach officer, Sarah Price, rung a ship's bell to begin a minute's silence to remember the suffering of the slaves. Pupils then attended workshops in Durham Cathedral that covered slavery and the rights of children in today's world. (www.dur.ac.uk)

⁓ JULY 14TH ⁓

1650: Oliver Cromwell, captain general of the Parliamentarian army, arrived at Durham on this day. He was met by Sir Arthur Haslerigg, Governor of Newcastle, along with Colonel Pride and other officers. Cromwell was then guest of honour at a 'sumptuous banquet' that took place at a house said to be part of the city's Royal County Hotel. After this a fast was maintained in order to implore God's blessing on the forthcoming campaign. Cromwell selected five companies from the Durham garrison to serve as reinforcements in his army before heading northwards to Newcastle and then to the Battle of Dunbar in early September. (Mackenzie, Eneas and Metcalf Ross, *An Historical, Topographical and Descriptive View of the County Palatinate of Durham* ... Newcastle upon Tyne: Mackenzie and Dent, 1834)

2012: Around 40,000 people filled the streets of Durham City for the 128th Miners' Gala and as light morning rain gave way to bright sunshine during mid-afternoon more than seventy colliery banners were paraded along the route to the Racecourse. Brass instruments, bagpipes and other exotic items featured in performances for dignitaries on the balcony of the Royal County Hotel. Ed Milliband became the first Labour leader to address the gala in twenty-three years and during an 11-minute speech he claimed that the next Labour government must 'rebuild Britain' using traditional values. (*The Northern Echo*, Darlington, 1870–)

— JULY 15TH —

1949: Trevor Charles Horn was born in Durham on this day and became famous as a pop music producer, songwriter, musician and vocalist. An early interest in music saw him become a bass player and member of the youth orchestra at Durham Johnston School before a move to Leicester, on leaving school, gained him work as a professional musician performing in local ballrooms while constructing a home studio. Session work in the early 1970s led to the formation of The Buggles with keyboard player, Geoffrey Downes, in 1978 in which Horn played bass, guitar and percussion as well as providing vocals. Later in the following year they were invited to form the rock group Yes but at the beginning of 1981 Trevor Horn left to concentrate on production work. His influence on popular music during the following decade led to him being described as 'The Man Who Invented the Eighties'. He was producer for a range of artists including Frankie goes to Hollywood, Tom Jones, Paul McCartney, Grace Jones, Pet Shop Boys and Charlotte Church. A series of awards such as Brit Awards and Grammy Awards followed and in 2011 Trevor Horn was appointed Commander of the Order of the British Empire (CBE) for services to the music industry. (en.wikipedia.org/wiki/Trevor_Horn)

~ JULY 16TH ~

2012: Officials at Durham University paid tribute to rock star and classical musician, Jon Lord, who died on this day after suffering from pancreatic cancer. The keyboard player was best known as a member of heavy rock band Deep Purple with whom he co-wrote the classic 'Smoke on the Water', but classical music remained his first love. In 2007 he released a concerto to mark the 175th anniversary of Durham University after six years of working on the project. The *Durham Concerto* was given its world premiere in Durham Cathedral during October 2007 when it was performed by the Royal Liverpool Philharmonic Orchestra and four soloists including Northumbrian pipes player Kathryn Tickell and Jon Lord himself on Hammond Organ. The concerto portrayed a musical picture of a day in the life of Durham and is comprised of seven movements with musical influences including jazz, ragtime, rock and folk which incorporates an old miner's lament. Professor Chris Higgins, vice chancellor of Durham University spoke of his sadness at Jon Lord's death and paid tribute to his musical talents which included composition of the *Durham Concerto* 'which captures the spirit and greatness of the City and the university so beautifully.' (*The Northern Echo*, Darlington, 1870–)

― July 17th ―

763: According to the Anglo-Saxon Chronicle, on this day Peohtwine was consecrated Bishop of Whithorn at Elvet. In that context Elvet would be the area around St Oswald's church as the district now referred to as Old Elvet was not established until the twelfth century. The consecration implies that Elvet was at that time much more important than nowadays, with the ceremony almost certainly taking place in a timber church with a small settlement of farmers and their families close by. The dedication of the church to St Oswald could indicate that he visited the area before his death in AD 642. (Clack, P.A.J., *The Book of Durham City*, Buckingham: Barracuda, 1985)

―――

1943: On this day the Sir John Priestman Hospital opened to cater for disabled servicemen returning from active service during the Second World War. The building had originally opened in 1935 as the Finchale Abbey Hotel and Roadhouse with a bed and breakfast rate of 10*s* 6*d* (53p) and a chauffeur for the day costing 10*s* (50p). It was advertised on the property market in January 1938 and was used by the War Department from the outbreak of war. In recent years it has become the Finchale College with facilities for unemployed and disabled people. (www.rotary-ribi.org)

~ July 18th ~

2012: On this day Queen Elizabeth II visited Durham during one of five stops in the North East. The visit was part of her diamond jubilee tour of the United Kingdom that ended in the south east region later in July. Accompanied by HRH the Duke of Edinburgh, the queen began the day by visiting Corporation Quay in Sunderland, the Tyne Tunnel and Saltwell Park in Gateshead. She wore a peach dress and coat by Stewart Parvin with matching hat by Rachel Trevor-Morgan and the morning's final engagement was to a sunny Durham City. Crowds stood three deep along Saddler Street and Palace Green as the royal party made their way to Durham Cathedral where they met dignitaries including the Bishop of Durham, Justin Welby. Lunch at Durham Castle consisted of ceviche of salmon with beetroot carpaccio, Kohlrabi salad and chilli caviar, home-smoked fillet of West Rackwood Farm beef served with epicure potato, cep dauphine, Lanchester asparagus and horseradish tuille, and Plawsworth strawberry delice with Langley Farm yoghurt sorbet and blood orange jelly. From Durham the royal couple travelled to the Tees Barrage to open The Queen Elizabeth II Diamond Jubilee White Water Course. (*The Northern Echo*, Darlington, 1870–)

⁓ July 19th ⁓

1821: Celebrations on this day to mark the coronation of King George IV saw a small ox roasted in Durham City at the upper end of Old Elvet. It was the gift of Lord Stuart, who later became the Marquis of Londonderry, and after being cut into pieces, along with an amount of bread, the portions of meat were thrown randomly to the public. Very soon, however, the assembled crowd gathered items of food and hurled them back at the platform party. The atmosphere of disorder was made worse when the contents of several barrels of ale were distributed free of charge. (Proud, Keith, *Durham City*, Chichester: Phillimore, 2003)

———

1919: The declaration of peace, following the signing of the Treaty of Versailles, was proclaimed today from the town hall balcony to a large number of citizens by the city's mayor, Alderman Proctor. Press reports indicate that in the Gilesgate and Milburngate districts residents paraded stuffed effigies of the Kaiser. During the afternoon children's sports events were held on the racecourse and in the evening a huge bonfire on The Sands was lit by the mayoress. (Richardson, Michael, *Durham: Cathedral City*, Thrupp: Sutton, 1997)

~ July 20th ~

1598: The will of Henry Smith which carries this date indicates that he possessed several coal mines and coal pits and that he 'devised the same to the City of Durham and thereby declared that he gave the same chiefly that some good trade might be devised for the setting of the youth and other idle persons to work, as should be most convenient, whereby some profit might arise honestly upon their trades.' This bequest was soon afterwards used to establish a cloth factory but the project failed and land and property was purchased with the remaining capital. After running costs were deducted amounts were handed out to those in need who were selected by trustees appointed by the Charity Commissioners. (Whellan, Francis, *History, Topography, and Directory of the County Palatine of Durham Comprising a General Survey of the County and a History of the City and Diocese of Durham …* , London: Ballantyne, Hanson and Co., 1894)

1904: *Buffalo Bill's Wild West Show and His Congress of Rough Riders of the World* was held on this day in the Engine Field near Elvet Colliery. The arena held 16,000 covered seats and the show included 800 men and 500 horses. Press reports indicated that 'Through the kindness of Col. Cody children at Durham Union Workhouse were permitted to attend the afternoon performance.' (Richardson, Michael, *Durham: Cathedral City*, Thrupp: Sutton, 1997)

– July 21st –

1703: By his will bearing this date, John Spearman left some property of which the rent was to be paid to the rector on condition that he performed Divine Service and administered the sacraments for the benefit of prisoners in the jail. This arrangement lapsed when the new prison was opened in Old Elvet in 1820 and a salaried chaplain was appointed. (Gibby, C.W., *St. Mary-le-Bow with St. Mary the Less, Durham … A guide to the Church and Parish.*, Gloucester: The British Publishing Company, 1958)

———

2009: On this day local residents at Shincliffe near Durham were surveying an enormous gulley that had been formed in a field belonging to Houghall Agricultural College, following a prolonged spell of torrential rain. The area experienced 3in of rain in 24 hours, ten times the average, causing millions of gallons of floodwater to surge from surrounding farmland towards the River Wear. Simultaneously the swollen waters of the Wear bust through the banks at exactly the same point to form a new tributary. No buildings were close enough to be affected and local residents soon named the new landscape feature 'The Durham Grand Canyon'. They speculated that the flood had exposed the original course of the Wear but experts believe it was simply a new gully formed by a huge amount of water. (www.dailymail.co.uk/news)

— July 22nd —

1434: On this day Bishop Langley of Durham was granted a faculty by Pope Eugene IV to make new rules and ordinances for Sherburn House. He appointed a priest as master along with four chaplains, four clerks or singing men and two boy choristers. Two lepers, if so many could be found, were to be maintained apart by themselves, and thirteen poor men were to be fed and clothed, to mess and lodge in the same house, and to attend mass daily. On the death of any brother the master was to choose a successor within fifteen days or forfeit a mark to the fabric of Durham Cathedral. A sober woman servant was to attend on the brethren at the master's expense to wash their linen and do other offices. The master was made responsible for the goods and buildings of the hospital and was bound by an oath to perform all his duties. (Page, William (ed.), *The Victorian History of the County of Durham, Vol. 2*, London: Constable, 1905)

1932: John Meade Falkner, novelist and poet died at Durham on this day. His best-known novel was *Moonfleet*, published in 1898. Following his retirement in 1921 he regarded Durham as his home and lived at Divinity House on Palace Green. A memorial monument is in the south cloister of the cathedral. (en.wikipedia.org/wiki/J._Meade_Falkner)

~ July 23rd ~

1503: On this day Margaret Tudor, the older of King Henry VII's two daughters, arrived in Durham on her way to Scotland where she was to marry James IV. The royal party had left Richmond Palace on July 2nd to journey northwards under the leadership of the Earl of Surrey with his countess as chaperone to the princess. The ladies rode on palfreys or were drawn on litters escorted by gentlemen, squires and pages with trumpeters, drummers and minstrels and the royal entourage passed through Grantham, Newark and York before reaching Durham where Bishop Fox entertained his guests in the great hall of the castle. From Durham they continued to Newcastle and Alnwick before crossing into Scotland. Margaret's betrothal, at the age of 13, to 30-year-old James IV was part of her father's negotiations of important marriages for his children. The marriage had been completed by proxy on January 25th 1503 at Richmond Palace and it was celebrated in person at Holyrood Abbey on August 8th of the same year. (tudorhistory.org/people/margaret)

1934: A DLI luncheon was given by the Mayor of Durham Councillor J.C. Fowler and members of the corporation to the 1st and 8th Battalions of the DLI in the town hall. (Richardson, Michael, *Memory Lane: Durham City*, Derby: Breedon, 2000)

– JULY 24TH –

1974: Andrew Charles Thomas Gomarsall MBE, international rugby player, was born on this day in Durham. Educated at Audley House Preparatory School and Bedford School, he developed into a fine scrum half and captained the 1992 England Schools U-18 team to their first Grand Slam triumph in eleven years. During the following season he joined London Wasps and went on to make his full England debut in 1996 against Italy. In 1997 he played in three Five Nations matches and made two appearances as a replacement on the tour of Argentina. Success in domestic competitions followed, first in 1999 as a member of Wasps' 1999 Powergen Cup winning side and then at Gloucester, where he enjoyed victory in the Powergen Cup in 2003. Andy Gomarsall's form led to an England recall in June 2002 when he played in the 26–18 success over Argentina in Buenos Aires and an impressive performance in England's 43–9 defeat of Wales at the Millennium Stadium led to his inclusion as one of three scrum halves in the 2003 Rugby World Cup Squad. He started all three of England's 2004 Autumn internationals at Twickenham before a series of injuries restricted his international appearances to the first two Six Nations games in 2008. (en.wikipedia.org/wiki/Andy_Gomarsall)

JULY 25TH

1588: The country house that formerly stood on Palace Green at Durham displayed the following inscription over a door on the upper floor. 'God preserve our gracious Queen Elizabeth the founder here of 25 July 1588'. This room within the timber building was used by jurors for their business while across the passageway, above the bishop's stables, was a courtroom for the judges of assize. The building was considerably altered by Bishop Cosin some eighty years later. (www.british-history.ac.uk)

1911: There was great excitement on this day when Colonel Cody's plane was forced to land at Pit House, Brandon Hill at about 5 a.m. Engine problems caused the unscheduled landing during a race from London to Newcastle and, after a two-day delay to repair the engine and wings, he took off again and finished second. Local schoolchildren were given a half-day holiday to see Col. Cody and his aeroplane. He had arrived in Europe during 1890 and appeared in Wild West shows before becoming the first man in Britain to fly a powered plane in 1908. Col. Cody was fatally injured in 1913 while testing a primitive sea plane. (Richardson, Michael, *Durham City*, Stroud: Sutton, 1996)

~ JULY 26TH ~

2012: Six people admitted their involvement in the theft of valuable Chinese artefacts stolen during a late-night raid at the Oriental Museum in Durham City on Thursday, April 5th 2012. Three men and three women pleaded guilty to a number of charges linked to the raid when they appeared at Durham Crown Court. They had been arrested in the days and weeks following the highly publicised raid which included coverage on BBC's *Crimewatch* programme, and the two Chinese exhibits valued at around £2 million were recovered intact by police officers eight days after the burglary. A Qing Dynasty jade bowl and an eighteenth-century porcelain figure had apparently been concealed in a field at Brandon near Durham. Sentences passed on the defendants at Durham Crown Court on February 8th 2013 ranged from eight years' imprisonment to suspended sentences and unpaid work.

The Oriental Museum which first opened in May 1960 as the Gulbenkian Museum of Oriental Art and Archaeology is undergoing a major redevelopment programme which will see all permanent galleries refurbished by the end of 2015. (*The Northern Echo*, Darlington, 1870–)

~ July 27th ~

1628: On this day Peter Smart, Prebendary of Durham, launched a vitriolic attack during his sermon against 'high church' ceremonial. In particular he called the altar a 'damnable idol' and all those who bowed before it 'spiritual fornicators' as well as stating that bishops were 'Rome's bastardly brood, still doting on their mother, the painted harlot of Rome.' A quorum of the high commission soon began proceedings against Smart. He was removed from his positions in the church, degraded from Holy Orders and imprisoned for about thirteen years. Subsequently he was vindicated and recovered his preferments. (Stranks, C.J., *This Sumptuous Church: The Story of Durham Cathedral,* London: SPCK, 1993)

2012: Possibly this country's first mustard-inspired restaurant opened in Saddler Street, Durham on this day. It was located within yards of the former site of a mill where a Mrs Clements is credited with inventing modern-day mustard. Her discovery of a method for grinding seeds into a powder saw Durham become the main centre for mustard-making until her secret recipe was discovered by Colman's of Norwich. For over a century Durham was renowned for mustard production but its last factory closed in the early twentieth century. Appropriately, the restaurant was officially opened by Durham cricketer, Phil Mustard. (*The Northern Echo,* Darlington, 1870–)

— JULY 28TH —

1899: On this day the foundation stone was laid for Durham Johnston Technical School at a site on South Street. Funding for the school building came from the bequest of a Scotsman, James Finlay Weir Johnston, who was born in 1796 and died in 1855. After graduating from the University of Glasgow, Johnston moved to Durham in 1826 and lived the rest of his life at No. 55, Claypath. He opened an academy in Saddler Street where students paid an annual subscription fee for tuition in English, reading, writing, arithmetic and geography. Although the school was successful it closed in 1829 as Johnston focussed his attention on chemistry. In the 1830s he became a founding member of the British Association for the Advancement of Science and a reader in Chemistry and Mineralogy during the formative early years of the University of Durham. He was highly regarded as a lecturer at venues such as the Literary and Philosophical Society meetings in Newcastle and at the London Lead Mining Company's premises in Middleton-in-Teesdale. His bequest facilitated construction of the city's first secondary school, Durham Johnston Technical School, which remained on the same site in South Street until the 1950s when it moved to its present location at Crossgate Moor. (Simpson, David, *Durham City*, Sunderland: Business Education Publishers, 2006)

~ July 29th ~

1964: Local press outlets carried a report on this day about the Mayor of Durham's pike-armed bodyguard which consisted of ten men but possessed only eight weapons. These comprised two pikes, two halberds, two lantern-carrier poles and two hefty staves and the mayor was appealing for anyone with a spare, unwanted pike or halberd to get in touch with him.

Mayors of the City of Durham are styled 'The Right Worshipful, The Mayor of Durham'. The first mayor of Durham took office in 1602 and the tradition of the Mayoral Bodyguard began at that time. Historically it is the oldest mayoral bodyguard outside the City of London and ranks as one of the oldest institutions in the City of Durham, as it was operating as early as the thirteenth century when members of the bodyguard protected the warden of the city. Mayors of Durham rank third in the local hierarchy after HM Queen and the Lord Lieutenant and claim to be fifth equal in civic precedence behind the Lord Mayors of London, York, Cardiff and Belfast. In March 2013 Durham County Council leader Simon Henig said having one person as mayor and council chairman would save hundreds of thousands of pounds and promised to pursue this issue if Labour won May 2013 elections. (Emett, Charlie, *A Century of Durham*, Gloucestershire: Sutton publishing, 2002)

~ July 30th ~

1655: John Duck married Ann Heslop, daughter or sister of his employer John Heslop, at a ceremony in St Nicholas' church, Durham marketplace, on this day. Born in 1634, probably at the village of Kilton, North Yorkshire, Duck had arrived in Durham in a destitute state seeking work as a butcher's apprentice. In taking him on for work John Heslop contravened rules of the guild and early in 1656 John Duck decided to leave Durham. As he was making his way along the banks of the River Wear towards Framwellgate Bridge he spotted a raven flying overhead with a shiny item in its beak. Swooping low the bird dropped what turned out to be a gold coin and Duck used it to buy two cows from a passing farmer. He soon sold the animals at a profit which he used to continue trading in cattle and built up business. In 1680 John Duck was elected as Mayor of Durham and received the freedom of the Butchers' Company. Some of his wealth was used to purchase coal mines and he also founded a hospital at Great Lumley. During 1686 he was created a baronet by King James II and both he and his wife were buried in St Margaret's church at Durham. (Proud, Keith, *Durham City*, Chichester: Phillimore, 2003)

~ July 31st ~

1809: On this day the foundation stone of Durham Prison was laid in a large field by Sir Henry Vane Tempest. During 1808 Sir George Wood had commented on the poor state of the House of Correction and County Jail and the Bishop of Durham promised £2,000 provided building work got underway before 1810. Bands played and soldiers from Durham Volunteers fired a volley of shots as the ceremony took place. (www.capitalpunishmentuk.org)

1888: Today Durham University conferred an honorary degree of Doctor of Divinity on Bishop Samuel Adjai Crowther, Bishop of the Niger Territories and ten of his fellow bishops. He was born in Osogun, West Africa, in about 1809 and carried off as a slave in 1821. After being rescued by a British man o'war he was put ashore at Sierra Leone and educated at Church Missionary Society Schools. Samuel Adjai Crowther was baptised in 1825 and ordained on Trinity Sunday 1843. Just over twenty years later, in 1864, he was consecrated as Bishop of the Niger. Along with the other bishops he arrived for the ceremony at Auckland Castle after attending the third Lambeth Conference. (www.dacb.org)

~ August 1st ~

2012: Baroness Valerie Amos, head of the United Nations office for emergency relief, addressed the opening session of a three-day conference at Durham University. The conference was organised by Professor Lena Dominelli, head of social, youth and community work at the university, under the title *Breaking the Mould: Humanitarian Aid and Empowering Local Communities* and was attended by speakers from Sri Lanka, South Africa and Mauritania. Debates considered whether it was time to alter the methods of delivering aid after a humanitarian crisis to improve outcomes. Professor Dominelli, Associate Director of the Institute of Hazard, Risk and Resistance Research maintained that it was time for humanitarian aid in time of disaster to be put on a more professional footing. She stated that although much fine work was done by aid workers through organisations such as the United Nations, the Red Cross and the Red Crescent, there were also many cases of exploitative or inappropriate interventions. Her proposal was for the establishment of an organisation of professionally qualified aid workers with multi-disciplinary skills whose efforts would be coordinated by an organisation such as the United Nations. (*The Northern Echo*, Darlington, 1870–)

~ AUGUST 2ND ~

1709: On this day 'Richard Simpson of Barnard Castle, currier, was tried at the Durham Assizes for breaking into the dwelling house of Michael Pudsey, merchant there and stealing a silver tankard, two pair of silver cock spurs, a silver chain, two silver seals, 19 yards of silver lace ... Pleaded his clergy and burnt in the hand.' (By entering a claim of benefit of clergy he was spared the gallows, but was marked so he could not claim it again.) (Sykes, John, *Local Records: or Historical Register of Remarkable Events Which Have Occurred Exclusively in the Counties of Durham and Northumberland, Town and County of Newcastle upon Tyne and Berwick upon Tweed; with an Obituary of Persons of Talent, Eccentricity, and Longevity,* Newcastle: T. Fordyce, 1866)

1940: On this day the cannon was removed from the battery at Durham's Wharton Park, in order to be melted down for the war effort. A formal park had covered this hillside setting on the north side of the city since 1858 and generations of local children had enjoyed climbing and sitting on the cannon. An unprecedented amount of metal was required to sustain the war effort with a single tank needing about 18 tons alone and scrap metal drives were organised by schools and community groups across the country. Items ranging from chicken wire to pots and pans, farm equipment and car parts were donated but in more recent times the effectiveness of scrap metal drives has been questioned as some weaponry such as aircraft needed virgin aluminium and in other cases historical items were needlessly donated. (Richardson, Michael, *Durham: Cathedral City*, Thrupp: Sutton, 1997)

‑ AUGUST 3RD ‑

1556: A number of cases dealt with at Durham Quarter Sessions on this day involved 'riotous assembly' and use of force during a robbery. These crimes took place during the later months of 1555 and the early part of 1556. Typical of these incidents was when 'Percival Lumley, late of Darlington, esq., Richard Lumley, late of Chester-le-Street, gen., Thomas Hussye of Sigston, Yorks., esq., James Bulloke, late of Darlington, Co. Durham., yeo., Stephen Key late of Heworth, yeo., and William Bryan of Aycliffe, on 12 November 1555 with force and arms assembled riotously at Bradbury and broke and entered the house of Robert Archer at Bradbury and attacked him and Agnes his wife so that their lives were despaired of and carried off 40 thraves of oats worth £3, 4 wainloads of hay worth 40*s*, 4 wainloads of coal worth 26*s* 8*d*, 4 hens worth 20*d*, a hatchet worth 7*d* and 2 iron forks worth 20*d* belonging to Robert Archer esq.' (Fraser, C.M. (ed.), *Durham Quarter Sessions Rolls 1471–1625*, Durham: Surtees Society, 1991)

—————

1726: 'Stephen Browne, Arthur Hewetson, David Steel, Ann Bone and Jane Browne were tried at the Durham Assizes for having, on 13 June preceding, robbed John Marshall of 32 guineas, on the King's highway, in the parish of Jarrow. They were found guilty and executed.' (Sykes, John, *Local Records: or Historical Register of Remarkable Events Which Have Occurred Exclusively in the Counties of Durham and Northumberland, Town and County of Newcastle upon Tyne and Berwick upon Tweed; with an Obituary of Persons of Talent, Eccentricity, and Longevity*, Newcastle: T. Fordyce, 1866)

— August 4th —

1819: The first prisoners were moved from the old House of Correction and Bridewell to the present prison on this day, although it is recorded that the execution shed was used in 1816 for John Grieg, a convicted murderer. (win1089.vs.easily.co.uk/pete/badrick)

1980: A fire was discovered at St Mary's church, Shincliffe on this day by Thomas Jobling as he approached the building to ring a special peal to mark the Queen Mother's birthday. Part of the roof, flooring, a stained glass window, pews and a book case containing hymn books suffered damage and the whole building was affected by the smoke. Total cost of the fire which had been started deliberately, totalled around £20,000. St Mary's church was opened in 1851 with a broach spire added about twenty years later. Three of its windows are filled with fine modern glass. One marks its centenary while the others are memorials linked to the Second World War and Frederick Sidney Dennett, a former rector. (Richardson, Michael, *Memory Lane: Durham City*, Derby: Breedon, 2000)

~ AUGUST 5TH ~

1927: Local newspaper the *Durham Chronicle* made a 'Special offer to Local Players' today with the explanation:

> As an incentive to cricketers in the field and to do the best for their side, the *Durham Chronicle* offers a weekly prize to members of clubs in various local leagues. The prize will take the form of a presentation bat, of first-class make, to be awarded each week, alternately to the batsman who makes the best individual score and the bowler who has the best performance to his credit. Only Saturday matches are covered by the awards. Two bats are being presented to players in the NORTH EAST DURHAM LEAGUE and this week's prize is for BOWLING. RULES. The claimant must be a regular playing member of the club, and where there is any doubt on this point the award will go to the club that first claims a bat for any player ... No individual shall be awarded more than one bat during the season. The decision of the Editor is final and no correspondence will be entered into regarding the competition.

(*Durham Chronicle*, 1820–1984)

~ August 6th ~

1638: At the assizes held before Judge Berkeley at Durham on this day:

> the singular spectacle of trial by wager of battle being offered and accepted for deciding the right to certain lands at Thickley, between Ralph Claxton, demandant, and Richard Lilburn, tenant. The defendant appeared at ten o'clock in the forenoon by his attorney, and brought in his champion, George Cheney, in full array, with his stave and sand bag who threw down his gauntlet on the floor of the court, with five small pieces of coin in it. The tenant then introduced his champion, William Peverell, armed in a similar manner, who also threw down his gage. The judge, after examining the champions, ordered them into custody of the two bailiffs of the court, till eight o'clock next morning, when they were ordered to put in pledges to appear at the Court of the Pleas on the 15 September following ... Means were found, however, to defer the trial from year to year, by finding some error in the record, till at length it was ordered that a bill should be brought in to abolish this mode of decision.

(Whellan, Francis, *History, Topography, and Directory of the County Palatine of Durham Comprising a General Survey of the County and a History of the City and Diocese of Durham ...* , London: Ballantyne, Hanson and Co., 1894)

‒ August 7th ‒

1843: John Bright MP for Durham between 1843 and 1847 made his maiden speech in the House of Commons on this day. He spoke in support of a motion calling for reduction of import duties and said that he was there 'not only as one of the representatives of the City of Durham, but also as one of the representatives of that benevolent organisation, the Anti-Corn Law League.' The motion was defeated but the movement of which Cobden and Bright were founders continued to spread and the Anti-Corn Law League became one of the most successful ever campaigning organisations. It raised enormous amounts of money, as much as £8 million in today's value, with a massive organisational ability to produce and disseminate literature in aid of 'the great principle' as John Bright stated. He worked closely with his great friend Richard Cobden to successfully achieve the repeal of the Corn Laws in 1846 and his campaigning approach continued when he was Member of Parliament for Manchester in almost single handedly opposing war in the Crimea. During 1858 Bright began his second great campaign – for parliamentary reform, by leading the campaign for the vote for the working class and household suffrage which led to the Reform Act of 1867. (Cash, Bill, *John Bright: Statesman, Orator, Agitator,* London: I.B. Tauris, 2012)

⁓ August 8th ⁓

2012: Dr Ruth Etchells, principal of St John's College with Cranmer Hall, Durham from 1979 to 1988 died on this day. She was the first lay person and the first woman to become head of a college devoted to the training of Church of England clergy. During a thirty year period she made a major contribution to various aspects of life at Durham University and in 2010 Dr Etchells was awarded the Chancellor's Medal. Following her installation as principal she introduced a far-reaching programme that included upgrading of the buildings, a more thorough admissions policy, a broader multi-disciplinary field of study and balancing of the college's books. Ruth Etchell's skills were soon brought to the attention of Church bodies and after election to the General Synod she was appointed to its Doctrine Commission and Crown Appointments Commission which during her period of office, appointed George Carey as Archbishop of Canterbury. In addition to her participation in central Church government Ruth Etchells was a member of the governing council of Ridley Hall, Cambridge and honorary vice-president of the Church Mission Society. Following her retirement from the university in 1988 she developed new skills in stained glass work from a studio based in the cellar of a cathedral building. (*Daily Telegraph*, London: Daily Telegraph, 1856–)

— August 9th —

1968: A conservation area covering the centre of Durham City was initially designated on this day (and extended just over twelve years later on November 25th 1980). The City of Durham contains more than 630 listed buildings, in addition to the castle and cathedral, of which 569 are located within the city centre conservation area. (en.wikipedia.org/wiki/Durham)

—

2012: Two historic stained glass windows were put on public display for the first time at Durham Heritage Centre and Museum on this day. They were created by William Collins and positioned, as part of a set of six, in drawing rooms at Brancepeth Castle during refurbishment by Matthew Russell and his family in the mid-nineteenth century. They are believed to date from 1824 and feature Lady Neville, the Rose of Raby and her husband Richard Plantagenet, Third Duke of York. During the Second World War the castle was requisitioned by the War Office and later served as the headquarters of the Durham Light Infantry. In 1961 Lord Boyne gave the windows to the City of Durham for display in Durham Town Hall and the most recent restoration work was funded by the Bow Trust and other local organisations. (*The Northern Echo*, Darlington, 1870–)

~ August 10th ~

1862: It was reported that:

> A most atrocious and cold-blooded murder was perpetrated early
> this morning, at a place called Broadmires, five miles north of
> Durham. The victim was an old woman named Ann Halliday, about
> 80 years of age. The deceased was a married woman, but separated
> from her husband, who kept a public house in the neighbourhood.
> The murderers were an Irishman and his wife called John Cox and
> Mary Cox who lived next door and were the first themselves to give
> information of the murder. The deceased, when discovered, was upon
> the floor of her cottage, and a coal rake and poker, smeared with
> blood were lying beside her. They were tried at the ensuing Durham
> Assizes before Mr Justice Keating, convicted and sentenced to be
> hung. John Cox was executed on December 23rd 1862. His wife was
> respited owing to her being in a state of pregnancy.'

(The hangman was Thomas Askern who was initially the
hangman for Yorkshire. It was common practice at that time to
draw hangmen from the prison population and he was in prison
for debt at the time. An efficient rail network allowed Askern to
travel to Durham where he carried out all five public hangings
between 1859 and 1865.) (Fordyce, T. (ed.), *Local Records; or,
Historical Register of Remarkable Events Which Have Occurred in
Northumberland and Durham … 1833 to [1875], Being a Continuation
of the Work Published by … Mr. John Sykes*, Newcastle upon Tyne:
T. Fordyce, 1867–1876)

‑ August 11th ‑

1093: Bishop William of St Carileph laid the foundation stone of the new cathedral at Durham in the presence of King Malcolm of Scotland and Prior Turgot of Durham. Carileph had recently returned from a three year period of exile in France and it could have been during that time that he formulated plans for the new building. The identity of the architect is unknown but it could well have been the bishop himself. After pulling down the stonework of the existing White Church work on the new cathedral progressed rapidly. Carileph had been amassing money for some time and, along with considerable amounts of cut stone from the White church, there was a plentiful supply from nearby quarries. It seems likely that he completed the choir from the East End and the nave as far as the second bay incorporating massive arches which would eventually support the tower. This initial phase saw the East End incorporating three apses, a central one circular on both inside and outside while the other two were circular on the inside and square on the exterior. (Stranks, C.J., *This Sumptuous Church: The Story of Durham Cathedral*, London: SPCK, 1993)

~ August 12th ~

1891: Cyril Edwin Mitchinson Joad was born in Durham on this day but during the following year his family moved to Southampton. In 1910 he began studies at Balliol College, Oxford and soon displayed considerable ability as a philosopher and debater. Graduating from Balliol College with a double first, Joad took up a position with the Board of Trade and continued in Civil Service posts until 1930 when he became Head of the Department of Philosophy and Psychology at Birkbeck College, University of London. His teaching skills and published books, *Guide to Modern Thought* (1933) and *Guide to Philosophy* (1936) helped to popularise philosophy and also brought him to the attention of the public. Joad was also interested in the supernatural and campaigned to preserve the English countryside. In January 1940 he became a member of the BBC radio programme *The Brains Trust* in which a small group of panellists discussed complex intellectual issues. Dr Joad soon achieved celebrity status and was widely regarded as the foremost philosopher of his era. However, in 1948 a conviction for fare-dodging led to his dismissal from the BBC and his health deteriorated. Shortly before his death on April 9th 1953 he renounced his agnostic views and adopted Christianity. (en.wikipedia.org/wiki/C._E._M._Joad)

~ AUGUST 13TH ~

1711: 'Thomas Wilson, John Brady, Andrew Miller, Andrew Langland and Robert Evans were tried at the Durham Assizes for having, in the night of the 19th of the preceding December, broken into the house of William Storey, a miller at Hedley, and stole therefrom ten guineas in gold, £59 5s in money. They were found guilty and executed.' (Sykes, John, *Local Records: or Historical Register of Remarkable Events Which Have Occurred Exclusively in the Counties of Durham and Northumberland, Town and County of Newcastle upon Tyne and Berwick upon Tweed; with an Obituary of Persons of Talent, Eccentricity, and Longevity*, Newcastle: T. Fordyce, 1866)

2012: Following the admission of women members for the first time some six months earlier, three more were welcomed on this day as City of Durham freemen. Sisters Barbara Samuel and Catriona Jackson were joined by Pamela Angus, taking the total of Durham women freemen, as they are known, to twenty-three. Mrs Samuel and Mrs Jackson were entitled to membership as their father is a freeman of the Drapers' Company. The family has discovered that their ancestors have been freemen since at least the eighteenth century, with one early relative made a freeman by birthright in 1747. Mrs Angus' family links to the Drapers' Company extend back more than a century. Freemen were expected to total more than 200 for the first time in living memory by the end of 2012. (*The Northern Echo*, Darlington, 1870–)

– August 14th –

1811: The Durham Assize Courts which formed the major part of the prison facade opened on this day with the first sitting of a criminal court. In those early days judges would travel twice yearly from London throughout the country to preside over sittings of the assize courts. (www.capitalpunishmentuk.org)

2002: A display featuring items belonging to a 3ft 3in Polish 'count' opened in Durham Town Hall after £1,500 of restoration work following damage caused by a leaking roof about a year earlier. Clothes, a violin and life-sized portrait were linked to Count Joseph Boruwlaski who was in fact a Polish commoner. He had travelled around the courts of Europe entertaining royalty and nobility by playing a miniature violin before he fell out of favour with his benefactors and moved to Durham in 1820. His popularity as a musician and raconteur soon spread around the city and he lived there until his death in 1837 at the age of 99. After his death, Count Boruwlaski's clothes and personal effects were bequeathed to the city and he became the only commoner to be buried in Durham Cathedral. His tomb is located inside the north door and is marked by a flagstone carved with the initials 'J.B.' (*The Northern Echo*, Darlington, 1870–)

~ August 15th ~

1683: Andrew Mills was executed at Durham on this day after being convicted of the murder of three children at Ferryhill. It seems that after his execution he was 'hanged in irons upon a gybett' and local folklore suggested that he survived for a while because his sweetheart fed him with milk through the bars of his iron cage. Another tale implies that when he was on the point of starvation a 'penny loaf' was hung on string in front of his face but just out of reach in order to add torment to his suffering. He finally expired, according to reports, with 'a shriek that was heard for miles around.' The gibbet remained on site and became known as Andrew Mills Stob, until the 1830s, when the site was enclosed and levelled. (Dufferwiel, Martin, *Durham: A Thousand Years of History and Legend*, Edinburgh: Mainstream, 1996)

1899: At Brandon 'C' Pit an explosion occurred when a powder shot was fired by the deputy, William Carr. It blew through a cavity in the stone and ignited some firedamp in an old working. The resulting explosions caused the death of six workmen. (www.dmm.org.uk)

‑ August 16th ‑

1960: A press report on this day described how customers of a new shop which had opened at Witton Gilbert were offered a free glass of Australian wine and each customer who ordered a minimum of 7s 6d worth of groceries would receive a free quarter-pound packet of tea. Mr N. Kelly's May Lea Stores had been opened by Mr W. Calvert Kirks, local director of Morris and Jones Ltd, wholesale grocers and provision merchants of Newcastle-upon-Tyne who traded under the Mace sign. Mr Kirks pointed out in his speech that his firm which was the largest wholesaler in the North of England, would be providing Mr Kelly with his consumer goods and, in addition, the local owner would be providing a local service, with due courtesy, that could only originate from an independent retailer who was running his own business for his own livelihood. He prophesied that both the shop and service would be to the customers' satisfaction and would be an asset to the district. Mr Kirks presented Mr Kelly, on behalf of the directors of Morris and Jones, with an electric wall clock. He then became the shop's first customer. (*Durham County Advertiser*, 1855–1968)

— AUGUST 17TH —

1715: 'Henry James of Ingleton, yeoman, was tried at the Durham Assizes for having at Ingleton, on the first of August, said – "The King is neither protestant nor churchman, and I will prove it, and he never did good since he came into England, and I hope in a short time to be quit of him." He was found guilty and sentenced to stand in the pillory at Wolsingham for one hour in open market, to be imprisoned for one year and to be fined 100 marks.' (Sykes, John, *Local Records: or Historical Register of Remarkable Events Which Have Occurred Exclusively in the Counties of Durham and Northumberland, Town and County of Newcastle upon Tyne and Berwick upon Tweed; with an Obituary of Persons of Talent, Eccentricity, and Longevity,* Newcastle: T. Fordyce, 1866)

———

1816: On this day John Greig was executed at Durham for the murder of Elizabeth Stonehouse. Until this time executions took place at Dryburn on the north side of Durham City but this hanging took place on gallows specially constructed for the purpose outside the courthouse. Once the new prison building was open (some three years later) the prisoner was brought along a passage and through a window to the gallows which were sited over the main entrance. Directly across the roadway house owners rented out their balconies to allow wealthy members of the public a better view of the proceedings. (www.dur.ac.uk/4schools/)

← AUGUST 18TH →

1821: On this day the local newspaper *Durham Chronicle* included an article criticising Durham's prebendaries for not allowing the cathedral bells to be tolled on the death of Queen Caroline. It criticised them for their political stance and maintained that in their political views in particular, they 'had lost all semblance to ministers of religion.' The argument spread as the bishop prosecuted the printer who was found guilty of libel and the case was then taken up by a former prebendary, Henry Philpotts, who was now incumbent of the richest living in England at Stanhope. His abrasive approach and command of combative vocabulary was directed towards the printer and publishers of the *Edinburgh Review* which had taken up the cause. (Stranks, C.J., *This Sumptuous Church: The Story of Durham Cathedral*, London: S.P.C.K, 1993)

1868: Mr J.E. Marshall, one of the oldest practising solicitors in Durham, died at his residence in Claypath on this day. A former member of the corporation, he sat in the Council Chamber for many years first as a councillor for the North Ward and then as an alderman. At the time of his death he held a number of posts including Clerk to the County Court at Sunderland and Chairman of Durham Gas Company. (Fordyce, T. (ed.), *Local Records; or, Historical Register of Remarkable Events Which Have Occurred in Northumberland and Durham ... 1833 to [1875], Being a Continuation of the Work Published by ... Mr. John Sykes*, Newcastle upon Tyne: T. Fordyce, 1867–1876)

~ August 19th ~

1856: The Durham to Bishop Auckland railway line opened to freight traffic on this day and served the coal mines on the western side of the county in particular. Construction work was directed by the North Eastern Railway's chief engineer, Thomas Harrison, a close associate of Robert Stephenson, and the route posed particular problems as it twice crossed the Wear and twice spanned other rivers. On the north side of the River Wear the line crossed via the nine-arch viaduct at Belmont which measured 649ft in length and stood 130ft above the water. A little further south was the 832ft-long eleven-arched Durham viaduct, where, according to the *Darlington and Stockton Times* newspaper, 'Piles of great length had to be driven through peat moss, quick-sand etc. by steam power.' South of Durham there were two timber bridges across the rivers Browney and Deerness before the line reached the impressive Newton Cap Viaduct. Building work began in 1854 and the completed bridge measured 828ft in length and stood 105ft above the riverbed on foundations with a depth of 20ft. (www.forgottenrelics.co.uk)

~ AUGUST 20TH ~

1948: Newspaper reports on this day described the:

Minister For War At Club Meeting … Performing a feat of diplomacy which would not have disgraced Solomon in all his wisdom, Mr Emanuel Shinwell, Secretary of State for War, at a special meeting of the County Branch, Working Men's Club and Institute Union at Durham, succeeded in having withdrawn a resolution of protest to the Government against the taxes on beer and tobacco … Mr Shinwell spoke to delegates for about 20 minutes, during which time he coaxed them, shouted at them and shook his fist at them, but in the end, achieved his purpose. He told them that the drinking of beer and the smoking of tobacco in the country could no longer be regarded as luxuries. They had both become virtual necessities. It had always been a matter of high policy with the Labour Party that taxation should be borne by those in a position to pay. It had to be imposed carefully without causing any excessive hardships … He suggested that in place of the highly worded protest they should approach their MPs and request them to meet the Chancellor with a view to affecting a reduction in the taxation at the earliest opportunity.

(Durham Chronicle, 1820–1984)

— AUGUST 21ST —

1938: Michael Philip Weston, England international rugby union player, was born on this day at Durham. During his early years at Durham School, he emerged as a fine all-round sportsman and played Minor Counties cricket for his home county before concentrating on rugby. Mike Weston's club rugby was played at Durham City and his international debut came on January 16th 1960 against Wales. In total he played 29 times for England between 1960 and 1968 and captained the side 5 times, firstly during the 1963 tour of Australia and then in his final two matches five years later. Although Mike Weston was primarily a centre, 5 of his international caps came as a fly-half and he was selected for the British Lions tours of South Africa in 1962 and Australia and New Zealand in 1966. Following his retirement in December 1968, he became a national selector and manager which included taking charge of the England team at the first Rugby World Cup in 1987. (www.espn.co.uk)

2012: The Royal School of Church Music's Millennium Youth Choir sang at the funeral service of pioneering academic Dr Ruth Etchells in Durham Cathedral. The singers, aged between 16 and 23, were drawn from all over the country. (*The Northern Echo*, Darlington, 1870–)

~ August 22nd ~

1941: A newspaper article on this day drew attention to a problem that seems to have existed for time immemorial:

> Litter in River Banks Deans Appeal to the Public. The river banks at Durham are among the most beautiful in the country and it is to be regretted that there are those careless, thoughtless people who leave litter wherever they go. Visitors have freedom to go just where they like in what are, in reality, private grounds for which the Dean and Chapter are responsible, and the least that visitors can do is to keep some semblance of order.
>
> Some years ago before Wharton Park was handed over to the Durham City Corporation there were reckless people who were in the habit of pulling branches from the trees and scattering them about with all sorts of litter. The position became so unsatisfactory that the late Col. C. W. Darwin had no other alternative but to close the park for some time.

A letter from the Dean of Durham, Dr C.W. Alington stated, 'May I make an appeal to those who use the Banks to help in keeping them tidy? ... It will be a great help if we can have the cooperation of those who use them.' (*Durham County Advertiser*, 1855–1968)

— August 23rd —

1891: 'At a Convocation of the University of Durham on this day a degree was conferred upon a lady for the first time in the history of that seat of learning, the recipient of the honour being Miss Ella Bryant, of the Newcastle College of Science.' On the same occasion, the honorary degree of DD was conferred upon Bishop Sandford and Bishop Tucker. The honorary degree of DCL was conferred upon Mr Gainsford Bruce QC and Temporal Chancellor of the County Palatine of Durham. Born in 1835 at Newcastle-on-Tyne, Gainsford Bruce was appointed as a Queen's Counsel in 1883 and contested several parliamentary elections unsuccessfully during the 1880s before winning the Finsbury (Holborn Division) seat in 1888. He was also successful in 1892 but before parliament sat Gainsford Bruce was appointed a judge and had to resign the seat. Knighted in 1892, he retired in 1904 and was appointed as a privy councillor in the same year. Specialising in shipping law, he was co-author of the standard work *Admiralty Practice*. Sir Gainsford Bruce died at his home near Bromley, Kent in February 1902 at the age of 77. (*Monthly Chronicle of North-Country Lore and Legend, Part LIV, August,* London: W. Scott, 1891)

~ 24TH AUGUST ~

1104: On this evening nine brethren, along with Turgot the prior, carefully opened the tomb of St Cuthbert for an examination. Inside they discovered a large chest overlaid with leather and further inspection revealed a second coffin covered with three layers of coarse linen. With encouragement from Leofwine they peeled off the linen to uncover a second lid with an iron ring at either end and beneath a copy of the Gospels, amid the sweetest of odours, and on his right side lay the body of St Cuthbert. (Stranks, C.J., *This Sumptuous Church: The Story of Durham Cathedral*, London: SPCK, 1993)

1953: Mr D.H. Dinsdale, Head of the Department of Agricultural Economics at King's College, Newcastle delivered a speech at St Mary's College on this day. On the subject of 'Agriculture in the Economy of County Durham' he explained that only 2¼ per cent of the county's population was engaged in agriculture compared with 5 per cent for the country as a whole. Mr Dinsdale stated that the main reasons for decline in the county's agricultural labour force were the more attractive wages and regular hours which industry offered. He added that this was one of the main factors behind the drive for increased mechanisation and many of the county's 4,600 farms were now mechanised. This was illustrated by there being seventy-one combine harvesters in the county during 1952 compared with nine in 1947. (*Durham County Advertiser, 1855–1968*)

~ August 25th ~

2012: A musical concert on this day in Durham Cathedral formed the highlight of the three-day annual Durham Streets Summer Festival. Events began the day before with film, music and street performances from the region and across the world before cabaret and a sing-along version of *The Rocky Horror Picture Show* was screened in the city's Gala Theatre. On the second day (August 25th) a range of free events were staged from noon in open areas such as the Millennium Square and Market Place with award-winning buskers, acrobats, jugglers and daredevils displaying their range of skills before the dramatic evening finale in the cathedral. First of all, the music of teenage vocalist Natasha Hows resonated around this magnificent building before the Lake Poets took to the stage and finally it was time for Sunderland band The Futureheads performing their distinctive brand of music. This included folk songs, cover versions such as Richard Thompson's 'Beeswing' and a number of their own tracks from the acoustic album, *Rant.* A choir from Sunderland University accompanied them on three songs and ended with an encore including *Hanging Johnny* and *Hounds of Love.* (*Evening Gazette,* Middlesbrough: Evening Gazette, 1869–)

~ AUGUST 26TH ~

1930: Details of a double mine fatality on this day were considered at the Durham inquest into events leading up to the accident at the Brockwell Seam of the Dean and Chapter Colliery, Ferryhill. The victims were named as Frederick Davison, aged 46, a deputy overman of No. 33 Barrington Terrace, Dean Bank and Parkinson Ovington, aged 47, a shifter of No. 78 Weardale Street, Low Spennymoor. It was revealed in evidence that the accident might have been caused by confused signalling in the pit which would have meant the tubs were tightened instead of slackened. Sam Kirby, a motor breaker, said that he received three distinct taps just before the accident occurred. This was a signal to tighten the set and this had been done. Referring to the system of signalling in the mine, Mr W. Wainwright, inspector of mines, explained that if two bare wires were brought into contact with each other they would ring the bell. He added that any slight vibration might give three rings instead of two. The coroner concluded that some irregularity with the signalling had taken place and a verdict of 'Accidentally killed' was recorded. (*Durham County Advertiser*, 1855–1968)

~ August 27th ~

2001: It was announced on this day that Durham Cathedral had been voted Britain's favourite building. Listeners to BBC Radio 4's *Today* programme took part in a survey to choose the best and worst examples of British architecture and the city's Norman cathedral which dominates the skyline, along with the castle, received more than 51% of the votes cast. A total of 15,819 people voted in the survey and other buildings that received a high rating included modern structures such as the Eden Project in Cornwall (22.5%), London's Tate Modern (11.9%) and Stansted Airport (7.02%). The most disliked building was Portsmouth's Tricorn Centre which was described by one critic as 'another 1960s consumer rat-maze.' (news.bbc.co.uk)

2012: Hundreds of people visited the region's largest gathering of military vehicles in the grounds of the DLI Museum and Durham Art Gallery. The show was organised by the North East Military Vehicle Club and featured around sixty skilfully restored vehicles and artillery dating from the 1930s to the present. These included a 1942 Austin Tilly pick-up, which is the same model as the one driven by the queen during the Second World War. (*The Northern Echo*, Darlington, 1870–)

~ AUGUST 28TH ~

1911: A garden party was held at 'The Laurels', Sherburn Road Ends, Durham on this day when the city's deputy mayor, Councillor W.H. Wood, owner of the mineral water works in Gilesgate, entertained a number of guests from local landed families as well as civic dignitaries. As well as the mayor and mayoress of Durham the party included Lord and Lady Londonderry, the Countess of Ilchester, Viscountess Castlereagh, Lord Stewart, Lord Staverdale, Lady Mary Fox Strangeways, the Honourable Maureen Stewart, Captain Apperley and Mr Malcolm Dillon. (Richardson, Michael, *Durham City*, Stroud: Sutton, 1996)

1919: A memorial plaque was unveiled in remembrance of those lost in the First World War at North Road Methodist church, Durham City on this day. The ceremony was performed by Mrs Thomas, wife of the church's minister, Revd J. Thomas, and the plaque, within a moulded wooden frame, was set on the landing wall of the front stairs. Seven names were listed, in two columns, below the wording: 'In loving memory of the men of this congregation who fell in the Great War 1914–18 "Pro Fide et Patria"' translated as 'For Faith and Country'. (www.newmp.org.uk)

— AUGUST 29TH —

1104: On this day the body of St Cuthbert was moved, with appropriate solemnity into the new church at Durham. Following an earnest *Te Deum* the grand procession moved off from the old church. At the front were many of the relics associated with the saints and next came a group of monks chanting hymns before the coffin of St Cuthbert. Covered with Bishop Ranulf Flambard's best cope, it was lowered to the ground in an open area within full view of everyone. Flambard then reputedly delivered an interminable address which included any number of irrelevant references before a heavy shower ended his discourse. A group of monks then lifted St Cuthbert's coffin and carried it, with some haste, into the church. Close inspection revealed that the rich vestments used in the ceremony had suffered no damage during the inclement weather and this was widely regarded as a miracle. This occasion marked the completion of the eastern half of the church apart from the vaulting of the North Transept which probably took a few more years. The eastern section of the nave was also built at this time as essential buttress to the western arch of the Crossing. (Stranks, C.J., *This Sumptuous Church: The Story of Durham Cathedral*, London: SPCK, 1993)

‒ August 30th ‒

1640: Scottish Covenanters defeated an English army at the Battle of Newburn, west of Newcastle and continued their triumphant march into Newcastle itself. Shops were looted and Viscount Conway withdrew English forces to Durham on this day. Again, trade was brought to a standstill and shops were pillaged as the Scottish troops seized Durham castle which had formerly been a Royalist stronghold. King Charles negotiated terms of a truce at York and the Scots disbanded on payment of £60,000 in 1641. (www.englandsnortheast.co.uk)

2012: On this day a £100,000 woodland burial site was launched close to South Road in Durham City. Located close to the crematorium, the area has a wooden lodge where services can be held or family members can shelter in poor weather, and up to 750 bodies can be buried on the 5-acre site. Research by Durham University indicated that Britain was leading the world in natural or woodland burials where people are typically buried in woods or fields in wicker or cardboard coffins. One reason for this is so that loved ones do not have to maintain a headstone or lay flowers and research findings indicate that we would much prefer that they enjoy a picnic on our grave. (*The Northern Echo*, Darlington, 1870–)

⁓ AUGUST 31ST ⁓

1831: A letter from the Dean of Durham to three prebendaries, Thorp, Durel and Prosser on this date outlined the first tentative move towards establishing a university in the city. He expressed a strong desire to extend the usefulness of the collegiate body to the public and, with this in mind, at the September audit he planned to place before the chapter details of an extended system of education . When the meeting took place on September 28th a considerable amount of discussion focused on measures for financing enlarged educational provision but the scheme was unanimously approved. (Stranks, C.J., *This Sumptuous Church: The Story of Durham Cathedral,* London: SPCK, 1993)

1911: Three thousand children and their teachers left Elvet Station at Durham on this day on four different trains. Their destination was Seaham Hall where Lord and Lady Londonderry were holding a summer fete. Each child was presented with a commemorative medal showing Lord and Lady Londonderry, mayor and mayoress of Durham, on one side and 'Seaham Hall, August 1911' on the reverse. The Sixth Marquess of Londonderry, Charles Stewart Vane Tempest Stewart (1852–1915) married Lady Theresa Chetwynd Talbot who was well known for her philanthropic and political work as well as being a splendid hostess. (Richardson, Michael, *Durham: The Photographic Collection,* Stroud: Sutton, 2002)

~ September 1st ~

1930: Local newspapers reported on the sad demise of 'Rip', a black and white collie dog who had made headlines some three weeks earlier during a serious fire in Coxhoe. Though small in size, Rip was an excellent guard dog and few people dared go near him while he was on duty at his owner's premises. Mr William Robinson, who had bred Rip in the first place, was the only person prepared to tackle the job of freeing him as the fire raged close by. Since then the dog had stayed with the Robinson household and was often seen playing with the family's children, but events were about to take a sinister turn. 'A vicious trait in his character' surfaced while one of Mr Robinson's sons was placing a collar around the dog's neck. Six-year-old Edith was standing alongside stroking Rip when he suddenly turned and attacked her. Edith suffered bites to her upper lip and chin as well as facial injuries caused by the dog's paws. Her wounds were reported to be 'severe' and dressings and bandages were applied at Dr Brown's surgery. Meanwhile, Rip met an 'ignominious end' when he was humanely destroyed the same evening. (*Durham County Advertiser*, 1855–1968)

— September 2nd —

1930: Two local youths were accused of stealing a billiard ball valued at 12s 6d from a billiard hall at Tudhoe Grange on this day. Magistrates heard that Eric Roper, age 19, of High Street, West Cornforth allegedly stole the ball from the billiard saloon of Mr Biago Coia but the defendant pleaded 'Not guilty'. In a written statement he claimed to have found a billiard ball in his pocket after making a visit to the saloon and that he fully intended to return the ball but lost it. The decision of the bench was to bind him over for 12 months and ordered him to pay costs as well as the price of the ball which totalled 27s 6d. A 14-year-old boy was charged with a similar offence and after pleading guilty he was bound over for 12 months. He was also placed under the care of the probation officers and ordered to pay costs. The boy said that he took the ball from Mr Biago Coia's in order that he could play billiards on his own table at home. Police Superintendent Foster pointed out that if one ball was stolen then the whole set became useless. (*Durham County Advertiser*, 1855–1968)

— September 3rd —

2010: On this day Michael Lassen, a stained glass artist, was fatally injured in a fall from a ladder while fixing a new window in the south choir aisle of the cathedral. The window which portrayed the Transfiguration of Christ had been created by Tom Denny and was one of the largest to be installed in Durham in recent years. Michael Lassen was working from top to bottom, fixing the glass he had leaded and had completed the main panels of Christ and his followers on the mountain. He was fitting a small panel on the lower left-hand corner, almost the final piece in the window, when he fell to the stone-flagged floor. Sadly, from the injuries that he sustained, Michael Lassen died some five days later, but his work in churches all over Britain bears testimony to his skills. Although English by birth, he trained in the Government School of Stained Glass at Hadamar in Germany and worked as a glazer and glass restorer before taking up glass painting and designing. Typical of his work are the windows at St Cadoc's chapel in Cowbridge, South Wales and the Church of St Peter and Paul at Great Somerford in Wiltshire. (*The Economist*, London, 1843)

∼ SEPTEMBER 4TH ∼

1290: A dispute broke out on this day between the Neville family of Raby Castle and monks based at Durham. The Nevilles held some of their lands from the abbey at a yearly rent of £4 and a buck was to be delivered to the monks each year on September 4th, the feast of St Cuthbert. On this occasion, Ralph, the third Lord Neville, claimed that when he arrived to present the buck, his retinue and as many supporters as he wished to invite should be entertained by the prior. In addition, he maintained that he should be waited by his own servants rather than those arranged by the abbey. When Neville's large party arrived and an attempt was made to carry the buck into the kitchen, the Prior Hugh Darlington refused to accept it. As the argument escalated, the monks were forced back into the church where they gathered the large wax candles from near the altar to resist Neville's men. When these unseemly events were investigated, John Balliol of Barnard Castle declined to support the Nevilles and Sir William Brompton, the Bishop's Chief Justice also ruled against the family's demands. Matters quietened down before the fourth Lord Neville again insisted on a lengthy and lavish stay at the abbey. (Stranks, C.J., *This Sumptuous Church: The Story of Durham Cathedral*, London: SPCK, 1993)

~ September 5th ~

1831: The banksman of Elvet pit narrowly avoided falling to his death in the pit shaft on this day. A corf of coal was accidentally lowered while he was working on it but fortunately, as he tripped, his feet caught on the edge of the shaft. Workmates were soon able to haul him to safety and as he reflected on his escape the banksman burst into tears. (Simpson, David, *Durham Millennium: A Thousand Years of Durham City*, Darlington: Northern Echo, 1995)

2008: It was reported on this day that the World Heritage Site, which included Durham cathedral and castle, had been extended to reflect its global significance. A recommendation by the International Council on Monuments and Sites (Icomos) had been approved by the United Nations Educational, Scientific and Cultural Organisation (UNESCO) World Heritage Committee and the future extent of the site would include Palace Green and a number of mainly seventeenth and eighteenth-century buildings surrounding it. The oldest property, Exchequer House, dates from the fifteenth century and is now part of the University's Palace Green Library. Icomos stated that extending the boundary would make the site continuous, strengthen its significance and make management simpler and more coherent. (*The Northern Echo*, Darlington, 1870–)

— September 6th —

1805: John Sell Cotman, one of the finest English artists of the Romantic era was staying in Durham and wrote to his patron, Francis Cholmeley on this day with the comment, 'Durham is a delightfully situated city' and later added that he found the cathedral 'magnificent though not so fine as York'. During his stay Cotman worked on two paintings of the cathedral and some experts argue that the view from the south west is the finest of all the topographical drawings of Durham cathedral. They point to remarkably accurate detail and compositional planning of light and dark areas which has an architectonic quality worthy of its subject. Laurence Binyon, author of *For the Fallen* stated, 'It has Girtin's largeness and serious simplicity and at the same time, a deeper comprehension of the grandeur of the architecture and an intense feeling for the actual moulding and essential character of the old stone.' Born in Norwich on May 16th 1782, Cotman moved to London in 1798 and although it seems that he had no formal art training, six of his watercolours were accepted for the annual Royal Academy exhibition during 1800. Between 1803 and 1805 he made sketching tours to Wales and Yorkshire and these resulted in some of his finest works. (Chilvers, Ian (ed.), *The Oxford Dictionary of Art and Artists*, Oxford: Oxford University Press, 2009)

~ SEPTEMBER 7TH ~

1960: Local newspaper reports on this day quoted Miss Alice Bacon MP for Leeds South East as saying 'Durham Jail is not at all bad' after she had spent 2½ hours 'inside' on a recent visit to the city. Compared with the older prisons she found Durham, 'quite bright' after much had been done to lighten it up. Miss Bacon, who made her visit as one of the Labour Party's spokesmen on home affairs, was accompanied by Mr Charles Grey, MP for Durham, and although 400 of its 1,000 male prisoners were housed three to a cell, she found it to be better than Armley Jail, Leeds, which she described as 'a glum place'. Miss Bacon spent most of her time in the girls' borstal wing and said that she was aware of criticisms by magistrates of conditions there as well as questions in parliament about the passing of love letters between girls and male prisoners. This traffic in love letters had been stopped, she claimed, and it was her opinion that officers were supervising things well. Miss Bacon added that she was impressed by the brightness of the girls' rooms and the individual interest shown by officers in the welfare of the 30–40 girls, though the real answer was to build a girls' borstal not attached to any prison. (*Durham County Advertiser*, 1855–1968)

— September 8th —

1477: Today a wrongdoer by the name of Oliver Branthywayt from 'Ireshopeburn in Werdale sought sanctuary at Durham Abbey on the Sabbath of September 8th 1477 – having murdered Thomas Lupton with a dagger at Sedbergh.' Two accomplices followed him on November 3rd, accompanied by Richard Fetherstonhalgh, a gentleman from Stanhope who acted as witness. Yet another accomplice appeared at the beginning of December. (Smith, Douglas *The Sanctuary at Durham*, Newcastle upon Tyne: Frank Graham, 1971)

————

2012: St Giles' church in Gilesgate, Durham City staged a medieval fair on this day as part of its year-long programme to celebrate its 900th anniversary. Archaeologist Louisa Gidney who runs 'Rent a Peasant', a Living History group, appeared at the event with her livestock which included chickens and her mule, Francis and a range of other activities included the Dunholm Living History re-enactment group, combat displays and textile demonstrations. (*The Northern Echo*, Darlington, 1870–)

————

2012: 'The Channel Challenge' took place in Durham marketplace in order to raise funds for the Trinity Special School in the city. Using rowing machines, firefighters from Durham City rowed the distance from Dover to Calais – 21 miles and finished a few minutes ahead of crew members from the city's adopted warship, HMS *Bulwark*. The event raised around £500 for the school. (*The Northern Echo*, Darlington, 1870–)

⁓ September 9th ⁓

1513: The Earl of Surrey visited Durham on his northern route to meet the Scottish army which had invaded England under the command of James IV. He is said to have assisted at Mass in the cathedral and borrowed St Cuthbert's banner from the prior to carry with him to the field of battle. A large troop was raised in the palatinate, commanded by Sir William Bulmer but when the armies met on the slopes of Branxton Hill James IV had superior numbers – around 35,000 to 40,000 men to the English forces 26,000. However, the Scottish force lacked experience and discipline and they were soon outmanoeuvred. The battle was ferocious and bloody as troops were cut down by artillery, arrows, pikes, bills and swords and after part of the English force had encircled the Scots position, James IV charged into the heat of the action. He was cut down 'within a spear's length' of the Earl of Surrey and became the last British king to die in battle. About 4,000 English troops died while Scotland lost up to 10,000 men. Following the victory at Flodden Field the Earl of Surrey was created Duke of Norfolk on February 1st 1514. (Whellan, Francis, *History, Topography, and Directory of the County Palatine of Durham Comprising a General Survey of the County and a History of the City and Diocese of Durham* ... , London: Ballantyne, Hanson and Co., 1894)

— September 10th —

1858: The parish of St Cuthbert in Durham City was formed out of the parish of St Margaret on this date. It included a major part of the Framwellgate area and gained a parish church on a site on North Road during 1862. The architect E.R. Robson designed a building with a nave and south aisle and a chancel with a semi-circular apse. A tower 'of peculiar yet attractive aspect,' at the north-west corner of the nave 'gives considerable effect to the appearance of the edifice'. The west front has several features worthy of attention, the most conspicuous being a large circular window, the outer portion of which is perforated in ten circles, the inner ring in six, whilst in the centre is a facsimile of the cross of St Cuthbert. An elegant feature of the building is the principal doorway, divided into two parts by a column, in front of which is placed a statue of the saint. Above the door is a figure of Our Lord within a vesica (oval with pointed head and foot). At the east end are five two-light windows, filled with stained glass, the principal figures representing the patron saints of all the churches of Durham. (Whellan, Francis, *History, Topography, and Directory of the County Palatine of Durham Comprising a General Survey of the County and a History of the City and Diocese of Durham* ... , London: Ballantyne, Hanson and Co., 1894)

~ SEPTEMBER 11TH ~

1650: A total of about 3,000 Scottish prisoners reached Durham on this day after a week of marching southwards with little food or water. They had been defeated by English forces under Oliver Cromwell at the Battle of Dunbar and tramped through Newcastle before crossing the River Wear into Durham, most probably across the twelfth-century Framwellgate Bridge. Durham Cathedral became a prison for captive Scottish troops while the adjacent castle was used as a hospital for sick and dying personnel. During their detention in the cathedral, prisoners and their guards destroyed much of the woodwork to fuel their fires and considerable damage was caused to the Neville tomb. This may have been in revenge for this powerful northern family's leading role in border warfare, most notably at Neville's Cross near Durham in 1346. Deaths resulting from starvation and outbreaks of dysentery may have totalled as many as 100 on some days. The overall toll among prisoners held at Durham has been estimated at about 1,600. During November 1650, 900 of the survivors were moved south and transported across the Atlantic to Virginia and Massachusetts while another 500 were enrolled in the French army. (www.scotwars.com)

— September 12th —

1597: John Bedforth, petty canon of Durham, made his will on this day, and the day after added to it the following nuncupative codicil (oral supplement) when walking in one of the streets. 'He willed and bequeathed to the parish church of St Mary, in the South Baily, his best surplice, having sleeves and being worth as he said 20*s*, before Robert Thompson and Mr Cuthbert Nicholl and divers others. Mrs Prentesse, Bartie Young, alias Drunken Bartie, and others heard when he those spoke and willed.' (Sykes, John, *Local Records: or Historical Register of Remarkable Events Which Have Occurred Exclusively in the Counties of Durham and Northumberland, Town and County of Newcastle upon Tyne and Berwick upon Tweed; with an Obituary of Persons of Talent, Eccentricity, and Longevity,* Newcastle: T. Fordyce, 1866)

1960: At a meeting of the Executive Committee of Durham Amateur Rowing Club on this day it was decided to investigate the possibility of a site for a new boathouse. The most viable alternative seemed to be an area of land that would become vacant between the proposed Leazes Road and the river channel once the road was completed. As the scheme progressed, however, the layout of the road was altered and spare land near the short course finish was too small for a boathouse. A total of £25 had been allocated to launch a boathouse fund and this amount was used to purchase premium bonds. (*Durham County Advertiser*, 1855–1968)

― September 13th ―

1869: Today 'At about half past nine o'clock two prisoners named Thomas Shield and Hugh Screenan contrived to make their escape from Durham Jail. The former was awaiting his trial for wilful murder at Shield Row, Annfield Plain, committed in August last year. It appears they managed to make a hole in the wall of their cell and so got out into the yard by means of their bedding and clothes which they made into a kind of rope to let themselves down. After arriving in the yard they had to get over an eighteen feet high wall which they did by the help of some timber lying in the yard. The prisoner Shield was captured during the night and taken back to Durham Gaol; the other prisoner escaped.'

Durham Jail had been completed during 1810 to replace an earlier prison in the Great North Gate that was causing serious traffic delays. Work began under the direction of a Mr Sandys but he was dismissed and replaced by an architect named Moneypenny. Unfortunately, Moneypenny died before the project was finished and Ignatius Bonomi finished the building which incorporated around 600 cells. The total cost of the building amounted to £134,684 15*s* 4*d*. (Fordyce, William, *The History and Antiquities of the County Palatine of Durham* …, Newcastle upon Tyne: T. Fordyce, 1850)

~ September 14th ~

1091: William de St Carileph was restored as Bishop of Durham on this day after a three-year period of exile. Royal approval was given for him to buy the political rights held by Mowbray, Earl of Northumberland between the rivers Tyne and Tees, leaving only the southern district of Durham, Sadberge, in Mowbray's holdings. As Prince Bishop, Carileph was able to raise an army, appoint sheriffs, administer laws, levy customs and taxes, set up markets and fairs, issue charters, salvage shipwrecks, collect revenue from mines, administer forests and mint coins. William de St Carileph had been nominated as Bishop of Durham by King William I in 1080 and during his term of office, in addition to the ecclesiastical duties he served as a commissioner for Domesday Survey and councillor and advisor to King William I and his son, William II. However, de St Carileph was implicated in a rebellion during 1088 and after William Rufus' forces had besieged Durham Castle he was put on trial for treason. A period of exile in Normandy followed and there he became a leading advisor to Robert Curthose, Duke of Normandy until his return to royal favour and England. (www.englandsnortheast.co.uk)

— September 15th —

1938: Coxhoe Hall was offered for sale by public auction at the Three Tuns Hotel in Durham and purchased by the East Hetton Colliery Company. It was requisitioned during the Second World War and housed Italian and German prisoners. During the early post-war years it was occupied by squatters, vandalised and then condemned by the National Coal Board. Pits had operated in the immediate locality since the early nineteenth century and it was claimed that underground coal workings had made it unsafe. The building was demolished in August 1952.

It had been largely the work of John Burdon who bought the Coxhoe estate in 1725 and added Gothic features to an earlier property. During a period of short ownerships and tenancies in the late 1700s and early 1800s it was held by Edward Moulton Barrett and his wife and their daughter, the poet, Elizabeth Barrett Browning was born there in 1806. (Meadows, Peter and Edward Waterson, *Lost Houses of County Durham*, York: Jill Raines, 1993)

1954: Durham City's mayor, Councillor Mrs E. Blyth signed the Salvation Army's National Youth Charter on this day. It had left London on January 1st 1954 and a logbook was signed by every leading dignitary at places where it stopped in England, Scotland and Wales before returning to London on January 1st 1955. (Richardson, Michael, *Memory Lane: Durham City*, Derby: Breedon, 2000)

— September 16th —

1998: During the early hours of this day a destructive fire swept through the church of St Brandon at Brancepeth near Durham City. The blaze was spotted by a routine police patrol but by the time the firefighters reached the scene flames, fanned by strong winds, were producing heat of about 1,200 degrees centigrade. Lead melted, stonework was reduced to dust and remains of a twelfth-century Frosterley marble font exploded at the heart of the raging inferno. Exquisite woodwork of the pews, pulpit and choir stalls which dated from the time of Bishop Cosin was reduced to ashes, while, in the nave itself, the lectern was one of few objects to survive relatively unscathed. A stone effigy of Robert Neville in the chancel was covered by massive charred oak beams that fell from the roof but survived with only minor damage. The fire also exposed more than 100 tombstones dating from between AD 1100–1300 which had previously been hidden in the church walls. Each weighed as much as half a ton and displayed symbols such as swords, books, chalices and shears but mystery surrounded a five point star design that has not been found anywhere else. (*Durham Times*, Durham: Newsquest, 2007–)

~ September 17th ~

1793: On this day an infirmary was opened by the Durham Chapter. Dr Dampier, one of the prebendaries and Dean of Rochester, was reported to have preached 'an excellent sermon' and a total of £54 6s 7d was raised by a collection at the door. A procession which included the bishop, the dean and the prebendaries along with the mayor and corporation, local gentry including Rowland Burdon and George Claverings Esq., clergy and many of the respectable inhabitants of Durham 'proceeded to the building and naturally dined together afterwards'. (Mackenzie, Eneas and Metcalf Ross, *An Historical, Topographical and Descriptive View of the County Palatinate of Durham ...* Newcastle upon Tyne: Mackenzie and Dent, 1834)

1895: The foundation stone of St John's church, Neville's Cross was laid on this day by Viscountess Boyne. Design work was carried out by Plummer and Burrell of Newcastle and Durham at a cost of £1,000 and the building was consecrated by Bishop Daniel Sandford, Assistant Bishop of Durham less than 7 months later on April 8th 1896. A chancel, vestry and organ chamber were added in 1908 as a memorial to Revd George S. Ellam, a former curate, who was killed nearby in a motorcycle accident. (Richardson, Michael, *Durham: Cathedral City*, Thrupp: Sutton, 1997)

— September 18th —

1855: James Finlay Weir Johnston, a Scottish agricultural chemist, died in Durham on this day. Born and brought up in Scotland, he embarked on a career devoted to studying chemistry and wrote *Catechism of Agricultural Chemistry* (1844) and *Chemistry of Common Life* (1853–55). Appointed as a lecturer at Durham University, his contribution to education in the city is further highlighted by a plaque on the wall of No. 56 Claypath which reads, 'James Finlay Weir Johnston, Applied Scientist and Scholar lived here 1826–55. From his bequest was founded the Durham Johnston School.' (en.wikipedia.org/wiki/James_Finlay_Weir_Johnston)

2012: Professor Peter Higgs was the focus of a special presentation from Durham University on this day. He had been invited to Durham to celebrate the tenth anniversary of the Ogden Centre, an internationally renowned research centre for fundamental physics. Newcastle born, Professor Higgs, now aged 83, gave his name to the Higgs boson which scientists at the Large Hadron Collider, based near Switzerland, believe they discovered during July 2012 after forming the concept in the 1960s. Professor Higgs was presented with a multi-coloured glass sculpture in the theoretical shape of the Higgs boson by Vice Chancellor Professor Chris Higgins. (*The Northern Echo*, Darlington, 1870–)

~ September 19th ~

2012: On this day three police officers, PCs David Robinson, Andrew MacLean and Gary Ramsey were each presented with Royal Humane Society certificates of commendation for their part in a rescue which took place on the outskirts of Durham City in March 2012. PC MacLean and a colleague were on patrol when they received a call to follow a Vauxhall Astra which had driven off after a routine stop in Langley Moor. Their pursuit continued along the A167 to a point near the Cock o' the North roundabout where the vehicle crashed through a fence. The driver ran into an area of woodland beside the River Browney and a police helicopter detected him in the river by using its infrared system. The man was beginning to suffer from hypothermia after being in the water for around 10 minutes, and when PC Robinson reached him his head was just above the surface. The other two officers then entered the water and managed to haul the unconscious suspect to safety before carrying him to an ambulance half a mile away. After emergency hospital treatment he made a full recovery and then faced prosecution. (*The Northern Echo*, Darlington, 1870–)

~ September 20th ~

2012: The Lordship of the Manor of Kelloe near Durham City was advertised for sale through the Manorial Auctioneers of London on this day. Although there was no land for sale with the title, the new lord or lady of the manor would be able to use the title on their passports, cheque books and credit cards as well as qualifying for membership of the Manorial Society of Great Britain. The earliest written reference to the manor appears in a return of knights' fees dating from 1283 to 1310 and at the beginning of the thirteenth century the Prince Bishop Richard Kelloe took his surname from the village. His brother, Patrick, commanded episcopal troops during 1312 when they took up arms against a dangerous band of freebooters named the Shavaldi, and Alexander Kelloe was a benefactor of the Hospital of Serburne (Sherburn) in 1260. By the early fifteenth century Kelloe was owned by the Forcer family, and it was later bought by the Tempest family of Broughton Hall, near Skipton. Sir Henry Vane-Tempest bequeathed it to his daughter, Lady Frances Vane, who married the 3rd Marquess of Londonderry. The title was sold by the 9th marquess in 1987. (*The Northern Echo*, Darlington, 1870–)

~ September 21st ~

1987: A sports hall was officially opened on this day at the Chorister School, Durham, by Colin Moynihan, the Minister of Sport. The building replaced a small wooden hut which had originally been used as St Mary's College chapel. Further work included enlargement of the adjacent yard though initial plans for a bigger play area had to be shelved when planning officers ruled that an early eighteenth-century pond must be restored in its existing location. (Crosby, Brian, *Come on Choristers! A History of the Chorister School, Durham*, Durham: B. Crosby, 1999)

2012: Residents and visitors to Durham gained an unusual glimpse of the city's past today when a video-screen in a shop window on Saddler Street displayed live images of the remains of Durham Castle's Medieval North Gate. The gate, demolished in 1820, was found in the cellar of the empty shop which was resealed after investigation. Before the shop was revamped a live video link was installed. Total cost of the project for Durham City Council amounted to £28,000 with further funding from the owners of the building, the Salvation Army. Later in the year the premises were due to be reopened by a clothing and footwear company. (*The Northern Echo*, Darlington, 1870–)

~ September 22nd ~

1711: Thomas Wright, astronomer and mathematician, was born at Byers Green on this day. Educated in Bishop Auckland, he took up an apprenticeship with a watchmaker in the town but left before his training was completed. Following a short time at sea he worked as a teacher in Sunderland before heading south to London. During the 1730s his skills as an astronomer led to the publication of an almanac for sailors and astronomers and the manufacture of scientific instruments for members of the nobility. In 1750 he turned down an invitation from the Russian court to take up the post of Chief Professor of Navigation at St Petersburg University and produced his hypothesis of the universe, which included his theory on the nature of Saturn's rings and his thoughts about the paths of comets. During 1780 Thomas Wright started work on Westerton Folly – a small round tower with small buttresses, cross-shaped arrow slits and low doorways – which served as an observatory, but he died before work was completed. Following his death on February 22nd 1786 he was buried in St Andrew's churchyard at Bishop Auckland. (Woodhouse, Robert, *County Durham: Strange but True*, Stroud: Sutton Publishing, 2004)

— September 23rd —

1826: On this day the old tithe barn at Shincliffe was consecrated as a Chapel of Ease for the Anglican community by the Bishop of Durham and services were held in it on the following day. Until this time Shincliffe was part of the ancient parish of St Oswald which spread around three sides of the City of Durham. In 1831 Shincliffe was consecrated a parish in its own right and during 1866 the benefice became a rectory. It seems that the tithe barn soon proved to be cold and draughty and a steady increase in the local population led to plans for a parish church. Reverend Isaac Todd, church officials and local residents initiated building work and the new church was commended in 1850 and ready for use the following year. A spire was added to the building in 1870 as a testimonial to the ministry of Revd Todd who served initially as a perpetual curate and then as rector for a period of forty-six years. (Brown, Reg, *A Brief History of Shincliffe*, Shincliffe, 1975)

2012: Beavers, Cubs and Scouts from Durham Scout County received their Chief Scout's awards during a ceremony at the Gala Theatre in Durham City on this day. (*The Northern Echo*, Darlington, 1870–)

~ September 24th ~

1679: On this day 'William Wall, amongst other legacies, bequeathed the yearly sum of 15s to the prisoners in Durham Gaol, which at the time of the Charity Commissioners' Report, was paid by Thomas Peacock, of Bishop Auckland.' (Whellan, Francis, *History, Topography, and Directory of the County Palatine of Durham Comprising a General Survey of the County and a History of the City and Diocese of Durham* … , London: Ballantyne, Hanson and Co., 1894)

1870: A destructive fire swept through the medieval Kepier Mill on this day. The blaze is believed to have started after the miller's son fell asleep and forgot to fill the hopper with corn. Sparks were then spread from the grinding of the stone millwheels to nearby timbers. The medieval mill building was one of several structures at this location that were under the ownership of the Heath family. The gatehouse had been built on the orders of Bishop Richard de Bury (1333–45) and the manor house dated from the late sixteenth century. This building later became the White Bear Inn and in its later years, before being demolition in 1892, it was renamed the Kepier Inn. The only remnant of the mill that still survives is the stone arch of the mill race further downstream from Milburngate Bridge. (Richardson, Michael, *Durham: The Photographic Collection*, Stroud: Sutton, 2002)

~ September 25th ~

2012: Durham City suffered severe flooding as the height of the River Wear rose several feet and burst its banks. One of the worst hit areas was Framwellgate Waterside and police officers blocked the riverside road between Milburngate House and the Radisson Blu hotel, where guests stood on the steps as water levels rose.

The hotel had previously flooded in 2009 but on this occasion the water stopped below the front doors. A nearby car belonging to one of the hotel's guests was slowly becoming submerged and so the hotel manager was summoned from his bed at home at 5.30 a.m. to put on a pair of swimming trunks and high visibility jacket in order to move the vehicle to safety. In other areas of the city, riverside footpaths slipped below the water, boathouses were flooded and members of staff at the Boathouse Bar had to wade through the deluge to remove picnic tables. At a lower level, rowing boats had to be lifted from the Wear and the *Prince Bishops River Cruiser* was forced to abandon its planned operations, while traffic through large areas of Durham was forced to slow down with part of the A690 westbound closed for a time during the afternoon. (*The Northern Echo*, Darlington, 1870–)

— September 26th —

2008: A public sculpture *The Journey* was unveiled in Durham City centre on this day by the Princess Royal. It was the work of Durham-based sculptor, Fenwick Lawson, whose work is exhibited at several locations across the city. These include *The Pieta* – a wooden sculpture depicting the body of Jesus and his mother Mary – which is displayed in Durham Cathedral and *Crucifixion, Resurrection and Ascension* which hangs in Grey College Chapel, one of four colleges within Durham University that display his work.

Fenwick Lawson was born at South Moor, County Durham in 1932 and grew up in the nearby village of Craghead before studying at the Sunderland College of Art and the Royal College of Art in London during the 1950s. He completed his studies in 1958 and in 1959 by visiting locations in France, Italy and Greece that had been influenced by sculptural masters such as Michelangelo and Donatello. In 1961 Fenwick Lawson was appointed to a lectureship at Newcastle upon Tyne College of Art and when it merged with the city's polytechnic nine years later he became Head of Sculpture before retiring in 1984. He was awarded an Honorary Doctor of Letters from Durham University in June 2008 and the Freedom of the City of Durham on 10 November of the same year. (www.dur.ac.uk/news/)

~ September 27th ~

2011: A bust of Sir Ove Arup, renowned structural engineer, was unveiled on this day during a ceremony at the Durham Students' Union. It replaced an original bronze bust by Diana Brandenburger which was stolen from a concrete plinth outside Dunelm House during 2006. Additional time had been needed to obtain planning permission to move the bust to a higher level and to receive permission to recast the head in a similar form to the original. According to the University's Deputy Vice Chancellor, Professor Anthony Forster, the new resin bust was bought by Durham University and the City of Durham Trust 'for a modest cost' and the event was accompanied by an exhibition organised by Durham postgraduate Natalie Proctor, which looked at the history of Kingsgate Bridge and Dunelm House and included photographs of construction work. Sir Ove, who was born in Newcastle in 1895, founded Ove Arup and Partners, one of the world's largest civil engineering practices and although he worked on Sydney Opera House, The Barbican Centre and the Penguin Pool at London Zoo, he considered Kingsgate Bridge to be his finest work. He died in 1988 at the age of 93 and his ashes were scattered from Kingsgate Bridge. (www.palatinate.org.uk)

— September 28th —

1684: A tanner from Framwellgate by the name of John Richardson, whose grave had been dug at Crossgate church on this day, was refused burial by the Bishop of Durham because he died while under the sentence of excommunication. He was buried on the following day in his garden at Caterhouse. (Simpson, David, *Durham Millennium: A Thousand Years of Durham City*, Darlington: Northern Echo, 1995)

1862: Isobel Violet Hunt, novelist and short story writer, was born in Durham on this day. When her family moved to London some three years later she was brought up in a Pre-Raphaelite group among contemporaries such as John Ruskin and William Morris. Her written works covered a number of literary forms, including short stories, novels, memoir and biography. Her novel *White Rose of Weary Leaf* is widely regarded as her finest work and she was also at the forefront in writers' organisations such as the Women Writers' Suffrage League which she helped to set up in 1908. Violet Hunt also staged literary salons at her home, South Lodge, in Campden Hill and numbered among her guests were Rebecca West, Ezra Pound, Joseph Conrad, Wyndham Lewis, D.H. Lawrence and Henry James. She died at her home at Campden Hill, London in January 1942. (en.wikipedia.org/wiki/Violet_Hunt)

~ September 29th ~

1930: Ratepayers in the parish of Broom sat for almost 2½ hours at the Roman Catholic School, Ushaw Moor, on this day, discussing the public lighting of the parish and even then no real progress was reported. Mr George Turnbull, Chairman of the parish council presided and the proceedings at times became somewhat lively. In a report on the subject, Mr J. Bradley, the clerk, explained that there were 170 lights in the parish, each of which cost the council £3 per annum to give a total of £510 per annum. A further sum was needed for the fire brigade and another sum for the maintenance of lighting and poles to make a total of over £550. He explained that raising £550 during the year would mean a 1s 2d rate but by switching the lighting contract from Messrs Cochrane and Co. to the Bearpark Coal Co. the rate had been reduced by 2d as the latter company had promised to charge only £2 15s per annum for each lamp. Cochrane and Co. had declined to make any reduction until the very last minute and would charge more per lamp for lighting a portion of the parish than for lighting the whole parish. (*Durham County Advertiser*, 1855–1968)

September 30th

1926: The chapel of Durham School was consecrated on this day by the Bishop of Durham, Dr H. Hensley Henson and the occasion also marked the presentation of school prizes. It had been built as a memorial to past pupils, known as 'Dunelmians', who had fallen in the First World War, with design work in the Gothic style by W.H. Brierley of Messrs Brierley and Rutherford of York. Construction work was carried out by Messrs Rudd and Sons of Grantham and covered just over two years following the laying of the foundation stone by Dean Weldon on July 3rd 1924. A total of ninety-seven steps leading up to the chapel represent the number of the fallen in the First World War. It was originally fashioned from wooden railway sleepers but these were replaced by concrete in memory of those who died in the Second World War. They were refurbished during 2006. Names of casualties from the First World War are engraved on a series of eight pillars in the chapel and those for the Second World War were added above them. A former pupil of the school (between 1905–11) the poet, William Noel Hodgson was killed on the first day of the Somme Campaign whilst serving with the 9th Devonshire Regiment. (*Durham County Advertiser*, 1855–1968)

~ October 1st ~

1628: Durham City's earliest known honorary tanner is George Clark who was admitted to the guild on this day and 'who doth faithfullie promise this dae that he will not at any tyme take any apprentice whereby the said trade and misterie of tanners may be preiudiced either by himself or any under color or pretence of his admittance.' One function of a trade guild was to regulate the number of apprentices (usually one to each freeman) who served for seven years (or nine for a tanner), to check that his work was of a suitable standard and then enrol him as a freeman of the guild for a fee providing he was 21 years of age (24 for a tanner). (Clack, P.A.J., *The Book of Durham City*, Buckingham: Barracuda, 1985)

1871: The final link for the East Coast Main Line between Reilly Mill Junction and the Leamside route towards Ferryhill at Tursdale Junction was completed and from this day the ECML services ran through Durham. (Aerofilms, *From the Air: Britain's Railways Then & Now*, Shepperton: Ian Allan Publishing, 2001)

2002: The first toll road in 100 years was introduced in Durham on this day. The so-called 'Congestion Charge' applied to a route along Saddler Street between the marketplace and the cathedral peninsula. (news.bbc.co.uk)

~ OCTOBER 2ND ~

1780: Following the guilds' petition for a new charter, Bishop Egerton, on this day, granted this last episcopal charter to the city which continued in force until the passing of the Municipal Corporations Act of 1835. The commissioners in 1835 reported that the Corporation exercised no jurisdiction, either criminal or civil, but that a manor court of very limited jurisdiction was held within the city. (*The Corporation of Durham: Official Guide*, Durham: G. Bailes, 1938)

1912: A ceremony to mark the laying of the foundation stone of St Margaret's parish church hall, Crossgate, Durham on this day included an address by Revd Ralph. Land had been purchased at a cost of £520 and the building, which was designed by W.H. Wood of No. 47 North Bailey, cost an additional £2,065 6s 11d. The Dean of Durham, Dr Herbert Hensley Henson, formally opened the hall on April 2nd 1913. After more than sixty years of usage, during which time St Margaret's Parish Hall had served as a base for many groups including the Church Lads Brigade and St Margaret's Billiard Club, it was demolished in September 1974. The site was cleared to build apartments for the Three Rivers Housing Association and a new church centre was opened in the former St Margaret's School on Margery Lane. (Richardson, Michael, *Durham: Cathedral City*, Thrupp: Sutton, 1997)

~ OCTOBER 3RD ~

1827: Bishop Van Mildert held a sumptuous banquet in the Great Hall of Durham Castle on this day and among the invited guests were Sir Walter Scott and the Duke of Wellington. Scott gives an account of the entertainment which displayed 'a singular mixture of baronial pomp with the grave and more chastened dignity of prelacy' and describes the demeanour of the host who showed 'scholarship without pedantry and dignity without ostentation.' The layout of the hall on this grand occasion was largely the work of Bishop Cosin who held office between 1660 and 1672. During the Civil War, Scottish prisoners had been held in the castle and a series of repairs were carried out in almost every part of the building. In addition to demolishing the barbican and partially filling the moat, Cosin oversaw two additions to the hall. In front of the original doorway to the hall he built an elaborate porch and added four great buttresses, while a portion of the hall which Bishop Neile separated was converted into a council chamber. Bishop Cosin took a personal interest in the work, as shown in a letter to his secretary from London in 1662, in which he ordered that they should wait until he returned to supervise the scheme. (www.british-history.ac.uk)

~ October 4th ~

1602: On this day Bishop Matthew granted a charter to the City of Durham. It stated that in future the city's affairs would be supervised by a mayor and aldermen instead of by a bailiff as had previously been the case. The first elected Mayor of Durham, James Farrales, was in office by this date and soon afterwards the city welcomed England's new monarch, King James I, during his journey south from Scotland to London. (Proud, Keith, *Durham City*, Chichester: Phillimore, 2003)

2012: On this day the Northern Education Trust was formally launched in Durham City. It was claimed to be the first multi-academy educational trust based in the North East and represented a major new initiative to improve struggling schools. Backing for the new agency came from the former Education Secretary, Estelle Morris, now Baroness Morris of Yardley, who was chairwoman of Northern Education, the leading education consultancy that was sponsoring Net. Initially it had four schools under its management with plans to run a total of twelve schools within a year. Strong leadership within schools was seen as critical to success and emphasis was placed on strong relationships with local government, industry, commerce and higher education as well as the sports and arts sectors. (*The Northern Echo*, Darlington, 1870–)

~ OCTOBER 5TH ~

2012: A new hospital, the Cambrian Appletree, was opened by Durham MP Roberta Blackman-Woods on this day in the Meadowfield district of Durham City. Owned and operated by the Cambrian Group, an independent provider of specialist mental health services, the premises were set up to provide care and treatment for women with enduring mental illness. The twenty-six bed rehabilitation centre takes referrals from the NHS and aims to assist women in regaining their place in the community and in rebuilding relationships with their families. It features facilities such as a therapy kitchen, beauty salon and dance studio. (*The Northern Echo,* Darlington, 1870–)

2012: Former World Cup winner Jack Charlton officially opened a new third generation (3G) artificial pitch at the Meadowfield Leisure Centre in Durham on this day. It had been funded with the help of a £78,273 grant from Football Foundation, the sports charity funded by the Premier League, the Football Association and the government via Sport England. Durham County Council co-operated with the Durham County Football Association to obtain funding from the Football Foundation and the new pitch, which is both full-size and floodlit, can be used for 11-a-side games, or divided into three to enable smaller teams to play in support of the FA's youth development plan. (www.footballfoundation.org.uk)

~ OCTOBER 6TH ~

1930: On this day a rate of 11*s* 3*d* in the pound was sealed for the next six months, at the monthly meeting of the Brandon and Byshottles Urban District Council held in the Board Room, Langley Moor, when Councillor Dickinson presided. This compared with 12*s* for the last half-year and provided a welcome reduction. The product of a penny rate is given as £170 and the amount required is £22,304 2*s* 9*d*. The County Council precept is £16,037 16*s* 0*d*. What was described as a serious issue was raised by the Rating Officer (Miss M.C. Salkeld). He stated that, according to the evaluation of colliery property by Messrs Michael Faraday and Partners, there would be a big reduction in the rateable value of the parish. This was due to the colliery assessments now appearing in the valuation list, which comprised more than 2,000 (or more than one half) of the rate book. An analysis was given of the old and the proposed new assessments. Commenting on the report, Councillor Carr said that the Willington Council had had a severe reprimand when they appeared before the Rating Authority with respect to provisional arrangements made on the assessments. The Chairman remarked that all they could do was await developments. (*Durham County Advertiser*, 1855–1968)

— October 7th —

1912: An advertisement in the local press stated that on this day in the window of R. Charlton, No. 103 Claypath, Durham, Miss Taylor, the lady expert from Messrs J. & J. Baldwin & Partners of Beehive Wool Frame, would be giving practical demonstrations in wool working. She would be giving special prominence to the knitting of the fashionable long coats by showing new stitches, etc. and in rug making she would introduce the new range of Turkish colourings and designs. Practical advice would be available from 10.00 a.m. to noon when Miss Taylor could be interviewed by ladies seeking advice or to discuss designs and how they could commence any work they may desire (free of charge).

In addition – A Great Show of Wools At Special Prices During The Week – Baldwin's Double Knitting Wool in all the New Shades now in large demand for knitted coats 3s 4d per lb. Baldwin's Turkey Rug Wool in a striking range of three dozen art shades. A detailed pattern would be given with all purchases of wool for rugs priced 1s 11½ d per lb. Various wools suitable for shawls, Giant Zephyr wool for making ladies capes, Beehive soft knitting for fingering and vest wools are also available.

Ralph Charlton, Draper, Durham.
(*Durham County Advertiser.*)

⚊ October 8th ⚊

1948: A newspaper report on this day stated:

> When Annie Metcalfe (47) Fairy Street, Hetton le Hole appeared on six charges relating to ration book offences, Mr V. H. Jackson for the Ministry of Food, stated that by this means she was actually using five books instead of three to which she was entitled. She pleaded 'guilty' to the two charges of using two duplicate ration books when the originals, reported lost, were in her possession; and guilty to two charges of using the reference leaf from the books in order to obtain two further books. She was fined £3 and £1 1s in each case and 5s costs, a total of £16 9s. Detective E.V. Peacock, MOF enforcement officer, stated that when interviewed with regard to the offences, the defendant at first denied all knowledge, then said she would tell the truth, and showed him three duplicates and two books which had been reported lost. She said 'So the Jackdaw has been talking.' (Mr Jackson said that this was some imaginary informer.) Metcalfe, in the witness box said that she could not find the three books when she made the application and after finding them did not return them as she was 'hard up for soap' at the time.

(*Durham Chronicle*, 1820–1984)

~ October 9th ~

1960: Local press reports on this day described how high winds and driving rain had transformed the River Wear into a raging torrent a few days earlier. The river had swept over the towpath and flooded the bus depot at Millburngate. Trees on the riverbanks had been uprooted and a haystack was seen floating downstream as the city suffered its worst flooding for eight years. The level of the river above Framwellgate was 10ft above the normal mark and below the river dams it flowed only 6in from the top of the 20ft high wall which rises from the river bed. The road at Millburngate looked more like a river than a busy thoroughfare on Monday. Traffic had to be diverted and there were lots of sightseers as the floodwater roared over the weir. At Durham Ice Rink water began seeping into the engine house at the Old Mill situated at the end of Framwellgate Dam. Workmen had to shut down the turbines which supply electricity to the rink because of the high water, but an emergency supply was used and it was skating as usual. With the return of colder and drier weather the river began to subside. It had been a near thing. (*Durham County Advertiser*, 1855–1968)

~ OCTOBER 10TH ~

1556: Sessions of the peace were held on this date at Durham before Henry, Earl of Westmorland, Robert Meynell, sergeant at law and a number of jurors. Cases heard include two separate incidents at Aislaby (near Yarm) where groups of local men 'riotously assembled' and carried out thefts. On September 29th 1556 more than twenty 'husbandmen', labourers and 'unknown malefactors' had entered land belonging to William Lambert and driven off three grazing cows to the village of Sadberge. Almost exactly a month earlier, on August 27th 1556, a smaller group of men had broken into land belonging to James Garnett and driven away 'half a wainload of hay worth 10*s* in a stack.' Two other cases involved the same small group of men who, on August 5th 1556, 'with force and arms' broke into the free fishery of Henry, Earl of Westmorland, at Blaydon and stole a boat and net worth together 4 marks, belonging to John Reppeth and also a boat and net worth together 4 marks belonging to John Bell and John Moreman. (Fraser, C.M. (ed.), *Durham Quarter Sessions Rolls 1471–1625*, Durham: Surtees Society, 1991)

1928: King George V and Queen Mary visited Durham on this day and were met by the city's mayor Councillor Moffatt Lynch, council officials and guests outside the town hall while 3,000 children sang the national anthem in the marketplace. (Richardson, Michael, *Memory Lane: Durham City*, Derby: Breedon, 2000)

~ October 11th ~

1930: The Browney Social Club Homing Society held their annual 'wind up' supper on this day in the Club Hall. Pie supper was catered for by Stoker and Co. and over 130 people sat down. After supper Mr W. Maddison, secretary of the Social Club, occupied the chair and awarded to Messrs Richardson and Son a handsome medal presented by Dr W.H. Denholme, the winner of the Cross-Channel race and also the beautiful vase given by the Club Committee for the best old bird's average. Mr Joe Cook was awarded the vase given for the best young bird's race and Mr W. Jobling for the winner of the Peterborough race. An interesting impromptu concert followed the presentations, songs were sung by Messrs A. Bone of Durham, Charles Edmondson, comedian of Ferryhill and local talent. On the same evening, the Langley Moor Wesleyan footballers held a successful social event in the North Brancepeth Council Schools where the proceedings consisted of games and supper 'There was a good company' and the Browney Page Boys' Jazz Band held a dance in the Scouts' Hut with music being supplied by the Ricardo Dance Band. (*Durham County Advertiser*, 1855–1968)

⁓ October 12th ⁓

1930: Concerts were held at several different venues in the Durham area on this day including the Brandon Social Club where the 'Broadway Five Concert Party' gave 'an enjoyable concert' with Mr J. Lidster presiding. Choruses were sung by the party, songs by Miss Milly Gillespie (soprano) and Jack Watson (tenor), and humorous items, patter and dances were led by Jimmy Bailey and Pat Hardy. Members of the Meadowfield Social Club enjoyed a 'capital concert' provided by Mr E. Franks and party from Sunnybrow. This comprised Messrs E. Franks and T. Cook (descriptive vocalists), Mr M. Bolam (humorist), Miss Trow (banjoist and dancer) and Mr R. Trow (accompanist). At the Langley Moor Social Club, 'Mr Bert Evans, an accomplished pianist and conductor from the New Herrington district visited with his orchestra and gave a very fine programme in the Club Hall before a crowded assembly. Vocal items were rendered by Mr W. Carr, Mr Spearman was solo violinist and Mr Evans accompanist Mr J. McKenna presided.' Meanwhile, Brandon Colliery 'was idle with the exception of the workmen engaged on special duties and Littleburn Colliery was again idle until further notice, the men 'signing on' for unemployment benefit last weekend at the Langley Moor Social Club.' (*Durham County Advertiser*, 1855–1968)

~ October 13th ~

1898: St Godric's RC School, Castle Chare, Durham City, was officially opened on this day by the mayor, Colonel Rowlandson. The architect was Mr C. Walker of Newcastle and the builder Mr Caldcleugh of Durham. Total cost of the site and building amounted to about £5,000. During 1996 the school was relocated to purpose-built premises at Newton Hall. (Richardson, Michael, *Durham: Cathedral City*, Thrupp: Sutton, 1997)

1951: This day marked the official opening of Ferens Park, home ground of Durham City FC. The club was originally formed in 1918 and gained membership of Division Three North of the Football League in 1921 before being disbanded in 1938. A meeting in the town hall on May 13th 1949 brought the first positive moves towards the formation of a post-war club with the appointment of Mr Raymond Appleby as chairman, Mr George Thompson as honorary secretary and Mr Harry Allison as honorary treasurer. Soon afterwards Alderman Ferens accepted the post of president and a temporary headquarters was set up in the home of a committee member, Mr J. Anderson. August 1950 saw the team playing Wearside League football before gaining admission to the Northern League in 1951. (*Official Opening of Ferens Park Saturday 13 October 1951 Souvenir Programme*, Durham, 1951)

~ OCTOBER 14TH ~

1973: Press reports on this day highlighted increasing debate about the future of Durham City Golf Club:

> The report in last week's *Advertiser* that ninety acres of the Durham City golf course may be sold for residential development has aroused a great deal of interest and speculation. We now understand from a reliable source that the Durham City Golf Club has decided to ignore a notice to quit the course. Served a few months ago on behalf of the lessors, the North of England Estates Company, the notice, it is understood, becomes operative this autumn. Despite such a serious threat, it is business as usual as far as the club is concerned. Even after the notice becomes effective the club is determined to carry on and members will continue to play golf … At present the Golf Club is undergoing one of the most turbulent periods in its lengthy history. It was founded at Pinkerknowle but in 1928 moved to its present course when the club took it over on a lease. In 1952 the lease expired and since that date the owners have not been prepared to grant a new lease but have allowed the club to remain in occupation.

(*Durham Advertiser*, 1968–2000)

~ October 15th ~

1930: On this day local citizens learned 'with deep regret' of the death of Alderman Robert McLean JP at his residence of Invergordon, The Avenue, Durham after a lengthy illness. For more than a year his health had been giving cause for concern but after a severe bout of illness he recovered sufficiently to take his familiar place in the Mayor's Chamber. At 72 years of age, Alderman McLean had been a prominent figure for many years in the public life of the city and county of Durham. He was born at Invergordon, Scotland and received his early education there, then, following a move to Glasgow, he became an apprentice in the drapery business. After settling in Durham as a draper in about 1895, he went on to own a tobacconist shop. In 1904 Robert McLean moved into local politics and was Mayor of Durham in 1912 and 1921 before becoming an alderman in 1925. For six years he was a member of Durham County Council and also served on the Board of Guardians as well as becoming a magistrate in 1921. Sporting interests led him to a directorship of Durham City FC and presidency of the City Bowling Club. (*Durham County Advertiser*, 1855–1968)

‑ October 16th ‑

1346: On this day forces from north and south of the Scottish border were converging on an area to the west of Durham City before the Battle of Neville's Cross broke out on the following morning. Scots, led by King David II, had crossed the border close to Carlisle and ranged along the Tyne Valley to plunder Lanercost Priory and capture Hexham and Corbridge. Continuing southwards they crossed the Tyne at the ford between Newburn and Ryton. Local legend suggests that King David had a vision warning him not to invade the lands of St Cuthbert but the advancing forces made their way across the river at Ebchester and set up camp on this day at Beaurepaire (Bearpark) just 2 miles from Durham City. In the meantime, English forces led by Ralph Neville, Henry Percy and the Archbishop of York gathered at Richmond before advancing to Bishop Auckland where they set up camp in Auckland Park. Henry Percy sent a message to King David warning him to withdraw but this plea was ignored as was the plea from two monks at Durham not to fight. On this night before the battle, St Cuthbert is said to have appeared before the Prior of Durham instructing him to carry the saint's banner to the battlefield. (Nixon, Philip and Dennis Dunlop, *Exploring Durham History*, Derby: Breedon Books, 1998)

~ October 17th ~

1346: On this day the Battle of Neville's Cross was fought between an English army numbering between 5,000 and 10,000 and Scottish forces totalling between 12,000 and 30,000. In the early stages, the Scottish right flank led by William Douglas, Earl of Moray, advanced but became stranded in boggy ground. This left them easy prey for English archers. The Scottish centre led by King David and the left flank under Robert Stewart advanced and pushed back the English right wing, only for the English reserve to move round and outflank the Scots. Soon afterwards Stewart withdrew his troops and English forces could now deal with David's central force. Eventually he was captured by John Copeland and the retreating Scottish forces were cut down between the battlefield and Findon Hill. Estimates of Scottish dead range from 1,000 to 15,000. (www.english-heritage.org.uk)

1799: Anthony Salvin, architect and expert on medieval buildings, was born on this day at Sunderland Bridge, south of Durham City. After an education at Durham School he worked on the restoration of Brancepeth Castle before moving to London in 1821. His work in restoring and replacing churches, cathedrals and castles led to him receiving the royal gold medal of the Royal Institute of British Architects in 1863. (www.victorianweb.org)

~ October 18th ~

1964: This day saw the ceremony of laying up the old colours in Durham Cathedral by warrant officers and Non-Commissioned Officers from the 8th Battalion of the Durham Light Infantry. Princess Alexandra, Colonel-in-Chief, was present and after the service in the cathedral a memorial garden was laid out in Cathedral Close. (Richardson, Michael, *Durham: Cathedral City*, Thrupp: Sutton, 1997)

2011: Multimillion pound plans to refurbish and extend Durham University's business school were approved on this day. The university's governing council backed the £16.6 million scheme for planned improvements to Durham Business School in Mill Hill in Durham City. As a result of increasing student numbers in recent years, university authorities planned to gather various offices that were currently spread across several buildings, under one roof. The plans for this extension included seminar rooms, offices and catering facilities while there were also alterations to existing lecture rooms, seminar rooms, a library, an IT suite and offices. At that time, the Durham Business School had more than 100 academic staff, 1,260 undergraduate students and 2,500 postgraduate students from the United Kingdom and overseas. (*The Northern Echo*, Darlington, 1870–)

~ OCTOBER 19TH ~

1932: The Chief Scout Lord Baden Powell (1857–1941) visited Durham on this day and purchased a calendar from the local association store at the County Scout Bazaar at Durham Indoor Market. A camp on Brownsea Island in 1907 and publication of *Scouting for Boys* are widely regarded as the beginning of the Scout movement. Lord Baden Powell had been in the North East for a jamboree that was held at Raby Castle and it was at the First World Scout Jamboree at Olympia that he was acclaimed 'Chief Scout of the World'. (Richardson, Michael, *Durham: Cathedral City*, Thrupp: Sutton, 1997)

———

2011: A campaign was launched on this day at Freeman's Quay Leisure Centre in Durham City with the intention of recruiting around 400 'Sports Makers' to encourage grass roots physical activity and exercise across the north-east region. The scheme was part of the national Sport Makers Campaign, funded by the National Lottery to recruit 40,000 volunteers by September 2013 and create a lasting legacy for the London 2012 Olympics, under the Places People Play initiative. At the Durham session forty-five young women from six schools and sixth forms in Durham and Chester-le-Street tried out Zumba, basketball, boxercise, football, tennis and fencing. (*The Northern Echo*, Darlington, 1870–)

~ October 20th ~

2011: During a school workshop at Durham Johnston School on this day, pupils tried out a new instrument, the didgeridoo. The session was led by Nick Burman, one of the foremost didgeridoo professionals in the United Kingdom and it formed an element of the children's study of *Riding the Black Cockatoo* by John Danalis for their English Language GCSE assessment. The book is the true story of one man's efforts to repatriate an Aboriginal skull which had stood on his parents' mantelpiece during his childhood. Nick Burman spent the day talking to pupils about his experiences of living with an Aboriginal tribe, playing the didgeridoo and demonstrating how the instrument is put together. (*The Northern Echo*, Darlington, 1870–)

2011: An exhibition in Durham Cathedral's Galilee Chapel celebrating the work of Harrison and Harrison (H & H) Durham-based organ makers closed on this day. The exhibition featured the company's history which began in Manchester in 1861 before a move to Durham nine years later. The business continued to grow and soon established itself as the biggest organ builder in the country. H & H has made or repaired organs for cathedrals in Durham, Belfast, Coventry, Edinburgh, Lincoln, Ely and Wells, Windsor Castle's St George's chapel and many other major churches overseas. (*The Northern Echo*, Darlington, 1870–)

~ OCTOBER 21ST ~

1930: Colonel G.H. Stobart CBE, DSO, DL of Helme Park, Tow Law was on this day re-elected chairman of the County Durham Territorial Army and Air Force Association and Col. F.R. Simpson was again appointed vice chairman. Other business included discussion on the future of units of the cadet force and following a report of the General Purposes Committee, who had carefully reviewed the position, it was decided to take no action on behalf of the British National Cadet Association with regard to the formation of a County Cadet Committee. It was decided to send the congratulations of the Association to the office commanding Durham Heavy Brigade RA, raised in Hartlepool, on their winning of the King's Cup in the National Artillery Association Competition. The Durham Heavy Brigade was congratulated on a further victory that was recently gained in competition with Northumberland and East Riding. The strength of the units administered by the Association were shown to be 96 per cent of the establishment with only 195 men being required to complete and, considering the period of the year, the position was considered to be very satisfactory. (*Durham County Advertiser*, 1855–1968)

~ October 22nd ~

1874: On this day Revd Joseph Waite MA, formerly master of Durham University College and newly appointed Vicar of Norham, was presented with his portrait and a silver plate by members of the university. The portrait was hung in the University Hall, where the portraits of other members of the university are displayed, and the silver plate has the following inscription: 'Presented, together with his portrait, to the Revd J. Waite, M.A., by the members of the University of Durham and other friends on resigning the mastership of the University and accepting the Vicarage of Norham, as a mark of their appreciation of his long and valuable services as a tutor and master, 1874.'

The presentation was made in the University Hall, and the gifts were a testimonial of the respect in which Waite was held both as a gentleman and as a scholar. Reverend Canon Cundill occupied the chair and after briefly stating the purpose of the gathering, called upon the Revd Mr Shafto, Rector of Brancepeth, who made the presentation. He remarked that Waite was well liked, above all for his loyalty to his University. (Fordyce, T. (ed.), *Local Records; or, Historical Register of Remarkable Events Which Have Occurred in Northumberland and Durham … 1833 to [1875], Being a Continuation of the Work Published by … Mr. John Sykes*, Newcastle upon Tyne: T. Fordyce, 1867–1876)

― OCTOBER 23RD ―

1915: A new Durham Miners' Hall was opened on a site at Redhills on this day. Statues of four miners' leaders that had stood in front of the original Miners' Hall (opened in 1875 in North Road) were removed to the new location where they were placed on pedestals close to the main entrance. The Miners' Association was primarily concerned with wages and working conditions in the coal mines but also took a close interest in the welfare of its members and played an important part in establishing the Aged Miners' Home. (Clack, P.A.J., *The book of Durham City*, Buckingham: Barracuda, 1985)

―――

1947: On this day Princess Elizabeth (later Queen Elizabeth II) made her first visit to Durham where she laid the foundation stone of St Mary's College. During the ceremony the city's mayor presented Mrs George Bull, wife of the town clerk, to the princess while his official bodyguard (composed of several men) remained in attendance wearing top hats for the occasion. After the official proceedings Princess Elizabeth was driven to Durham Castle for lunch. St Mary's College building was designed by Vincent Harris and was completed in 1952. (Richardson, Michael, *Durham: Cathedral City*, Thrupp: Sutton, 1997)

~ October 24th ~

2012: The Palatine Centre at Durham University was officially opened on this day by Sir Paul Nurse, a Nobel-Prize-winning scientist and President of the Royal Society. Built at a cost of around £50 million, this headquarters development accommodates student services and an administrative base as well as a law school and enlarged library on a site adjacent to Stockton Road in Durham City. Completion of the project followed four years of planning and brought together all the university's 'student facing' services for the first time, with inclusion of its careers service, international office and IT and finance departments. It replaced Old Shire Hall, the university's headquarters for fifty years, which was then advertised for sale. The library extension, which cost £11 million, provided 500 extra study places, 30 study rooms, computer suites and 11.5 miles of shelving. It was renamed 'The Bill Bryson Library' in honour of the popular travel writer who stepped down from the office of university chancellor during 2011. Current spending by the university included £12 million on sports facilities, £10 million on World Heritage Site properties, and £16.6 million on rebuilding Durham Business School which extended its total investment to almost £100 million. (*The Northern Echo*, Darlington, 1870–)

~ OCTOBER 25TH ~

1766: In celebration of the king's accession to the throne, the bells in Durham Cathedral were rung for the first time after being rehung on one level. The eight bells had been framed and rehung by Mr Francis Ellis. The exactness of the new bell, both in tune and tone, to the peal, the construction of the frame and the easy ringing of the whole set were agreed by all competent judges to have been completed in a masterly manner. The length of each side of the new frame measures 16in shorter than the old one in which the bells were hung at two different heights. (Sykes, John, *Local Records: or, HistoricalRegister of Remarkable Events Which Have Occurred in Northumberland and Durham, Newcastle upon Tyne, and Berwick upon Tweed from the Earliest Period of Authentic Record, to the Present Time ...*, Newcastle, 1833)

1809: The jubilee of King George III's coronation was celebrated in Durham on this day, with a collection for the benefit of poor families and the chapter appropriated 'a large sum for the liberation of prisoners confined for smaller debts'. George III had become monarch in 1760 and although he is often regarded as 'the tyrant' who lost the American Revolution (1783–1815) he remained popular with his subjects and the fiftieth year of his reign saw countrywide celebrations during 1809–10. During 1811, illness robbed him of his sight, hearing and sanity so on February 5th 1811, his son, George, Prince of Wales was appointed regent. George III died on January 29th 1820. (Stranks, C.J., *This Sumptuous Church: The Story of Durham Cathedral*, London: SPCK, 1993)

~ OCTOBER 26TH ~

1950: Patrick Turnage pleaded guilty to murder at his 7 minute long trial held at Durham on this day. His victim was a prostitute, Julia Beesley. Turnage, a merchant seaman, had come ashore for drink and sex on July 22nd 1950 but after their sexual encounter the pair quarrelled over her proposed charge and he had strangled her. Turnage was arrested the following day and confessed to killing Julia Beesley. A conviction for manslaughter rather than murder was strongly suggested but Patrick Turnage refused to accept this approach. He insisted on pleading guilty to a charge of murder so that he would be hanged and not have to serve a probable fifteen-year sentence for manslaughter. He was executed on November 14th 1950. (www.capitalpunishmentuk.org)

2012: A concert to mark the centenary of the organ at St John's church in Neville's Cross, Durham was held on this day. The pipe organ was built in 1912 by the celebrated Durham organ-makers Harrison and Harrison and cost £300. Initially, wind had to be pumped in by hand but an electric blower was installed in 1941. Currently the organ has 540 pipes ranging from a few inches to 8ft in length. (*The Northern Echo*, Darlington, 1870–)

⬗ OCTOBER 27TH ⬗

1597: By this date a total of 844 people had died of plague in Durham City, 'There was dead in Elvet, more than four hundred; in St Nicholas' parish one hundred; in St Margaret's two hundred; in St Giles sixty; in St Mary's in the North Bailey sixty. Twenty four prisoners died in gaol ... Many of these persons were buried on the moor, or in St Thomas' Chapel, beyond Claypath ... The Bishop of Durham retired to his castle at Stockton as a place of refuge.' (Richardson, M.A., *The Local Historian's Table Book, of Remarkable Occurrences, Historical Facts, Traditions, Legendary and Descriptive Ballads, &c., &c., Connected with the Counties of Newcastle-upon-Tyne, Northumberland and Durham*, Newcastle upon Tyne: M.A. Richardson, 1841–1846)

2012: Durham City Food Festival which opened on this day featured a gourmet food marquee on Palace Green that featured more than 100 food retailers. Among these was master chocolatier, Paul A. Young, who trained at New College, Durham and Leeds Metropolitan University before working his way through the ranks to become head pastry chef for Marco Pierre White at Quo Vadis and Criterion restaurants in London. After specialising in chocolate, he opened three chocolate shops in London and won awards for his chocolates which are handmade in the kitchens of his shops. Other demonstrations included Bill Oldfield, Bob Arora and Jean-Christophe Novelli who hosted the television programme *Chef Academy*. (*The Northern Echo*, Darlington, 1870–)

~ October 28th ~

2011: The new Bishop of Durham was formally consecrated on this day at a service in York Minster. Right Revd Justin Welby, formerly Dean of Liverpool, was commissioned for his new role, along with the Venerable Robert Freeman, new Bishop of Penrith, by Dr. John Sentamu, the Archbishop of York, in a celebration service that mixed English and African styles. A congregation of more than 1,000 people witnessed Bishop Welby make oaths to the queen and the archbishop and promises to serve and lead his diocese whilst carrying out his duties as bishop. During the ceremony other bishops laid their hands upon him to pray for him, he was anointed with oil and presented with a pastoral staff, which symbolised his mission to lead his Christian flock. During a sermon, Josiah Fearon, Bishop of Kaduna in Nigeria, brought congratulations for Bishop Welby from Olesegun Obasanjo, former President of Nigeria, and after stating that the worldwide Anglican community was 'very badly divided' he called for unity among Christians. The service lasted around 2 hours and included hymns partly written by Dr Sentamu, John Cosin, a seventeenth-century Bishop of Durham and Michael Sadgrove, Dean of Durham. (*The Northern Echo*, Darlington, 1870–)

~ OCTOBER 29TH ~

1968: On this day John McVicar, an armed robber from London, escaped from the E wing of Durham Jail. This section of the building was described as 'a prison within a prison' and was widely regarded as escape-proof until McVicar's successful bid for freedom proved otherwise. After chipping his way through the brick wall of a shower room, he worked his way into a ventilation shaft and out into the exercise yard. From there he was able to continue his flight to freedom over the roof and although two fellow convicts were recaptured, McVicar successfully clambered over the prison wall and headed along adjacent streets. According to the account of this episode in his autobiography, it seems that he used the cover of darkness to edge his way along a roadway that led to a church and adjoining graveyard (in all probability this was St Oswald's church). At this point he swam across the river and then walked along a riverside route for around half a mile before swimming past the Framwellgate area. After sleeping overnight on derelict land he was able to cross open ground to the east of Durham and eventually reach Chester-le-Street where telephone contact was made with associates in London who arranged his return to the capital. (*Durham Times*, Durham: Newsquest, 2007–)

~ October 30th ~

1873: On this day Mr David Lambert, a well-known bass singer, 'expired in a most sudden manner' while performing his duties as a chorister in Durham Cathedral. As the members of the choir were assembling for afternoon service at 4 p.m. Mr Lambert was absent, but joined them as they marched through the cloisters and had evidently hurried to the cathedral in order to be in time to perform. As the service got underway it became clear to other choristers that Mr Lambert was unwell and as he got to his feet to sing the psalms he fell against the shoulder of the next choir member. The Dean of Durham, who was sitting almost opposite, rushed from his stall to assist and as Archdeacon Bland moved across to offer further aid the service was immediately suspended. It was obvious that Mr Lambert's condition was critical and 'in order to obtain more air for him, he was carried to the marble step outside the communion rail, where he was laid down, with his head supported on cushions. He rapidly sank, however, and died within ten minutes of the first appearance of his illness. The service was not afterwards proceeded with.' (Fordyce, T. (ed.), *Local Records; or, Historical Register of Remarkable Events Which Have Occurred in Northumberland and Durham ... 1833 to [1875], being a Continuation of the Work Published by ... Mr. John Sykes*, Newcastle upon Tyne: T. Fordyce, 1867–1876)

~ OCTOBER 31ST ~

2012: It was reported on this day that a landmark clock in Durham City centre had been reset after failing to keep time for many years. The marketplace clock was installed in the spire of St Nicholas' church in 1871 'by special appointment to the Queen and HRH the Prince of Wales' of No. 61 The Strand, London. Local residents recalled that the clock was altered manually, on a daily basis, by a designated workman employed by Durham County Council. Following his retirement the clock became an unreliable timepiece and a campaign was launched to bring about necessary improvements. This led to the installation of a pendulum regulator at a cost of £2,100 from council funds.

St Nicholas' church was constructed during 1857–58 by J.P. Pritchett of Darlington and was described at the time by the *Illustrated London News* as 'the most beautiful specimen of church architecture in the north of England'. Initial plans show the church with a tower, but no spire, and it was at the insistence of the vicar, Revd George Townsend Fox, who met building costs, that the spire was incorporated. (*The Northern Echo*, Darlington, 1870–)

— November 1st —

1956: Her Majesty Queen Elizabeth the Queen Mother paid a visit to St Mary's College at Durham on this day. During a tour of the building which was led by the principal, Miss E.M. Williamson, Her Majesty spent time talking to members of the kitchen. Following dinner the senior college woman, Jennifer Haynes, presented the Queen Mother with a specially bound *Album of Durham*. As she left the building, at the end of her visit, Her Majesty was given a special cheer from the college's maids. (Richardson, Michael, *Memory Lane: Durham City*, Derby: Breedon, 2000)

1965: James Wood, literary critic, essayist and novelist was born on this day at Durham, where his father was Professor of Zoology at the University. He was educated at Durham Chorister School and Eton College before graduating from Jesus College, Cambridge in 1988 with a first class honours degree in English Literature. In 1990 he won the title 'Young Journalist of the Year' at the British Press Awards and between 1991 and 1995 James Wood was chief literary critic of *The Guardian*. A move to the United States in 1995 saw him become senior editor at *The New Republic* and in 2007 he took up a post as a staff writer at *The New Yorker*. (en.wikipedia.org/wiki/James_Wood_(critic))

~ November 2nd ~

1660: The restoration of King Charles II to the throne of England was greeted with widespread celebrations around Durham City. The County Palatine and Bishopric of Durham were also restored to the Bishop John Cosin. He had already begun the refurbishment of the castle at Durham which suffered an amount of damage and neglect during its ownership by the Lord Mayor of London. (Simpson, David, *Durham Millennium: A Thousand Years of Durham City*, Darlington: Northern Echo, 1995)

———

1761: On this day the corporation of Durham repealed legislation that had been in effect since 1728 and which had prevented members gaining election through illicit practices. At that time the city's governing body was composed exclusively of freemen of trade guilds who were elected through patrimony and apprenticeship. Members were determined to influence the result of a parliamentary election in the city after the death of the sitting member, Henry Lambton. Freemen of the city held exclusive voting rights for choosing the Member of Parliament and the corporation swore in 264 new freemen in order to influence the outcome of the vote. About 215 were eligible and they duly achieved the election of the corporation's favoured candidate, Major Ralph Garland. (Simpson, David, *Durham Millennium: A Thousand Years of Durham City*, Darlington: Northern Echo, 1995)

~ November 3rd ~

1894: Margaret Savage, *née* Bone, died on this day and her husband, Robert Savage of No. 56, Hallgarth Street, Durham, a shoe-maker and later cow-keeper passed away five days after his wife. He is buried in St Oswald's cemetery, Durham City where a large four-sided granite column lists generations of family deaths. (Richardson, Michael, *Durham: The Photographic Collection*, Stroud: Sutton, 2002)

2012: On this day Durham Cathedral's shop was officially opened in the western undercroft, beside the Cathedral Cloister and opposite the Undercroft Restaurant. Reached by a new accessible foyer, it brought visitor amenities and a new shop together in one location and was part of a major development project aimed at transforming a range of Cathedral buildings. The opening ceremony was performed by paralympian Baroness Tanni Grey-Thompson who spoke of the importance of making historic buildings such as Durham Cathedral accessible and in particular providing access for visitors with different needs. With this in mind, steps into the area have been remodelled to make space for a visitor lift so that visitors who are unable to manage steps now have a direct route. The Dean of Durham, the Very Revd Michael Sadgrove commented that during a year when the achievements of disabled athletes had been so well publicised, it was appropriate that someone who championed disabled rights and inspired others was able to celebrate the opening. (*The Northern Echo*, Darlington, 1870–)

— NOVEMBER 4TH —

1850: A letter from the Prime Minister, Lord John Russell, written on this day to the Bishop of Durham appealed for help to stop the 'aggression' of Rome and the increasing popularity of High Church practices among members of the clergy of the Church of England. He stated that:

> Clergymen of our own Church have been most forward in leading their flocks, step by step, to the very verge of the precipice. The honour paid to Saints, the claim of infallibility for the Church, the superstitious use of the cross, the muttering of the liturgy so as to disguise the language in which it is written, the recommendation of auricular confession and the administration of penance and absolution, all these things are pointed out by the clergymen of the Church of England as worthy of adoption, and are now openly reprehended by the Bishop of London in his charge to the clergy of his diocese.

A sustained offensive was underway against anyone showing support for the Roman Church and serious reprisals followed any manifestation of Catholicism. Among those who suffered were advocates of Tractarian ideas such as W.G. Ward whose degree was withdrawn after publication of his study *The Ideal of a Christian Church*. (Lane, Richard, J., *Functions of the Derrida Archive: Philosophical Receptions*, University of Sussex, 1997)

— NOVEMBER 5TH —

2011: The Durham police headquarters at Aykley Heads was the setting for a bonfire and fireworks event on this day. Organised by Durham Constabulary and County Durham and Darlington Fire and Rescue Service, it marked the thirty-sixth consecutive year that the event had taken place at this location, attracting thousands of spectators on each occasion. It represented one of the largest such events in the North East and, once organisers had covered expenses incurred, proceeds from ticket sales each year were distributed to local voluntary projects and charities. Following the display in 2011 twenty charities within the County Durham and Darlington area received a cash handout from the overall total of almost £9,000. Recipients included Brandon United FC who intended to use the funds to improve facilities and access for more young and disabled people, Bishop Auckland Cycling Club, who were attempting to recruit and retain more young members, the Durham branch of Guide Dogs for the Blind and Durham Heritage Centre and Museum where two stained glass windows dating from 1822 originally at Brancepeth Castle were being restored. (In 2012 the bonfire and display was switched to Beamish Museum's events field because of redevelopment of the Aykley Heads site.) (www.aycliffetoday.co.uk)

‒ November 6th ‒

1930: A gloom was cast over Hetton and district on this day when news spread that two men had lost their lives at Elemore Colliery. The victims were John Seymour Mann, master shifter of No. 53 Lilywhite Terrace, Easington Lane and James Moss, a stoneman of Hornsey Terrace, Easington Lane and they had been at work in the Five Quarter Seam shortly after Wednesday midnight. Early reports indicated that Mann was in a sitting position issuing instructions for the timbering of the area when, without the slightest warning, several tons of stone, in small pieces, fell from the roof and completely buried the master shifter and his workmate, Moss. Another workman named Mortimer had a miraculous escape. Two hours elapsed before the bodies were retrieved and neither man showed signs of serious external injuries; initial findings were that in each case death was due to suffocation. Moss' lamp was between his knees and still burning when debris was removed. In accordance with usual practice, the colliery, which is in the Lambton, Hetton and Joicey Colliery Group and employs some 1,200 men and boys, was laid idle for the rest of the day. (*Durham County Advertiser*, 1855–1968)

~ November 7th ~

1966: Closure of the Durham City goods station on this day marked the conclusion of an element of the district's early railway history. The buildings served as Gilesgate station when the city was first linked into the developing railway network of the mid-nineteenth century. A branch into Durham was opened off the Newcastle and Darlington Junction Railway on June 18th 1844, leaving the section between Darlington and Rainton Crossing at Belmont Junction Station and terminating on the east side of the city at Gilesgate. Both Belmont Junction and Gilesgate stations were closed to passenger traffic on April 1st 1857 when the current Durham station was opened. Completion of the Gateshead–Newton Hall and Relly Mill– Haggersgate sections between 1868 and 1871 formed the current East Coast main line and placed Durham on the main line rather than a branch. As the other end of the branch line, Belmont Junction, there was a watering point for locomotives in addition to passenger facilities. The original water tank displayed the inscription 'Losh, Wilson & Bell, Walker Iron Works, 1845' which was the year after the original opening of the line. (Hoole, Ken, *Forgotten Railways: North East England,* Newton Abbot: David and Charles, 1973)

NOVEMBER 8TH

1969: On this day Roger Whittaker's recording of 'Durham Town (The Leavin')' entered the British singles charts at number twelve in the 'Top Twenty' to become the singer's first UK hit. Born on March 22nd 1936 in Kenya, he moved to England in September 1959 and gained a Bachelor of Science degree at Bangor University before signing a contract with Fontana Records in 1962. Some four years later he switched from Fontana to EMI's Columbia label and his self-written recording of 'Durham Town (The Leavin')' which was his fourth for the Columbia label led to further success with songs such as 'The Last Farewell' and 'New World in the Morning'. (rogerwhittaker.com/bio.htm)

———

2011: Today experts were completing an archaeological excavation in Hawthorn Terrace, Durham on a site which was formerly occupied by Byland Lodge, a base for the former Durham City Council. The land which was to be developed as a thirty-three-house estate through the Durham Villages Regeneration Company, lies about 2 miles from the place where English and Scottish forces clashed at the Battle of Neville's Cross on October 17th 1346. The excavation which was led by TWM Archaeology of Newcastle uncovered Victorian bottles and jars along with evidence of medieval plough soil but no direct evidence of the battle. (*The Northern Echo*, Darlington, 1870–)

— NOVEMBER 9TH —

1610: The medical bill for Robert Carnaby, a servant of Durham St Nicholas, indicates that he was visited by a physician on this day. Another physician named Mr Lamb provided a second opinion and each was paid just 1s for their services. It was probably at their instigation that an apothecary named Bartholomew Barnard supplied ointment and some aqua vitae during the following day. When these costs are considered in the context of Carnaby's personal estate, the list seems to include a disproportionately large number of expenses linked to his care, funeral and wake, and his employer Edward Nixon, a wealthy Durham cordwainer, is careful to claim £2 2s against his servant's estate for his other servants watching over him, for spoiled bedding and for the cost of losing these servants' labour during their vigil. (familyrecords.dur.ac.uk)

2012: The Rt Revd Justin Welby was confirmed as the 105th Archbishop of Canterbury on this day. He was to replace Rowan Williams who was stepping down from the post of leader of 77 million Anglican Christians after ten years. His appointment looked increasingly likely during weeks leading to the announcement and it was believed that Bishop Welby would be the first person to move directly from being Bishop of Durham to Archbishop of Canterbury. (*The Northern Echo*, Darlington, 1870–)

— November 10th —

1673: Dr Nathaniel Crewe (afterwards Lord Crewe) was translated from the See of Oxford to Durham. He held the See of Durham forty-seven years and died on September 18th 1722 aged 88 leaving a considerable portion of his property for charitable purposes. (Richmond, Thomas, *The Local Records of Stockton and the Neighbourhood; or, a Register of Memorable Events, Chronologically Arranged, Which Have Occurred in and near Stockton Ward and the North-Eastern Parts of Cleveland*, Stockton: William Robinson, 1868)

———

1735: Granville Sharp, a leading British abolitionist was born on this day in Durham. At the age of 15 he was apprenticed to a London linen draper and then worked as a civil servant and also developed a wide range of interests including theology and music. During 1765 Sharp became involved in the issue of slavery when he successfully campaigned for the release of a slave, Jonathan Strong, whose former owner was attempting to sell him back into slavery in the Caribbean. He then channelled his efforts into securing a definitive legal statement on whether a slave could be forced to leave Britain and the outcome was a ruling in 1772 by Lord Chief Justice William Mansfield that slave owners could not legally demand the return of slaves to the colonies once they were in Britain. Granville Sharp also supported other contemporary campaigns, such as parliamentary reform and improved wages for agricultural workers. He died in London on July 6th 1813. (www.bbc.co.uk/history)

~ November 11th ~

1858: The death occurred on this day of William Green at No. 55 Old Elvet, Durham. A career in medicine saw him gain membership of the Royal College of Surgeons on May 1st 1812 and he was elected as a fellow of the same institution on August 26th 1844. During his time at Durham he was in partnership with Edward Kane Jepson and also surgeon to the Durham Infirmary. (livesonline.rcseng.ac.uk)

1919: A war memorial located near the north wall of St Mary Magdalene church, Belmont, was unveiled on this day by Rt Revd Handley Moule, Lord Bishop of Durham. The ceremony was attended by a considerable number of relatives of the fallen along with parishioners, and wreaths were laid by the Belmont Working Party and the children of Gilesgate School. (www.newmp.org.uk)

2011: A First World War memorial outside Durham Cathedral was used for the first time in thirty years on this day. The memorial cross had remained hidden until major repairs were carried out to the east end of the cathedral. During the ceremony 'Durham Pals' – a re-enactment group – joined Chorister School pupils and others in observing 2 minutes silence next to the cross. (*The Northern Echo*, Darlington, 1870–)

ᓚ NOVEMBER 12TH ᓚ

2011: On this day Durham University Athletics and Cross Country Club staged their annual 'Past *v.* Present' Cross Country Fixture starting from the Graham Sports Centre at Maiden Castle on Durham's southern outskirts. The route for the race was mainly confined to Houghall Woods, close to Maiden Castle and apart from a short paved section it was predominantly off road. The Women's Race, which started at 2 p.m., covered around 3 miles and the Men's Race, which began half an hour later, was some 4 miles in extent. The events traditionally represented a contest between past and present Durham University Students but in 2011 the event was extended to include outside University and Club teams as well as other sporting and collegiate clubs from within the University of Durham. In fact, on the day there were no entries from other universities. The women's race was won by a new Durham University Athletics and Cross Country Club member and Great Britain athlete, Jen Walsh, who completed the course in the highly commendable time of 16 minutes 51 seconds. Fifteen of the sixteen finishers were DUAXC members and the college points race was won by Hild Bede. The men's winner was Harry Coates of the 'Past Members' team but the college title went to Van Mildert. (www.duaxc.co.uk)

— NOVEMBER 13TH —

1810: Jimmy Allen, a colourful but shadowy character, died on this day at the age of 77. Plagued by illness later in life he spent his final days in a dungeon below Elvet Bridge after earning a reputation as a gypsy piper. Allen's early life was cloaked in mystery but he was probably born at Rothbury in about 1733 before being adopted by the Faa or Faws family from a gypsy clan in the Border area. From about the age of 14 he was given tuition in playing the Northumbrian pipes and, as his talent blossomed, Jimmy Allen became official piper to the Countess of Northumberland. However, he soon earned a reputation for his drinking and gambling exploits as well as horse-thieving. After enlisting in the army, he deserted and travelled to parts of Europe and the Far East as well as making frequent forays to Dublin and Edinburgh. During 1803 Allen stole a horse in Gateshead and after being captured at Jedburgh he was convicted at Durham Assizes and sentenced to death or transportation. Reprieved of these punishments on account of failing health and old age, he spent his final years in the confines of the dungeon below Elvet Bridge. (Simpson, David, *Durham City*, Sunderland: Business Education Publishers, 2006)

– November 14th –

1569: On this day a force of rebels under the command of the Earls of Northumberland and Westmoreland entered Durham, after marching from Brancepeth, and celebrated Mass in the cathedral. This insurrection became known as the 'Rebellion (or Rising) of the North' '… having for its objects the liberation of Mary Queen of Scots and the restoration of the Catholic religion. After the suppression of this outbreak, forty-four persons who had taken part in the revolt were executed in the marketplace at Durham; amongst these was Thomas Plumtree – an old Queen Mary's priest … who refused to conform to the new doctrine and liturgy.' (Whellan, Francis, *History, Topography, and Directory of the County Palatine of Durham Comprising a General Survey of the County and a History of the City and Diocese of Durham* … , London: Ballantyne, Hanson and Co., 1894)

1728: Jane Finney, by her will bearing this date, devised a close, in or near Claypath, to trustees to pay the profits thereof to the minister of this parish for the time being, to be by him distributed yearly among such poor people of the said parish not receiving alms as he should think most proper objects of charity. She also gave a house, garth and garden for the support of the charity of Bluecoat boys and girls in Durham. (Whellan, Francis, *History, Topography, and Directory of the County Palatine of Durham Comprising a General Survey of the County and a History of the City and Diocese of Durham* … , London: Ballantyne, Hanson and Co., 1894)

NOVEMBER 15TH

1936: The German Ambassador to the Court of St James, Joachim von Ribbentrop visited Durham on this day as a guest of the city's mayor. Von Ribbentrop was staying at Wynyard Hall between November 13th and 17th with Charles Stewart Henry Vane-Tempest, 7th Marquis of Londonderry, who served as the Secretary of State for Air during the 1930s and was a strong advocate of the appeasement policy towards Nazi Germany. During their visit, the official party walked up Owengate for a civic service in the cathedral as thousands of local people lined the streets. After the Second World War, Von Ribbentrop was put on trial at Nuremberg and hanged as a war criminal in 1946. (Richardson, Michael, *Durham: Cathedral City*, Thrupp: Sutton, 1997)

2011: An exhibition of forty examples of Egyptian quilting and textile art was displayed at St Mary's College in Durham City. The centrepiece was a 10ft square wall hanging by Egyptian craftsman, Hany Fattoh, which used traditional tent-making and embroidery techniques to illustrate events in Cairo leading to the overthrow of former President Hosni Mubarak earlier in the year. The exhibition resulted from collaboration between Durham University's Centre of Advanced Study of the Arab World and its School of Government and International Affairs with St Mary's College. (*The Northern Echo*, Darlington, 1870–)

— November 16th —

1940: This day marked the beginning of 'War Weapons Week' in Durham which lasted from the November 16th to the 23rd 1940. A feature was the positioning of a captured German Messerschmitt aircraft in the city's marketplace pointing towards St Nicholas' church and a total exceeding £174,000 was raised by residents of Durham City, Brandon and Spennymoor Districts during the week. (Richardson, Michael, *Durham: Cathedral City*, Thrupp: Sutton, 1997)

——

2012: News reports on this day stated that a Catholic order had established a new community in Durham City. Three friars from the English Province of the Order of Preachers, also known as the Dominicans, accepted an invitation from the Rt Revd Seamus Cunningham, Roman Catholic Bishop of Hexham and Newcastle to take over operations of Durham University's Catholic Chaplaincy and St Cuthbert's RC church on Old Elvet. Establishment of the community was marked by a celebration of Mass on Catholic Feast of All Saints of the Dominican Order and the new religious house represented the order's first base in Durham. Dominican friars had first arrived in north-east England in AD 1239, less than twenty-five years after their order was founded and a medieval priory building still stands on Friars Street, Newcastle. (*The Northern Echo*, Darlington, 1870–)

∽ November 17th ∽

1771: Torrential rain on the Pennines in mid-November sent flood waters surging down north-east rivers and the torrent reached Durham City on this day. Although the brown waters of the Wear had spread over marshland and fields around Durham the river still held enough power to wreck the wooden footbridge that predated the current Prebends Bridge. Constructed in 1574, the timberwork was no match for the force of the flood and it was soon swept away. (A temporary replacement was installed until the present stone-built bridge was completed between 1772–77 to designs by George Nicholson, architect to the dean and chapter of the cathedral. It was restored during 1956). Before they began to subside the flood waters destroyed three of the arches of Elvet Bridge, which in those days had fourteen arches, and a house at the end of Framwellgate Bridge was also wrecked. The high water mark for the Wear in Durham is reported to have exceeded the highest previous point by 8ft. (www.british-history.ac.uk)

1883: A statue of Alexander MacDonald, former President of Durham County Miners' Association, was unveiled on this day in front of the Miners' Hall on North Road, Durham. (Whellan, Francis, *History, Topography, and Directory of the County Palatine of Durham Comprising a General Survey of the County and a History of the City and Diocese of Durham* … , London: Ballantyne, Hanson and Co., 1894)

– November 18th –

1559: Bishop Cuthbert Tunstall of Durham died on this day during imprisonment at Lambeth Palace, becoming one of eleven bishops to die in custody during the reign of Elizabeth I. He had spent thirty-seven years as a bishop during a career that spanned the reigns of Henry VIII, Edward VI and Mary I before he fell from grace under Elizabeth I. His demise resulted from his refusal to take the Oath of Supremacy and to participate in the consecration of Matthew Parker as Archbishop of Canterbury. (www.elizabethfiles.com)

1975: The traffic control box in Durham marketplace moved on this day after becoming obsolete when new bridges at Millburngate and New Elvet radically altered the flow of traffic through the centre of the city. It had become the first such installation in the world to be fitted with television screens for controlling traffic when it became operational on December 31st 1957. Television cameras at the bottom of Silver Street, directed towards Framwellgate Bridge and another positioned in Saddler Street facing Elvet Bridge, directed images back to the control box to allow the police officer to direct the flow of traffic. (www.east-durham.co.uk)

— NOVEMBER 19TH —

2011: Today huge crowds flocked to Durham City for the third evening of Lumiere 2011, a spectacular arts festival organised by 'Artichoke'. Commissioned by Durham County Council, it followed a similar event two years previously which attracted 75,000 visitors and generated £1.5 million for Durham's economy. This extended event was made up of thirty-five installations with contributions from more than thirty international and local artists such as Tracey Emin and included artwork across a wide area, taking in the peninsula, Elvet, Walkergate and Wharton Park. The festival featured four major installations – Peter Lewis' *Splash*, an illuminated waterfall descending from Kingsgate Bridge into the River Wear, the *I Love Durham* snowdome which engulfed the *Lord Londonderry on Horseback* statue in Durham marketplace, Compagnie Carabosse's *Spirit* and *Crown of Light* by Ross Ashton which saw huge images from the Lindisfarne Gospels projected on to the walls of Durham Cathedral. In addition, the four day event included talks, workshops, a children's lantern parade and a seminar for sharing experiences and meeting industry experts. 'Artichoke' was set up in 2005 by Helen Marriage and Nicky Webb and their previous projects included *Telectroscope* and Anthony Gormley's Trafalgar Square *Empty Plinth* set. (www.bbc.co.uk)

— November 20th —

1807: A meeting held on this day reviewed the question of financial remuneration for Durham Choristers. The outcome was a decision to set a qualifying age so that boys who left the choir before the age of 13 would not be entitled to an apprentice fee. Those who stayed after their thirteenth birthday would have their annual 'salary' increased by £6 to £16 and if their progress was satisfactory they would receive a substantially increased fee of £20 when they left. Accounts indicate that two boys received the salary increase that term and three others were added during the course of the financial year. (www.thechoristerschool.com)

2012: On this day Lieutenant Edward Drummond-Baxter became the first soldier in living memory to be awarded a funeral with full military honours at Durham Cathedral. He died on October 30th alongside Lance Corporal Siddhanta Kunwar from Nepal at a checkpoint in Nahr-e-Saraj, Helmand, Southern Afghanistan when a man wearing an Afghan police uniform opened fire. Both soldiers were from the 1st Battalion the Royal Ghurkha Rifles. As the cathedral bells tolled, six Ghurkhas carried Lt Drummond-Baxter's coffin, covered in a Union flag, into the cathedral, led by a bagpiper playing the *Flowers of the Forest* lament. (*The Northern Echo*, Darlington, 1870–)

NOVEMBER 21ST

1861: The enthronement of the Rt Revd Charles Baring DD the newly appointed Bishop of Durham took place in that cathedral this morning. The event attracted great interest, and there was a large attendance, not only of the inhabitants of the city, but of the clergy of the diocese. About 10 a.m. his lordship arrived at the northern entrance of the cathedral, where he was received by the Very Revd G. Waddington DD, Dean of Durham, and a large number of the chapter. On arriving at the altar the bishop offered the prayer usual on such occasions and was then conducted by the dean to his throne, on which he remained during the morning service. The throne occupies a greatly elevated position on the south side of the choir, the ascent to it being fourteen steps. The throne was built in the year 1370 by Bishop Hatfield, for the double purpose of an episcopal seat or chair of state and a canopy over his own tomb. The arms carved on the oaken doorway are those of Bishop Crewe, by whom it was repaired in the year 1700. It is said to be the most elevated episcopal seat in Christendom. (Fordyce, T. (ed.), *Local Records; or, Historical Register of Remarkable Events Which Have Occurred in Northumberland and Durham … 1833 to [1875], being a Continuation of the Work Published by … Mr. John Sykes*, Newcastle upon Tyne: T. Fordyce, 1867–1876)

— NOVEMBER 22ND —

1939: At a scouting presentation event on this day held in Durham town hall, scout patrol leader F. Keeling handed over a cheque for £5 to the mayor Councillor S. Kipling. The cash had been raised by collecting waste paper and cardboard from local businesses and it was to add to the Red Cross Fund. As an acknowledgement of the 5th Durham Scout Group's effort, patrol leader Keeling was presented with a scouting book by the district commissioner. (Richardson, Michael, *Durham: Cathedral City*, Thrupp: Sutton, 1997)

2012: On this day retired policeman Ron Hogg began work as the new Police and Crime Commissioner for County Durham and Darlington, and became one of five former police officers across the country to be elected to the post. Born in Scotland, his family moved to Northamptonshire when he was 6 and after gaining an honours degree in politics he taught at a Northamptonshire comprehensive school before joining the police in 1978. Progressing through the ranks he became chief superintendent with Northumbria police and then joined Durham as assistant chief constable in 1998. Further promotion saw him join Cleveland Police as deputy chief constable in 2003 and he continued in the post until his retirement in 2008. (*The Northern Echo*, Darlington, 1870–)

~ November 23rd ~

1946: A press report on this day gave details of a dramatic meeting involving skilled workers from the mining industry:

> The eagerly-awaited meeting of the Council of Durham Colliery Mechanics Association, held at the Miners' Hall, Durham, was remarkable for the fact that by a two to one majority the delegates rejected an explanatory report by the secretary (Mr W. S. Hall), the purpose of which was to show the utter futility of moving for an advance of wages in face of Clause 4 of the national agreement. The next step apparently rests with the lodges. The proceedings, lasting for three hours and presided over by Mr Thomas Clark of Ferryhill, were devoted entirely to discussion of the report presented by the secretary on behalf of the executive committee. The meeting was private. At the close Mr Hall told our representative '... The delegates refused to accept the situation. The next move must come from our lodges. The position seems to me to one of stalemate. I expect that the lodges will consider the reports of delegates who attended the Council meeting and forward their views to the central office at Durham.'

(*Durham Chronicle*, 1820–1984)

— NOVEMBER 24TH —

1883: An incident involving Canon Evans, the professor of Greek, at Durham Cathedral on this date highlighted the absent-mindedness of the learned cleric. He was in the habit of forgetting what was taking place and nonchalantly sidling away and the precentor used Cicero's address to Catiline 'Excessit, evasit, enepit' ('He escaped, evaded, eluded us') to describe his behaviour. On another occasion, according to reports, he was being led out to preach but became so deeply involved in his own thoughts that he proceeded beyond the pulpit and made his way home. (Stranks, C.J., *This Sumptuous Church: The Story of Durham Cathedral*, London: SPCK, 1993)

———

1928: The County War Memorial was unveiled at 12 p.m. on this day outside the east end of Durham Cathedral. An unveiling ceremony was performed by Lord Londonderry, Lord Lieutenant of the County, after some ten years of controversy about its location, funding and design. The Grade II listed stone column, which is carved with modern artefacts such as helmets, water bottles, a Mills bomb and rifle grenades, stands on an octagonal base which is set on a square plinth with the dates '1914–18' inscribed in Roman lettering. (www.newmp.org.uk)

~ November 25th ~

1699: Dr Thomas Comber, Dean of Durham Cathedral and chaplain to the queen, died on this day. In addition to his reputation as a preacher and writer, Dr Comber was also associated with a number of projects in the Durham area. He initiated afforestation of wasteland belonging to the cathedral at Bear Park, completely overhauled the water supply to houses in the college area from an octagonal stone tower at the western edge of the green and also made an unsuccessful attempt to mine coal at Bear Park. Church lands at Croxdale and Stainforth were successfully reclaimed during Dr Comber's period of office and he also cooperated with magistrates and the Bishop of Durham to appoint a schoolmaster, with payment of £40 annually, to teach fourteen poor girls how to read and spin. (Stranks, C.J., *This Sumptuous Church: The Story of Durham Cathedral*, London: SPCK, 1993)

2011: The new Bishop of Durham, the Rt Revd Justin Welby, was welcomed into his diocese during a ceremony on Croft Bridge which included presentation of the Conyers falchion (an ancient broadsword). Before 1790 this took place at several other nearby locations and although it lapsed for much of the twentieth century, it was revived in 1984 for Dr David Jenkins. (*The Northern Echo*, Darlington, 1870–)

NOVEMBER 26TH

1910: On this day, less than three weeks before his death, Charles Hodgson Fowler took a leading part in deliberations of the local Ruri-decanal (linked to a dean or deanery) Conference. Fowler is chiefly remembered for his work in building and especially restoring churches but this episode highlights his involvement as a layman, in the day-to-day work and politics of the church with which he felt such a strong bond. His obituary in the *Durham County Advertiser* states that he was a member of the house of Laymen of the Province of York, that he had a seat on the Durham Diocesan Conference and was a steward of the Durham Diocesan Sons of the Clergy Society. (Wickstead, John, C., *Hodgson Fowler (1840–1910): Durham Architect and his Churches*, Durham: Durham County Local History Society, 2001)

2011: The enthronement of the new Bishop of Durham took place on this day as the Rt Revd Justin Welby hammered three times with his staff on the cathedral door to request entry as his predecessors had done for generations. Leaders of other Christian denominations played key roles, children took part and modern hymns were sung during the service in which Bishop Welby called Christians to live 'revolutionary' lives which broke every mould and rekindle the Christian faith in the North East. (*The Northern Echo*, Darlington, 1870–)

— NOVEMBER 27TH —

1902: George Henry Camsell, footballer, was born on this day at Framwellgate Moor, Durham City and played for local teams Esh Winning, Tow Law and Durham City before joining Second Division Middlesbrough for a fee of £500 on October 6th 1925. In his first full season, Camsell scored a record 59 league goals and Middlesbrough gained promotion to the First Division.

Camsell played his last league game for Middlesbrough against Leicester City at Ayresome Park on April 10th 1939 and scored the opening goal in a 3–2 victory. He also won 9 caps for England, scoring 18 goals including a hat-trick in a 6–0 win against Wales on November 20th 1929 in the British Home Championship and four goals in a match against Belgium on May 11th 1929. The outbreak of war in 1939 effectively ended George Camsell's football career but in 419 games for Middlesbrough he had scored 325 goals. During the post-war years he worked as coach, chief scout and assistant secretary before retiring in December 1963. George Camsell died on March 7th 1966. (www.spartacus.schoolnet.co.uk)

~ November 28th ~

1986: On this day Durham Cathedral, Castle and surrounding buildings were designated a World Heritage Site by UNESCO (United National Education, Scientific and Cultural Organisation.) They described the cathedral as one of the finest examples of Norman architecture anywhere in the world and stated that, 'The innovative audacity of its vaulting foreshadowed Gothic architecture.' (whc.unesco.org/en/list/370)

———

2011: News reports on this day indicated that heat generated by the Durham Crematorium could be fed back into the National Grid to supply electricity. Plans under consultation included installing turbines in two of the three new furnaces which were being installed at the crematorium in South Road, Durham City, which is run by Durham County Council. If it was approved, the crematorium would be the first in the United Kingdom to carry out the process. Improvement work at the fifty-year-old crematorium, which was operating at five times its original rate, was being carried out in two phases, enabling it to remain open during the switch over. The project resulted from a change in the law which meant that mercury must be removed from crematorium emissions by January 2012. (*The Northern Echo*, Darlington, 1870–)

~ November 29th ~

1838: A poster for this date stated:

> To be sold by Auction on Thursday, 29 November, 1838
> By Mr Walker, At the Rooms, in the Queen's Court, near the Public
> Sale and Exhibition Room, North Bailey, Durham, Household
> Furniture, Books and Other Effects, of the Late Celebrated Count
> Boruwlaski THE SALE TO COMMENCE AT SEVEN O'CLOCK
>
> Catalogues of the above will be ready on Monday 26 November
> and may be had of the Auctioneer, Durham.
>
> Count Jozef Boruwlaski, a Polish dwarf, died in Durham on
> 5 September 1837 at the age of 97 years ten months. He spent the
> latter decades of his life living in a cottage in the South Bailey and is
> buried in Durham Cathedral close to the north-west tower.

(Heron, Tom, M., *Boruwlaski: The Little Count*, Durham: City of Durham, 1986)

1971: On this day licensing magistrates for County Durham granted a Club Registration Certificate to Durham Amateur Rowing Club and members began a concerted effort to complete work in time for a Christmas opening. When the bar opened for business on December 23rd it marked completion of a building project which had been underway since February 1968, during which time spending on land and building amounted to £9,700. (www.nerowing.com/darctimeline.html)

~ November 30th ~

2011: At evensong on this date, St Andrew's Day, feast day to the Scottish patron saint, a memorial plaque was unveiled alongside the altar to Queen Margaret of Scotland at the east end of Durham Cathedral. The memorial was a tribute to hundreds of Scottish prisoners who died in the cathedral following defeat in the Battle of Dunbar in September 1653. Thousands of prisoners were held by Oliver Cromwell's victorious Parliamentarian troops and although many died during a seven-day march south, it was recorded that about 3,000 prisoners were detained in the cathedral. At that time the cathedral was largely empty and unused after the dean and chapter had been dissolved and worship suppressed during the period of the Commonwealth. During the next few weeks a combination of cold weather, shortage of food and outbreaks of illness led to the deaths of many prisoners before around 1,200 were transported overseas as bonded labour in the colonies. It is believed that the dead were buried in mass graves which have never been accurately located. Installation of the plaque followed a campaign by Scottish historians to remember the 'Durham Martyrs' as they have become known. (*The Northern Echo*, Darlington, 1870–)

December 1st

1906: The complicated administrative workings of the Durham Great Chapter are illustrated by the outcome of a meeting on this day. They ruled that, at the current Master of the Choristers' resignation, the post should be offered, subject to certain conditions, to Revd Arnold D. Culley, who was quite unusually already precentor. The condition included the requirement that his duties as precentor and a minor canon should come first, that an assistant would be needed who would train the choir and play at services as approved by chapter and that the post of assistant should be offered to a man named Ellis with a salary of £200 per annum. The decision to offer the position of Master of Choristers to Revd Culley was repeated when the ordinary chapter gathered on March 2nd 1907. It was also agreed that when the current Master of Choristers retired on May 13th 1907 he should be awarded the title, 'Honorary Organist', and it was clearly stated that this title did not bring with it any duties, but was in recognition of his long and distinguished years of service. The formal offer of the post to Revd Culley was deferred several times before it was approved by the Great Chapter on November 20th 1907. (Stranks, C.J., *This Sumptuous Church: The Story of Durham Cathedral*, London: SPCK, 1993)

~ December 2nd ~

1861: The statue of the 3rd Marquess of Londonderry was unveiled on this day in Durham marketplace. It was the work of Raffaelle Monti (1818–81), an Italian by birth who moved to England in 1848 and is widely considered to be his finest work. Installation of the statue was deferred when five local tradesmen filed a lawsuit against the siting of the statue. Their claim was that the location would restrict access to the marketplace and although their action failed there was a further delay when Monti was declared bankrupt. Creditors seized the statue and it was left to the marquess' widow to raise an additional £1,000 before it was released for the unveiling ceremony surrounded by rifle volunteers from Seaham, Sunderland and Durham City. The double life-size statue was lifted from its plinth on the morning of Sunday April 1st 1951 and transported by road to London for repair work. Almost one year later, on March 3rd 1952, it was returned to Durham where the 8th Marquess of Londonderry and members of his family gathered to watch it being reinstated on the plinth. (Simpson, David, *Durham City,* Sunderland: Business Education Publishers, 2006)

- December 3rd -

2011: An exhibition that opened in Durham on this day included skeletons which were believed to be the remains of Roman gladiators. They had been discovered among nearly 100 skeletons in a linear cemetery, measuring almost 2 miles in length that spread alongside the main route in York. The remains seemed to indicate a defined section of the burial ground which included a larger-than-anticipated number of young men. Many had trauma injuries and, overall, there were many more decapitations than in wider Roman society. The excavation leader, Kurt Hunter-Mann explained that detailed analysis showed the skeletons came from a range of backgrounds. Some were native Yorkshiremen, others lived near the North Sea and a number were from the Alps, Mediterranean, Africa and Germania which was outside the Empire. Some were buried with many honours and grave goods or had a very impressive gravestone, while others revealed what could well have been scars of the arena such as blunt trauma wounds or animal bites from a beast such as a tiger. The brutal decapitations may well have resulted from losing a bout and it was hoped that further analysis might prove or disprove the theory that they were gladiators. (*The Northern Echo*, Darlington, 1870–)

― December 4th ―

1864: A destructive fire swept through the church building of Sherburn Hospital on this day. Located at the east end of the hospital's north side, it was perhaps exposed to the worst elements of wintry weather, and late during the previous evening Revd J. Carr, Master of the Hospital had banked up the fire in order to warm the chapel for Sunday worship. Unfortunately, the flue became blocked and the wood panelling caught fire in the early hours of Sunday morning. The blaze spread and the whole building was gutted. It was not until the January 3rd 1869, that the rebuilt chapel was opened to designs by Austin and Johnson, which included the addition of a full length north aisle. A press report described it as 'a magnificent instrument which has elicited the warmest expressions of approbation from the subscribers.' (www.duresme.org.uk/NEorgans/shbhosp)

1883: A public meeting was held on this day in Bishop Cosin's Library in order to discuss the establishment of a High School for Girls in Durham City. The school opened during April 1884 in premises at Claypath and two years later it moved to The Bailey. During September 1912 the school moved again to the former residence of John Henderson and in January 1968 a purpose-built school opened at Fairwell Hall. (Richardson, Michael, *Durham: Cathedral City*, Thrupp: Sutton, 1997)

‒ December 5th ‒

1688: The final weeks of 1688 saw events surrounding the Glorious Revolution impact on the northern counties and on this day Lord Lumley entered Durham City along with fifty horsemen and accompanied by gentry from a wide area of Durham and Yorkshire. After declaring his support for William, Prince of Orange, he sent Captain Ireton and ten troopers to seize the dean's horses and to order Dean Granville himself to stay in his own home during Lord Lumley's time in the city. As events gathered pace, the dean determined that Durham was not a safe place in view of his own strong belief that the Church of England was irrevocably committed to the 'Divine Right of Kings' – and he set out for Carlisle where the governor was still loyal to James. Before long, however, William's supporters controlled Carlisle and Dean Granville departed for Scotland only to be arrested and robbed of possessions on the way. After being taken back to Carlisle his valuables were returned and, although ordered to return to Durham, he stayed two more weeks and preached in the cathedral before travelling to Edinburgh. From there he journeyed to France and his refusal to swear an oath of allegiance to William and Mary made a return to England impossible. (Stranks, C.J., *This Sumptuous Church: The Story of Durham Cathedral,* London: SPCK, 1993)

~ December 6th ~

1946: A press report on this day described an incident which might have had serious consequences but ended with only minor damage when a horse attached to a milk float loaded with hundreds of bottles of milk for house delivery ran amok at Shotton Colliery.

In the course of their roundsmens's duties Mr N. Train and his assistant were issuing the milk to customers when the horse apparently received a fright. Bolting, unattended from the top of Lee Terrace, it continued its mad career for nearly half a mile downhill, finally crashing into the front of a house at the bottom of a cul-de-sac in Hopper Terrace. A motor car, parked in the front, just missed being demolished by a foot margin, immediately prior to the impact. The horse crashed under the window, which is only 3ft from the ground, and Mrs Robson, her child and father were in the front room at the time. Menfolk of the area quickly rendered first aid and liberated the horse, which they found to be suffering from minor injuries, from the broken shafts. From the small river of milk and the maze of broken bottles it must be presumed that a number of people did not get their daily ration. (*Durham Chronicle*, 1820–1984)

⁓ December 7th

1966: Colin Murray Archer, musician, was born on this day in Durham and began his career in a group called The Edge during the early 1980s. There were several changes in personnel but they released two singles before 'Gem' Archer, as he became known, moved to London in 1987. He formed The Contenders and wore a distinctive stage outfit in the form of a black boiler suit with the group's name written down the sides in large white lettering. During the 1990s Archer worked with groups such as Whirlpool and Heavy Stereo before he returned to Durham to care for his mother. Once she had recovered, he took up an invitation to join Oasis as rhythm guitarist and appeared on the 'Go Let It Out' video playing lead guitar. As his career with Oasis became established Archer was officially described as the group's rhythm guitarist but he also contributed songs, beginning with 'Hung in a Bad Place'. Following the departure of Noel Gallagher from Oasis in August 2009 the group folded and Archer joined other members of the group in Beady Eye who released a debut album *Different Gear, Still Speeding* in late February 2011. (en.wikipedia.org/wiki/Gem_Archer)

~ December 8th

2011: Sophie, Countess of Wessex, visited Durham on this day. Although bad weather delayed her arrival in the North East, she was able to visit Gilesgate Armoury in Durham City in her role as Colonel-in-Chief of 5th Battalion The Rifles (5 Rifles). Later she joined about 1,500 visitors at a Carols of Light concert in Durham Cathedral which raised a total of £80,000 for the Sunderland Association Football Club's (SAFC) Foundation and Durham Cathedral's Music Endowment Fund. Before the event got underway the Countess of Wessex signed the Durham Cathedral visitors' book and then delivered a reading from a lectern during the service which featured a host of personalities including Joe McElderry, Sir Thomas Allen, Rick Wakeman, Barbara Dickson, Kate Adie and Steve Cram. The evening followed the traditional Nine Lessons and Carols format with contributions from the recently appointed Bishop of Durham, the Rt Revd Justin Welby, former Foreign Secretary David Milliband and TV presenter and architect George Clarke. Overall production was in the hands of Sir Tim Rice and featured a premiere performance of 'If I Could Wish for One Thing', a new carol written by school children of the North East. (*The Northern Echo*, Darlington, 1870–)

— December 9th —

2011: An exhibition featuring the work of one of Japan's most famous artists opened at Durham University's Oriental Museum on this day. Katsushika Hokusai was born at Edo in 1760 and during a lifetime that spanned 89 years he is credited with some 30,000 paintings and wood engravings. Most of his typical woodblock prints, silk-screens and landscape paintings were completed in the decade between 1830 and 1840, and show an emphasis on the common man and his surroundings rather than aristocratic settings. His best known work is probably *The Great Wave off Kanagawa* a colour woodcut measuring 10in x 15in which was produced in about 1831, while other highly regarded creations include the thirteen-volume sketchbook *Manga* (meaning *Random Sketches*) which he started in 1814 and the series of block prints known as *The Thirty Six Views of Mount Fuji* which included *The Great Wave*. Japanese artists chose to sign their work with seals (stamps) based on Chinese calligraphic symbols and often adopted a range of different names linked to a current style. During his working life Hokusai used more than twenty different names. (www.ee.umanitoba.ca)

~ DECEMBER 10TH ~

1637: A decision was made on this day to pull down the ruins of St Mary-le-Bow church and carry out a complete rebuild. Several weeks earlier the tower had crashed to the ground bringing down most of the walls of the nave and prompting this new resolution. In fact, nothing happened. In all probability this was because of the turmoil resulting from the Civil Wars and disruption of church life during the Commonwealth period. Building work finally got underway in 1683 and the church reopened two years later with costs amounting to £117. (Owen, O.T., *St. Mary-Le-Bow, Durham*, Gloucester: British Publishing Company, 1958)

1831: Moves towards establishing a university at Durham continued on this day when the dean reported to the chapter that Prebendary Thorp had been provisionally appointed as warden of the new university. Later in the same month, Thorp prepared an outline of staffing requirements to cover subjects offered in a university and at the same time the appropriate legislation was being channelled through the House of Lords by bishops and through the Commons by Sir James Scarlett. After an amount of discussion it was also agreed that non-conformists could attend lectures but not receive degrees. (Stranks, C.J., *This Sumptuous Church: The Story of Durham Cathedral*, London: SPCK, 1993)

— December 11th —

1875: At Durham Assizes a youth was charged with highway robbery of the most aggravated type in and around Durham. The prisoner was but 18 years old but the calendar showed his career of crime to have been a notorious one. He had fallen into the hands of the police at the early age of 13 and from that period he had spent the greater part of his time in prison. He was now sentenced to penal servitude for life, a sentence which seemed to take him very much by surprise. (Fordyce, T. (ed.), *Local Records; or, Historical Register of Remarkable Events Which Have Occurred in Northumberland and Durham … 1833 to [1875], being a Continuation of the Work Published by … Mr. John Sykes*, Newcastle upon Tyne: T. Fordyce, 1867–1876)

2011: More than 600 people assembled in Durham Cathedral on this day to pay tribute to loved ones. The occasion was the annual 'Light up a Life' memorial service of St Cuthbert's Hospice which is based at Merryoaks in Durham City. The evening service, which included readings and music from the Durham Miners' Association brass band and Galilee Choir, marked the end of the yearly appeal through which hospice authorities invite people to remember a loved one by making a donation to the centre which provides free care for people with life-limiting illnesses. (*The Northern Echo*, Darlington, 1870–)

∼ December 12th ∼

1298: Edward, King of England, then at Durham, gave to the prior and convent of Durham the sum of £1,012 9s 11¼ d, their arrears of subsidies. (Sykes, John, *Local records; or, Historical register of Northumberland and Durham, Newcastle-upon-Tyne, and Berwick-upon-Tweed*, Stockton on Tees: Patrick and Shotton, 1973)

1894: John Wharton Darwin was born on this day at Dryburn Hall, near Durham, to Charles Waring and Mary Dorothea Darwin. He was educated in Germany, Switzerland, Broadstairs and Winchester before joining the army in 1912. During 1916 he transferred to the Royal Flying Corps which became the Royal Air Force some two years later. He was an adviser to Churchill at the Paris peace talks that followed the end of hostilities and in 1918 was appointed as one of the first flying instructors at RAF Cranwell. He resigned his commission in 1928 but remained on the staff of the Secret Intelligence Service.

A move to the Bristol Aircraft Company and later Sauders Roe saw him travel all over the world, with some probable assignments for the SIS, and in 1939 he played a part in setting up Bletchley Park before journeying through Europe to brief agents and set up a network of radio transmitters. John Darwin left the SIS in 1940 and rejoined the RAF, but after illness the following year he died on December 26th 1941. (www.elstonheritage.org.uk)

~ DECEMBER 13TH ~

1949: A double execution took place on this day at Durham Jail after two local men had been convicted separately of murders that took place within two days of each other. John Wilson's crime came to light when he called at his sister's house in east Durham and announced that he had murdered a woman. His story was not believed but when he repeated the confession at his father's home the police were called and he handed over his victim's watch and ring that had been removed from her body. Wilson, a married man, had recently met Lucy Nightingale and, after touring pubs in Murton, they were walking through a cornfield when an argument developed. He became enraged about her demand for 10s in return for sex and strangled her. It was similarly a crime of passion, on August 14th that same year, when Benjamin Roberts ended the life of Gillian Vickers in Chilton. Jealous of her association with another man, he blasted her with a double-barrelled 12 bore shotgun. An attempt to end his own life with a gunshot was not fatal and he was convicted of murder in late October. Both men were hanged by Stephen Wade, assisted by Syd Dernley. (www.capitalpunishmentuk.org)

~ December 14th ~

2011: Publication of a study by Durham scientists in the journal *PLoS One* on this day provided a revealing insight into the sex lives of goats. The research project was funded by the Natural Research Environment Council and involved data from 15,000 hunted male chamois (or antelope), a species of wild goat. Durham-based researchers worked in collaboration with ecologists from the University of Sassari in Italy to prepare findings which showed that male chamois pursue different mating strategies in different groups. Some exert themselves at a young age, while others wait until they are much older to dominate, and the study, which was carried out in northern Italy, is regarded as the first to prove that the waiting strategy, known as terminal investment, exists among animals. It is considered that this phenomenon could be the result of hunting which means that if too many larger, older males are killed then younger males may start breeding earlier. Years of rutting could leave them in a poor state in old age. Co-author of the report, Durham University PhD student Tom Mason, commented, 'Males have different strategies, which might be related to resources, climate or competition.' (*The Journal*, Newcastle upon Tyne, 1958)

~ December 15th ~

1913: An entry in the official records of Durham Choristers' School for this day indicates that nine choristers were selected. Parents of those chosen then received a formal letter which stated that they would be contacted again as soon as a vacancy occurred through voices breaking. When this happened events moved rapidly with the pupil usually leaving immediately (if he was continuing his education the headmaster would arrange a place). The incoming pupil's parents may well have been contacted on a Tuesday and told to prepare their son for attending school just three days later. The stipulated items of clothing to be worn by choristers included Norfolk suits and plain purple ties along with Eton suits, which were required on Sundays, and black cassocks for services. (Crosby, Brian, *Come on Choristers! A History of the Chorister School, Durham*, Durham: B. Crosby, 1999)

1936: A civic party assembled on the balcony of Durham town hall on this day to hear the mayor, Lord Londonderry, proclaim the accession of King George VI. The rest of the group was composed of Lady Londonderry, Dean Arlington, the deputy mayor, Councillor W.R.H. Gray and several other councillors along with Durham County deputy chief constable, Mr R. Gardiner and several sword and mace bearers. (Richardson, Michael, *Memory Lane: Durham City*, Derby: Breedon, 2000)

— December 16th —

1902: Samuel Walton, aged 31, was executed at Durham Jail on this day after being found guilty of triple murder at Middlestone Moor on September 11th. His victims were his wife, Isabella, whom he had shot, his mother-in-law who was also fatally wounded by a gunshot and his 11-month-old daughter, Esther Jane. It seems that Walton had attempted to take his own life by cutting his throat, but he recovered to fulfil his promise to his mother-in-law that he would 'swing for the lot of them'. At the time of the murders Walton was in possession of his marriage certificate and on the back he had scribbled what seemed to be an attempt to compose a will: 'His mother gets all, (signed) Samuel Walton', which shows that his mother was still alive at that time. Another hanging, on the same day, involved Thomas Nicholson, a 23-year-old man from Bill Quay, who had been convicted of murdering Mary Ina Stewart, aged 7, on August 16th. She lived in Joel Terrace and a memorial to her was installed at St Mary's church, Heworth. (Thompson, Albert A. (1998) *Classic Murders of the North East*, London: True Crime Library)

~ DECEMBER 17TH ~

1958: The fifty-fifth and last execution took place at Durham Jail on this day when 20-year-old Private Brian Chandler of the Royal Army Medical Corps was hanged for the murder of Martha Dodds of Darlington during the course of theft. On Sunday 8th June 1958 Private Chandler went absent without leave from his army base at Catterick and made his way to Darlington where he befriended two local women. After spending the day together they arranged to meet up again the following lunch time and as night fell they found an overnight stop in an old bus. By Tuesday the three friends found themselves short of cash and decided to approach Mrs Dodds, who was known to one of the women, about completing odd jobs for her. When this offer was declined, discussion among the threesome took on a sinister tone with talk of robbing the elderly lady. During the early afternoon of Wednesday 11 June, Chandler returned to Mrs Dodds' home in Victoria Road where he brutally attacked her with a hammer and stole just £4. After neighbours alerted police, Brian Chandler was arrested at Catterick on Friday 13 June and convicted of capital murder on October 29th. (www.capitalpunishmentuk.org)

⊸ December 18th ⊸

1875: A miner named Thomas Green, accompanied by his 12-year-old son, was proceeding from Shotton Colliery to Haswell when passing Shotton church he picked up on the footpath a curious looking thing resembling a lead pencil. After examining it slightly he handed it to his son, who drew his attention to a split at one end of it. When the lad pricked this with a pin some milky fluid oozed out into the hollow of his hand. An instant after and without any warning, the curious looking thing burst with a loud explosion, blowing off the finger and thumb by which the youth was holding it at the time and one portion of it narrowly missing the side of his head as it flew past The lad afterwards received medical assistance. What the nature of the article Green picked up could not even be guessed at. (Fordyce, T. (ed.), *Local Records; or, Historical Register of Remarkable Events Which Have Occurred in Northumberland and Durham … 1833 to [1875], being a Continuation of the Work Published by … Mr. John Sykes*, Newcastle upon Tyne: T. Fordyce, 1867–1876)

1998: The Prince Bishops' Centre was opened on this day by the MP for Durham, Gerry Steinberg. It was constructed to effectively provide two extra streets to the city in keeping with its existing design, but green tiles on the eastern stairwell aroused any amount of debate. (Nixon, Philip, *Portrait of Durham*, Tiverton: Halsgrove, 2006)

– December 19th –

1978: Press reports on this day announced:

Durham County Council is to involve the public in a planned opencast coal mining programme for the future. The council has a massive publicity and consultation exercise which will last until January 12. The move by the council follows talks with the National Coal Board and district councils on possible sites throughout the county. A leaflet describing the council's approach to the problem will be available from all libraries and planning offices between now and the closing date for comments. People will also be able to refer to a large plan and other details about each site. County Planning Officer Mr Jim Wilson said this week:- In addition to seeking the comments of the general public, district councils and parish councils, 400 groups and organisations of various kinds are being consulted for their views. The leaflet is entitled *Is this the right approach to opencast in County Durham?* and lists sites which the council feels should be in the programme, those which should not be included at the present time and others which are yet to be decided.

(*Durham Advertiser,* 1968–2000)

— December 20th —

1921: A rail crash occurred on this day at Belmont Junction to the north east of Durham when an express locomotive class Z4-4-2 No. 720 travelling from Aberdeen to Penzance with eleven coaches collided with four standing coaches which were being shunted into a siding. Fortunately no one was killed in the accident. At this time alterations were being made to the main line at Langley Bridge with the result that all rail traffic had to be rerouted via Leamside. (Richardson, Michael, *Durham: The Photographic Collection*, Stroud: Sutton, 2002)

1996: Following a major programme of refurbishment Durham Market Hall was officially reopened on this day by Rt Hon. Tony Blair MP, the Leader of the Parliamentary Opposition. By the beginning of the nineteenth century overcrowding in Durham marketplace had become a considerable problem and traders joined local businessmen in petitioning for construction of a purpose built market hall and more efficient running of markets. During May 1851 the Durham Markets Company Act was passed and during the late nineteenth century fairs for sheep and horned cattle were regularly held in the market hall with servants' hirings taking place twice yearly. Originally the hall was only open on Saturdays but following the refurbishment it operated for trading from Monday to Saturday. (en.wikipedia.org/wiki/Durham_Indoor_Market)

— December 21st —

Over several years: On or around this date, the ghost of a 'white lady' has been spotted on a flight of stone stairs in the Jacobean Room at Crook Hall on Frankland Lane just outside Durham City centre. This eerie apparition is said to be the niece of a fiery character, Cuthbert Billington, who inherited the manor in 1615, but there is no rational explanation for her fleeting supernatural intrusion. The earliest stonework of Crook Hall dates from around 1286 on land that was at the time part of Sydgate Manor and it was later named after Peter de Croke, the owner during the early years of the fourteenth century. Only the great hall and a screen passage remain from the early medieval building although it is possible to see where old medieval doorways have been blocked in. The screen passage runs through the Jacobean addition with the flight of stairs dating from the earliest phase leading nowhere and serving no useful purpose (the upper floors are now reached via an outside tower staircase). Surrounding the hall are 4 acres of attractive garden settings which include a Shakespeare garden, secret walled garden, cathedral garden, silver and white garden and grass maze. (ghosts.org/crook-hall-durham-england)

~ December 22nd ~

1430: A formal agreement completed on this day states that John Steel agreed to serve the Prior and Convent of Durham as cantor for the rest of his life. In effect, he had to instruct, to the best of his ability, eight secular boys and an indeterminate number of monks in all aspects of music. This included coaching them in organ playing and aspects of singing which covered 'Pryktenote, Faburden, Deschaunte, and Counter'. Although he was a member of the lay community, John Steel was expected to be present at Mass and Vespers in the choir area where he would be involved in the services either by playing the organ or by singing one of the parts as required by the precentor. His duties also included singing one of the parts at the Mass of St Mary which was celebrated daily in the Galilee chapel, while Steel's annual salary totalled £3 6s 8d, to be paid in two equal instalments. In addition he received food and clothing along with the offer of a house 'within the Bailey'. Provision for the future stated that if his wife died and he did not remarry then he would be offered an 'honest room' in part of the monastery. (Crosby, Brian, *Come on Choristers! A History of the Chorister School, Durham*, Durham: B. Crosby, 1999)

~ December 23rd ~

1946: Newspaper columns on this day reported on:

A happy ceremony at Pelton Fell Miners' Welfare Hall, when in recognition of the generosity of the directors of Mid Durham Coal Company in providing a Christmas tea for aged people of the village, workers at the colliery made gifts to Mr A. Kellett (managing director) and Mrs Kellett. The tea was the 18th provided by the directors, it being originated by Mr Kellett's father, the late Mr M.H. Kellett, and also the last of the series because of the advent of nationalisation. Mr T. Davidson presided at the ceremony, and Coun. J. Miller handed to Mr Kellett a cut glass writing set and to Mrs Kellett a gold bracelet. Replying to a tribute paid to the continued generosity of the Kellett family, Mr Kellett recalled his father's interest in the annual Christmas event and said it would give him many happy hours. He would prize the gift which would remind him in the years ahead of a happy association with the workers of his colliery. A company of 250 aged people were entertained to tea and a concert, and a Christmas gift of 10*s* from the workers of the colliery was presented to each.

(*Durham Chronicle*, 1820–1984)

— DECEMBER 24TH —

1285: Bishop Anthony Bek was enthroned at Durham on this day in a service conducted by his brother, the bishop of St David's. He took a keen interest in military matters and hunting where he favoured the forests of Weardale because of their close proximity to his residence at Auckland Castle. Nor did he avoid controversy as when he clashed with the Archbishop of York after refusing orders to excommunicate some Durham monks. The Archbishop was so infuriated that he decided to excommunicate Bek himself and the argument went to the king who was persuaded to reinstate Bishop Bek on the grounds that an archbishop had no right to excommunicate a 'Prince Bishop' without permission of the king. (www.englandsnortheast.co.uk)

2012: On this day a serious landslip occurred on the banks of the River Wear behind Church Street at Durham. It removed a section of the garden of Revd Peter Kashouris, the priest in charge at St Oswald's church and represented one in a series of landslips along both riverbanks in Durham area. Experts were called in to conduct monitoring and a full geotechnical assessment to discover reasons for the continuing movement and to identify long-term solutions. (*The Northern Echo,* Darlington, 1870–)

~ December 25th ~

1345: On this day:

> Thomas Hatfield, the King's secretary, and keeper of the privy seal
> was enthroned as Bishop of Durham. Under his firm and vigorous
> administration the see of Durham lost nothing of its ancient dignity
> and splendour. Like his predecessor, Bishop Bury, he maintained
> a princely hospitality and dispensed daily and extensive charity.
> Generous, open and sincere, he was just and beneficent to his subjects,
> and to his dependants liberal and indulgent. The cathedral of Durham
> is indebted to the prelacy of Bishop Hatfield for some of its fairest
> ornaments. He rebuilt or repaired many edifices belonging to the see
> and also erected a sumptuous palace in the Strand, London, for the
> residence of himself and his successors whilst attending Parliament;
> he also caused the survey to be made which bears his name.
> Bishop Hatfield died at his manor of the Alford near London, on
> 8th May 1381. His body, attended by the Bishop of Hereford and a
> numerous train, was brought to Durham and interred in the tomb, on
> the south side of the choir, which he had prepared during his lifetime.

(Whellan, Francis, *History, Topography, and Directory of the County
Palatine of Durham Comprising a General Survey of the County and a
History of the City and Diocese of Durham* … , London: Ballantyne,
Hanson and Co., 1894)

~ December 26th ~

1960: A Boxing Day pools win raised hopes of a huge payout for Mr John Beattie, steward of New Durham Workmen's Club. When Mr Beattie checked his pools coupon he found he had 1 first dividend and 24 thirds. A payout running into tens of thousands seemed in prospect but many other forecasters had also obtained all correct lines (after most of the Boxing Day matches went according to form). This meant that on December 29th Mr Beattie received a cheque for £2,363 8s 0d. This followed a win the previous year of £280 on the pools and he invested 27s 6d each week. (*Durham County Advertiser*, 1855–1968)

1972: Durham City triumphed 14–8 in the Boxing Day rugby fixture against Sunderland at Hollow Drift. Following pressure by Sunderland in the opening stages, back row forward Miller scored an unconverted try only for Barry Dickinson to kick a penalty goal for Durham. This score inspired City who added tries from Blakey, converted by Dickinson and McCall. In the second half Nicholson burst through the Sunderland defence for another unconverted try and although Sunderland came back strongly in the final minutes their only success was a try by Robson which Wilson converted. (*Durham County Advertiser*, 1855–1968)

‒ December 27th ‒

1946: Newspaper reports on this day gave extensive coverage to the 'Five Day Week For Miners':

The decision of the government through the Coal Board, to concede a five day week to miners as from May next has occasioned immense satisfaction in the Durham coalfield. Mr Sam Watson, secretary of the Durham area of the National Union of Mineworkers has described it as 'The greatest single concession ever to be secured by the coal mining industry'. He also noted that it had been gained without recourse to strike action or limitation of output but added that as every reasonable person must realise, the shorter week would entail great responsibilities upon colliery managements and workmen. For example, the loss of the Saturday working will mean a loss of approximately 300,000 tons of coal per week. This would have to be made up during the five working days and to do that will obviously necessitate the very minimum of absenteeism …

Conditions to be attached to the five day week were to be negotiated with the Coal Board. If agreement could not be reached the points of disagreement were to be referred to arbitration and the decision would be final and binding upon the parties.

(*Durham Chronicle*, 1820–1984)

~ December 28th ~

1946: Newspaper reports on this day indicated that Christmas proved a jolly season for the young patients, all boys, and staff of Earl's House School, Durham. The hospital was gaily decorated and each wing had its own glittering Christmas tree. On Christmas Eve, members of Witton Gilbert church choir, led by Revd W. James, sang carols at the school and on Christmas morning members of the nursing staff were also 'waits'. Santa Claus paid a nocturnal visit whilst the patients were asleep and gave each a big Christmas stocking, filled with presents and other good things. A really sumptuous dinner was enjoyed on Christmas Day, the menu including turkeys, chickens, plum puddings, trifles, jellies, mincemeat and 'pop' with Christmas crackers to pull. The nursing staff had their dinner at night and the domestic staff on Boxing Day. The highlight of the festivities was a grand party where Dr Ian McCracken, county medical officer of health, disguised as Santa Claus, presented each child with a gift from the Christmas tree. A delightful marionette show, given by pupils of Waldridge Fell School, Chester-le-Street was well-received by an enthusiastic audience. Guest of honour, Councillor T. Benfold proposed a vote of thanks to all who helped to make the party so successful. (*Durham Chronicle*, 1820–1984)

DECEMBER 29TH

1752: Richard Trevor, Bishop of St Davids, succeeded Bishop Butler, and was enthroned at Durham on this day. The bishop held the see for nineteen years, during which time he resided alternately at Durham or Auckland. His contemporaries describe him as a sincere friend, a generous patron, and a splendid and munificent prelate. He died in London, after a long and painful illness on June 9th 1771. (Whellan, Francis, *History, Topography, and Directory of the County Palatine of Durham Comprising a General Survey of the County and a History of the City and Diocese of Durham* ... , London: Ballantyne, Hanson and Co., 1894)

1815: During the late hours of this day:

> ...the paper mill belonging to Mr Lumley at Butterby near Durham was blown down. The building extended across a valley and was about 100ft long, the upper part being constructed of wood and brick pillars, the lower floor of stone. The wind, sweeping along the vale and taking the building at its broadside, tore away the roof and the whole of the upper storey, or drying rooms; nothing remained standing but the two gable ends and the walls of the lower rooms. The fall of the roof forced in the pillars of the drying rooms, breaking some beams and involving in the general ruin a quantity of paper in an unfinished state, all the vats and the various utensils used in the mill.

(Sykes, John, *Local records: or, Historical register of remarkable events which have occurred in Northumberland and Durham, Newcastle upon Tyne, and Berwick upon Tweed from the earliest period of authentic record, to the present time* ..., Newcastle, 1833)

~ December 30th ~

1960: The annual New Year Ball for Durham Amateur Rowing Club was held in the city's town hall on this day and continued until 2 a.m. the following morning. This year was special as it was 100 years since the foundation of the club and a Centenary Dance followed on December 31st. This time there was an earlier finish, at 11.30 p.m., as New Year's Day happened to fall on a Sunday. A further event was a members' 'Smoker' which was staged in the Garden House Hotel. Earlier in the year, on May 28th, a special Centenary Regatta had been held which included senior fours, senior clinker fours, junior clinker fours and maiden fours events – all over the usual short course. (www.nerowing.com/darctimeline.html)

2011: On this day the Bishop of Durham, the Rt Revd Justin Welby, set out his thoughts in a message for 2012. During his speech he called for confidence, optimism and hope based on God's love and urged generosity and courage to combat the downturn in the economy and the impact on jobs. The bishop's New Year message was delivered as the North East faced further difficult economic and social hardship, with the unemployment rate anticipated to reach 8.8 per cent nationally in 2012. (*The Northern Echo*, Darlington, 1870–)

— December 31st —

1539: On this day Prior Hugh Whitehead and his staff handed the abbey at Durham to King Henry VIII's commissioners, though Whitehead remained in charge until revised arrangements were made. It was stipulated that all outstanding debts were to be paid and all unnecessary servants discharged with six month's wages. (Stranks, C.J., *This Sumptuous Church: The Story of Durham Cathedral*, London: SPCK, 1993)

2011: Bill Bryson, Durham University's 11th Chancellor, stood down from his post on this day. He had succeeded Sir Peter Ustinov in April 2005 and earned a reputation for his commitment to engaging with all aspects of life in Durham. Apart from his ceremonial, pastoral, scholarly and ambassadorial duties as chancellor, he appeared in a Durham student film (the sequel to *The Assassinator*) and joined students as a litter picker to help keep the city clean. Bill Bryson's charitable activities in Durham included the 'My Friend Oli' campaign which encouraged people to sign the NHS Organ Donor Register. His affection for Durham is illustrated by a reference in *Notes from a Small Island* where he writes about 'a perfect little city'. (www.dur.ac.uk/bill.bryson)